Secre
Martial Arts Masters
Volume II

Secrets of the Martial Arts Masters

Bohdi Sanders, Ph.D.

Secrets of the
Martial Arts Masters

Library of Congress Cataloging-in-Publication Data
Sanders, Bohdi, 1962-
Secrets of the Martial Arts Masters
ISBN – 978-1-937884-22-2

1. Martial Arts. 2. Self-Defense. 3. Karate. 4. Asian Arts 5. Title

Kaizen Quest Publishing

Endorsements

When asked by Dr. Bohdi Sanders, to write a chapter for his new book, titled, *Secrets of the Martial Arts Masters*, I was, at first, a little skeptical, mainly due to the fact that there are already so many books and magazines promoting so called "wisdom" from various masters of the martial arts. So my first question was, "So who are these masters that have committed to providing chapters in this work?" Well, the answer was all it took for me to become very excited at the prospect of contributing, as when I was made aware of the incredible list of the "who's who" of the martial arts world, who were in fact sharing their knowledge and wisdom, I truly felt humbled to be asked to be a part of this illustrious group.

Having been privy to a great deal of the chapters already written by these masters, *I can honestly say that it is one of the most comprehensive collections of thoughts on all things martial arts, from some of the most respected instructors, that I have ever read.* Some of these masters are teachers that I have idolized and been guided by, and continue to be guided by, in my martial arts journey.

To have *one* such diverse volume of writings, which has managed to capture so many insightful, personal, and introspective thoughts on our arts, would literally be a gift to our martial arts community. But to have *three* such volumes of the knowledge and insights of some of these amazing teachers, that can quite honestly, inform and illuminate the understanding and journey of every martial artist, especially our younger students, is indeed *an incredible gift to our industry*. Again, I am honored to be a part of such a wonderful collection of writings from some of our greatest practitioners. Well done, Bohdi! I don't know how you managed to bring such an amazing group of people together, Bohdi, but I am so glad you did. Thank you for your passion in making this happen.

Richard Norton Sensei

~

Many of us long for our martial arts to be something bigger than mere punching or choking. We look for something grander than us that we can be a part of. *Bohdi Sanders does his part, providing inspiration to those who are ready to grow past the lessons in physical technique alone.*

Offering thoughts from leaders of the martial arts in the 21st century, he has gathered *quite an inspiring collection* for you. Study, consider, and grow!

Grandmaster Stephen K. Hayes

~

I think that Bohdi Sanders has done the martial arts world a great service with the Secrets of the Martial Arts Masters series. He has been able to bring together many of the world's greatest martial artists to share their knowledge together, without any egos, competition, or debates over styles and techniques, which in itself is a huge accomplishment in today's martial arts world. He has brought together world champions, box office movie stars, well-known masters, and more, all for one purpose – to share their knowledge. This is how the martial arts world should be, sharing and caring, without all the overblown egos.

Secrets of the Martial Arts Masters brings together 80 something martial arts masters, each writing about a specific martial arts topic. ***These books are absolutely packed with martial arts knowledge! These are books that I think every martial artist should read and take to heart.***

I stayed in close contact with Bohdi during his work on this humongous project. I personally know how much work went into putting these books together – the time, the triumphs, the frustrations, the challenges, and the successes. Through it all, ***Bohdi was determined to make this 3-volume anthology the best, most complete martial arts books ever published. And I think that he succeeded. These books are exceptional!*** And to say the list of martial arts masters included in these books is impressive, is a giant understatement.

I highly recommend *Secrets of the Martial Arts Masters* to every martial artist and anyone who is interested in martial arts. ***The amount of knowledge and information in these books is staggering.*** I think it is around 1,200 pages total. Some of the chapters alone are worth the price of the whole set! Get them! You won't be sorry.

Master Alan Goldberg

~

All martial artists, whatever their martial arts political views, will find much to stimulate their thinking and training methods in this *awesome collection of martial arts knowledge and wisdom* titled, *Secrets of the Martial Arts Masters*. Its breadth, insights, the variety of data explored, and its stark nature of views, will provoke both deep thought and emotions.

As Dr. Bohdi Sanders has done throughout his martial arts writing career, in his great books and articles, he once again helps us think more clearly about the important issues in the vast world of martial arts, by bringing together the brightest and most distinguished masters of the arts. ***I highly recommend the Secrets of the Martial Arts Masters series to every martial artist!***

Sifu Al Dacascos

~

Imagine if you were gifted with a martial arts book that inspires you and embodies the minds of the masters, and their experiences, in words of wisdom – sagacity and knowledge bound and collected in a massive three volumes. *This is the anthology that you've been waiting for! Bodhi Sanders' new book series, Secrets of the Martial Arts Masters, is great!*

When I was a young, aspiring, martial arts student, I devoured everything that had anything to do with martial arts – books and magazines of Karate, Tae Kwon Do, Kung Fu, Judo, etc. The techniques that were shown were great, but most of the time they didn't reveal the personal encounters of the masters. That's the difference with this book series. It contains the firsthand experiences of the masters who trained arduously all their lives. The reason this is so valuable is that the sage aphorism, "hindsight is 20-20," is accurately proven here. The masters have reflected on their experiences, good and bad, and they share their intimate thoughts in these wonderfully revealing books of martial arts wisdom.

Furthermore, what is amazing about these books is that all disciplines came together to contribute to the *Secrets of the Martial Arts Masters*. Who wouldn't want to read about Chuck Norris' life of Zen, Richard Norton's *Longevity in the Martial Arts*, and even the esoteric Tactical Special Forces' Grandmaster Harry Greene's *Brutal Reality of Blade Fighting*, just to name a few. I am also truly honored to be a small contributor this anthology.

These books belong on the shelves of every martial artist's library. I highly recommend them. I wish I had these books growing up as a young, impressionable, martial arts student. I hope these books will inspire and connect with young and old students of this current generation, and future ones to come.

Master Jino Kang

~

I have known of Dr. Bohdi Sanders for some years, often stumbling across his daily wisdom teachings across social media which resonated with traditional values and the code of Bushido echoing through his thought-provoking teachings across the globe. I have had the pleasure of immersing and nurturing my mind through his enlightening publications and his *Wisdom Warrior Blog*.

I was very honored and pleased to have been asked to contribute to *Secrets of the Martial Arts Masters*. It was an opportunity to express my thoughts, wisdom, knowledge, and expertise of my life-long study of martial arts and sports over several decades, alongside some of the greatest masters of today.

By far, most books and publications I have read over the years gave me an insight, technical and mechanical, to understanding the system, as perceived by one individual, the author. Dr. Bohdi Sanders created a platform, and a source of information, which *offers a multitude of perspectives through a multi-dimensional immersion in the theories and teachings of some of the most renowned martial arts masters of today.*

Every problem has multiple solutions, just as every journey can take many different paths. Familiarizing ourselves with multiple schools of thought, disciplines, theories, and philosophies will enable us to see a broader picture and draw upon us a better conclusion. *Secrets of the Martial Arts Masters is an absolute MUST READ for every martial arts enthusiast who wants to have a deeper understanding of one's self through their martial arts practice.*

Master Silvio Simac

~

The *Secrets of the Martial Arts Masters anthology is exactly that – Compelling! Insightful! Inspiring! Educational!* I can tell you from my some 50 plus years of training in the arts, to master level in several disciplines, that the *Secrets of the Martial Arts Masters Series* is a very rare opportunity for both a beginning student or the seasoned master to get glimpses into the world of Budo that cannot be viewed with only one pair of eyes.

Learn from some of the great masters of this arts. Study their perceptions, their insights, and their knowledge from decades of their hard training. It is very rare to get this many martial arts teachers to share their deepest secrets and insights of the arts. In fact, that's why this is a three volume set. I was honored when Dr. Bohdi Sanders asked me to contribute my insights on the personal development and spiritual nature of the Martial Path.

It takes almost a lifetime of study to even get a portion of the glimpses that you will learn by reading and carefully studying what other masters on the path have learned. I invite you to read carefully and diligently. Above all take what really inspires you and embody it into your Budo and deeply in your life. To me Budo is life; and it begins and ends with respect.

Grandmaster Richard Van Donk

~

As I thumb through the hundreds of pages of the book series, *Secrets of the Martial Arts Masters*, it brings to mind the thousands of years of experience and insight that has been gleaned and applied from all the masters noted within these pages. *All the various mindsets and styles that mesh within the three volumes is simply amazing!* The purpose of these books is to educate the next generation of martial artists who want to glimpse into the lives of accomplished masters who came before them. Read about them in their own words and what it takes to become proficient in their own martial arts styles.

Every time I turn the page to a new chapter, I sense I am entering a different world. It is absolutely amazing how we all have different martial arts styles, but at the same time, share the same practical foundations and techniques. It is to every martial artist's advantage to look into their styles, and thus, learn from these great masters. I, myself, have spent decades traveling throughout the world to learn from these same masters.

Instead of traveling all over, one can now relax in the comfort of his or her own home, reading and gaining insight from the *Secrets of the Martial Arts Masters*.

Shihan Dana Abbott

~

It is without hesitation, my honor to endorse Shihan Bohdi Sanders' latest book series, *Secrets of the Martial Arts Masters*. I've had a chance to read the pre-release version of his latest book series and I definitely have to admit that it was captivating to say the least. *I found it hard to put down. Any true martial artist, no matter what your rank, will feel the same way.*

After reading several of his previous books, I knew right away that Bohdi Sanders, who I was honored to have awarded the title of Shihan in 2017, was a true martial artist and truly understood the concept of Budo. He writes with such passion and sincerity about his understanding of Budo, that teachers, such as myself, and many others, cannot ignore it. I have always told my good friend to never stop writing, no matter what, because he inspires teachers like myself to stay focused and to continue to teach the old ways.

My friend *Bohdi is one of the few true martial artists and authors who has caught the attention of so many masters and grandmasters, who read and learn from his wisdom and knowledge of the arts. I highly recommend that everyone get the Secrets of the Martial Arts Masters series*, and even take the time to look back at all of his other books. Consider getting them all! He is definitely a rarity in today's world of the martial arts.

Soke Richard Hallman

~

Once again, Dr. Sanders has put together an amazing piece of literature. These books have allowed the reader to see into the minds of some of the most revered and knowledgeable martial artists, with literally hundreds of years of combined experience. It provides information that can only empower those who want to enhance their skillset. I see this as a tool and reference for beginners to very advanced practitioners.

Experience, which has taken a lifetime to assemble, can now be captured by simply studying, not just reading, these wonderful books. If we think about how we learn and why we learn, we find there are two ways to achieve knowledge. One method is by what we call the school of hard knocks or old fashioned experience.

An example would be the first person that fell off a high platform, such as a roof, provided the, "I don't want to do that" experience for the observer. That person who fell was the "hard knocks" learner and the observer was the beneficiary! The second method is to become the observer and student of history. This is how most people can achieve a high level of intellect without the suffering that comes with that information.

The final step in the process is how one uses this new information. If you only observe and never apply any of the information, you have a full vessel that remains unsampled. You need to drink from this vessel of gathered knowledge to make the most of what is assembled in the books. I know that you will be empowered by the information in these books, but don't forget to drink in the knowledge and put these books in your reference library, after you have tattered the pages reading them repeatedly!

Grandmaster Dan Tosh

~

Acknowledgements

I want to thank each and every one of the Grandmasters and Masters who shared their time, wisdom, knowledge, and secrets in this massive undertaking. Without them, *Secrets of the Martial Arts Masters* would never have been published. There are too many to list them all here, but you are ALL appreciated!

I want to give special recognition to Master Alan Goldberg, who was a great help to me in getting some of these masters on board, as well as providing me with contact information, putting in a good word for me when needed, and his constant support during this project. Your help was invaluable, my friend!

In addition, I want to thank Grandmaster Bob Gomez for his work on the covers for each of the books in this series. Not only is GM Gomez a great martial artist, but he is also a pretty amazing graphic designer and lives with the Budo spirit!

I want to thank Grandmaster Richard Hackworth for stepping up and doing a lot of work for me while I was both in the hospital and recovering from my surgery. He is, not only one of the most knowledgable martial artists I know, but also a real friend and blatantly honest, which is a rare quality in this world!

I want to also thank Cheryl Wheeler Sanders, as she went out of her way to both support this project and to get some of the other masters on board. Thank you for all of your support!

I want to thank Gena O'Kelly Norris and Master Doug Marcaida, whose help and support are greatly appreciated. Without their help, this project would have been incomplete, missing several invaluable chapters.

I also want to thank Michael DePasquale, Jr., who took time out during a very trying time in his life, and was gracious enough to enable me to include a chapter by both his father, Michael DePasquale, Sr. and the great Joe Lewis in this work.

And finally, I want to thank my beautiful wife for her patience while I spent countless hours, weeks, and months working in my office, on the phone, on the computer, and traveling to complete this gigantic project. She also contributed dozens of hours to this project by editing each of the books. Without her love, patience, and support, I could have never finished this amazing project. I love you, sweetheart!

Table of Contents

Foreword: Grandmaster Eric Lee…………………………...xv

Introduction……………………………………………xviii

Casey McPartland – Life or Death: When Seconds Count……..1

Al Dacascos & Bohdi Sanders – Loyalty and Integrity………11

Jino Kang – Overcoming Fear on the Mat and in the Streets...23

Bob Allen – Festival of the Naked in Japan………………… 33

Eddie Mapula – Training to Win……………………….. 41

Rick Moneymaker & Mike Patrick – The Hidden Code…....... 47

David Hansen – Strategy versus Skill………………………...59

Bohdi Sanders – Simplifying Your Martial Arts……………. 65

John Duncan – 20 Survival Secrets from a DEA…………….75

Dave Johnson – Tactical Firearm Training…………………...91

Nicholas Moreno – Watered Down Martial Arts...................103

Mike Mather – Fighting Multiple Attackers…………….....111

Don Newbill – 16 Year Old Black Belts……………………123

Richard Hackworth – The Psychology of Self-Defense……. 131

Vincent Marchetti – Effects of Hard Core Conditioning……141

Richard Van Donk – The Path to Empowerment………….. 149

Carol Womack – Maai: Distancing……………………165

Bohdi Sanders – The Internal Warrior Spirit………………...175

Tak Wah Eng – Balance: Unifying Mind and Heart………...187

Col. Phil Torres – True Leadership………………………...195

Bill Kipp – Importance of Full Speed Reality Training……..213

David Nelson – The Way of Healing is found in Death……. 223

Steve Cooper – Dim Mak……………………………...235

Peter Freedman – Hard Core Martial Arts vs Competition... 247

Harry Mok – Internal Healing.....................................255

Dana Lynn Hee – The Good, the Bad, and the Ugly........... 271

Alan Goldberg – Out of Control Egos in the Martial Arts.....283

Malia "Dacascos" Bernal – The Road to the Top...............291

William Powell – Revealing that which is Hidden.............305

Bill Logan – Realistic Training and Mindset....................321

Frank Dux – The Martial Arts Hater Mentality.................327

Bohdi Sanders – Don't Teach Undesirable People.............333

Rondy McKee – What it takes to be a Master.................. 341

Max Massiah – Importance of Effective Self-Defense........349

Jeff Scott – MA Revolution and Mind Control Theory........357

Marc Stoner – Consequences of Fighting.......................367

David Furie – The Psychology of Street Survival.............. 377

About the Dr. Bohdi Sanders....................................381

Looking for more Wisdom.......................................382

For Your Consideration...383

Foreword

When Dr. Bodhi Sanders asked me to write a foreword for his new book, *Secrets of the Martial Arts Masters*, at the Elite Black Belt Hall of Fame in 2017, I said of course, I would be honored. I will have Lady L. Reed help me send him what he needs from me.

I did not expect the books to have so much wisdom or that so many martial arts masters could be put together for one book series. What a great effort and much hard work it must have taken Bohdi to get this one project done! He covered a lot of martial arts topics that I never thought could be possible to read in one book set.

Secrets of the Martial Arts Masters is full of life stories of well-known martial artists, their teachings, and explanations of martial arts topics, that are written for people to easily understand. Even a white belt can understand the meanings behind some of the complex topics in these wonderful books.

I believe that it is up to each individual person to interpret the martial arts as he sees fit. I don't judge another person's decisions regarding his or her martial arts style. Styles, for me, are like personalities. Everyone has their own.

I like the fact that Dr. Sanders has allowed each martial arts master in this book series to approach the topics from their own point of view. We all see things through our own perceptions. This book series definitely gives readers a wide variety of ideas and point of views about martial arts.

Dr. Sanders has done the martial arts community a great service by bringing all of these martial arts masters together to share their knowledge and experiences. I am for harmony among all brothers and sisters of the martial arts. We need more harmony within our martial arts community. These books work to promote harmony to the martial arts by allowing many masters, from many styles, to work together in harmony.

Since a book series like this has never before been done in the martial arts, this is a historic book series that I believe will be read for many generations to come. I am honored to write the foreword for this amazing martial arts publishing accomplishment. The teachings in this book will live on for years to come and I am honored to be able to be a small part of this book series.

Grandmaster Eric Lee

Grandmaster Eric Lee was born in Chung Shan Village of Canton Province in 1946, China. Eric Lee's family came to the United States in 1962. His family owned a Chinese restaurant in Oakland. They lived several years before that in Hong Kong. His main interest was to study martial arts and pursue his interest in acting. So he became the "King of Kata." He raised the level of tournament kata to such a new level of excitement and skill, that his mastery was recognized when he was named United States Champion in both 1972 and 1973. He won over seventy first place titles, as well as two Golden Fist Awards for Outstanding Kung Fu Kata and Outstanding Chinese Weapons Stylist.

His martial arts training began in traditional Kung Fu in 1966 under See Chung Ball. He also trained under Grandmaster Al Dascascos in the styles of Wun Hop Kuen Do and Kajukenbo. Wing Chun and JKD are among the styles he also trained in with other martial artists in Oakland, California. He started playing small parts in films like The Killer Elite, The Death Machine, Good Guys Wear Black, Rambo 2, and Big Trouble in Little China. His starring role in Falcon's Claw, and the lead roles in The Shinobi and The Master Demon, were just a few of the films that made him a successful actor. He is currently the President of Dragons Network Productions, LLC. His mission is to live in harmony with others before his expiration.
(GM Eric Lee's bio is written by Lady L. Reed)

xvi

Introduction

I was talking with my dear friend, mentor, and teacher, Sifu Al Dacascos one day, as we do quite often, and he was inviting me to come stay with him for a while in Hawaii for some much needed rest and relaxation, as well as more training, of course. He had been inviting me to come for a long visit for years, but because of surgeries and health issues, I hadn't been able to make it.

During the conversation, he jokingly told me that he was not getting any younger and I better come for a long visit. That got me thinking about the fact that many of the martial arts pioneers in the United States are getting older, as we all are. It also made me wish that I had recorded some of the conversations that Sifu Al and I have had over the years, as Sifu Al has so much amazing martial arts knowledge that he has shared with me. Sifu, when I come for that visit, my digital recorder *will be* coming with me for sure!

After our conversation a lightbulb went off, and I started thinking about putting, not only Sifu Al's vast martial arts knowledge down in writing, but also compiling teachings from many of the other great, old school martial artists' wisdom and knowledge. And from that, *Secrets of the Martial Arts Masters* was born.

I started to compile a list of martial arts masters that I thought would add traditional, old school, martial arts knowledge to my new book. Since my book, *Modern Bushido*, hit #1 on Amazon several years back, I have met more and more of the martial arts greats, who I have admired for years. I started by contacting many of them, and my idea was met with enthusiasm across the board.

In 2017, I was inducted into the Elite Black Belt Hall of Fame and also given a Lifetime Achievement Award for my contributions to the martial arts world. That gave me the opportunity to meet and become friends with many other martial arts legends, as well as to do some training with my dear friend, Grandmaster Harry Greene and his top student, Master Ray Kodani, who by the way, is without a doubt, the most respectful martial artist I have ever met, as well as a deadly combative knife instructor.

I also had time to have another conversation with my friend, Grandmaster Eric Lee, and during our conversation, I mentioned my idea to him and asked if he would be interested in writing the foreword to *Secrets of the Martial Arts Masters*. He graciously agreed to do so, and the new project was starting to come together.

Secrets of the Martial Arts Masters was originally going to be a single book, filled with unique martial arts wisdom. It soon became obvious that it was going to be much more than that! The list of martial arts Masters and Grandmasters started to take shape and then began to explode across the martial arts world. It went from one large book to two volumes, and then, to three volumes, as more and more grandmasters and masters wanted to be a part of this historic project.

I call *Secrets of the Martial Arts Masters* a historic project simply because there has never been a martial arts book series like this in the history of the martial arts. This series has martial artists from many different styles and countries, all sharing their time, wisdom, knowledge, and even secrets to the martial arts community.

When I first mentioned that *Secrets of the Martial Arts Masters* was going to be a historic book, several martial artists on social media took it the wrong way and unfriended me because I "Had no humility." That was a great example of people taking something the wrong way because of their erroneous assumptions, instead of postponing judgment until they were able to judge the work for themselves. I was not bragging on *my* work, but merely stating a fact. There has never been any published martial arts book series which brought together this many of the great martial arts masters, all for the purpose of sharing their knowledge and wisdom; and that, indeed, is historic.

Secrets of the Martial Arts Masters has martial arts masters from the United States, Japan, Mexico, the United Kingdom, the Phillipines, Europe, Australia, China, South Korea, Portugal, South America, and India, hopefully I did not miss any countries. If I did, please forgive me; it was not intentional.

They all united to share their knowledge to the martial arts world. This project has many World Champions, retired Special Forces warriors, ex-DEA agents, ex-law enforcement experts, Special Forces instructors, SWAT instructors, martial arts movie and television stars, Olympic Champions, ninjas, Grandmasters, martial arts legends, and more, sharing their teachings in one humongous project.

At this point, you might be thinking, "Wow, this sounds like an overwhelming job to organize and get all of these people together, and put all of their teachings together in this one project." And, you would be right! It was a gigantic project, definitely worth all of the effort.

Looking back, if someone would have given me the list of names of the martial arts masters in this series, and told me that I had to get teachings from them all and put those teachings into a book series, I would have probably said that it could not be done. It would have sounded virtually impossible! It would have seemed so overwhelming that my mind would have simply discounted it right then and there. After all, these are very busy people, sought after all over the world for their seminars and teachings.

Luckily, it didn't happen that way. I just started working on putting my next book together, adding one Grandmaster, then another, then another. Then I would think, what if...? The question, "What if" is a marvelous question, as it can lead you to places that you never thought possible, *if* you have the courage to follow it up with *action*; otherwise, it is merely daydreaming.

I asked, "What if I could get Grandmaster Fumio Demura on board?" So I set out to find GM Demura's contact information. I ran into many dead ends, but continued to try until I was successful. I contacted GM Demura, and I was honored that he actually remembered meeting me about a year earlier. Not only did he remember me, he said that he, "Was honored to be asked to be a part of my book."

We talked for about an hour about the book and personal issues. I was extremely excited that GM Demura was going to be a part of the book, but I was completely shocked by what happened about a month later.

I had started organizing this project a couple of months before I was scheduled to have a major surgery. I had briefly mentioned my surgery in conversation with GM Demura the night we spoke. My surgery was just after Thanksgiving in 2017. About a week before Christmas, I received a call from GM Demura. I was not taking any calls at that time, as I was really sick and having a hard time with my recovery, but when GM Demura calls, I don't care who you are, you answer the phone, period!

To my surprise, Grandmaster Fumio Demura called just to see how I was doing after my surgery, as he was concerned about me and wanted to check up on me. Talk about an honor! This is the character of a true Grandmaster! He not only listened intently to everything in our conversation, but remembered it weeks later and made a point to call and ask me how I was doing after my surgery!

That is the exact character of the people that I wanted in *Secrets of the Martial Arts Masters,* to teach today's students of the martial arts. Not every martial artist has that kind of character or the Budo spirit – the true spirit of the martial way. Many martial artists have forgotten that the ultimate goal of martial arts is spiritual, ethical, and moral self-improvement or perfection.

That is exactly what Grandmaster Demura exhibits, at least in my humble opinion.

I now have many stories like that, as I made a point of searching out martial arts masters who truly live by the true martial arts ideals, who work to perfect their character, as Master Gichin Funakoshi taught. I have been honored over and over again by the masters who so graciously agreed to be a part of this project.

One after another, martial arts greats joined my project and it started to grow bigger and bigger. And, time and time again, I was honored when many of these martial arts masters told me how much they have enjoyed and appreciated my writings, teachings, and what I am doing for the martial arts community.

I tell you what, there is no trophy or rank promotion that is any bigger honor for me than to hear iconic martial arts Grandmasters and Masters tell me that they enjoy my teachings and appreciate what I am doing for the martial arts world!

It got to the point that, each time I took a chance, I was having more and more success in getting really well-known masters on board with the project. People would tell me, "There is no way he will give you the time of day. He is too big of a celebrity and you won't even get close." But I didn't get to where I am by being disheartened by naysayers or listening to their negative energy. As Wayne Gretzky stated, "You miss 100% of the shots you don't take."

If I wanted someone in the book, I simply asked, asked again, and persisted to ask, until I got a firm answer. Did it take some work to get some of the big name martial arts celebrities on board? Of course! Everything worth doing takes some work. This whole project took a tremendous amount of work. If you are not willing to put in the work, you don't deserve success; that's the bottom line, as far as I am concerned.

So when I thought, *I wonder if I could get Doug Marcaida on board. That would be really cool! And maybe I could I get one of my all-time favorite television action stars, Adrian Paul, the Highlander, to write a chapter? I love his television show, as it really taught the value of honor and character. What about Chuck Norris? Would that even be possible?* I followed those thoughts up with action.

Each time I ask myself these questions, my mind would almost immediately tell me, "That is ridiculous! You won't even get close." But instead of listening to my negative thoughts, I decided to just go for it and take a chance.

Now, several months later, Doug Marcaida, Adrian Paul, and Chuck Norris, along with dozens of other martial arts greats, are on board with this project. Doug Marcaida calls me from time to time and his depth of knowledge, and the way he sees life, always captivates me during our conversations. His television show, *Forged in Fire*, does not do him justice; his martial arts wisdom is simply amazing, as is the way he sees life.

In addition, I have had personal correspondence with Adrian Paul, and we will be discussing an exciting venture when I am back to 100%. I have always enjoyed his television show, *Highlander*, as it was one of the few television shows which taught traditional values of honor, integrity, and character, along with great martial arts actions. In fact, it is probably my all-time favorite action series. And now, I have been honored to have him write about honor in *Secrets of the Martial Arts Masters*.

And, I was honored to have Chuck Norris and his beautiful wife, Gena, who personally helped me a lot during this process, and personally prayed for me as I went through an unexpected brain surgery while working on this project. Not only did they both pray for me, but were genuinely concerned for my well-being and followed up to find out how I was doing. Grandmaster Chuck Norris is another well-known television and movie star which I have a lot of respect for. And I am tremendously honored that he was willing to help a martial artist, whom he had never met, by agreeing to be a part of this project. I have too many stories like this to list them all here.

Never listen to your negative thoughts when they tell you that something is impossible! You are only limited by the thoughts that you believe and accept. As Buddha taught, "We are what we think. All that we are arises with our thoughts. With our thoughts we make the world." If you think you can't, you probably won't; if you think you can, at least you will give it your best shot.

I was determined that nothing was going to stop this amazing project. When I was hit with the unexpected news that I had to have emergency brain surgery to remove a brain tumor, just as I was getting ready to put the last chapters in the manuscript, it was very disheartening. But I was determined not to allow that to stop these teachings from being published. I made arrangements for everything to go forward, with or without me.

I made it through the surgery, but had to spend five days in the ICU in the University of Colorado Hospital in Denver. The endocrinologist was shocked when she came into my room one night and I had gotten a stack of copy paper from one of the nurses and was hand writing one of my chapters while I was in the ICU. I got scolded for not resting, as I just had a "major brain surgery." So I didn't tell her about the other chapter, which I had written the night before and stuffed into my bag.

Hey, in my defense, there was not a lot to do in the ICU room, so writing seemed like a good way to pass the time and get my mind off all the needles stuck in me. I already had all of my chapters in the books, but now, thanks to five nights in the ICU, there are two extra chapters included in the series as a bonus. It just continued to grow!

Plus, I was determined to keep my word and get this book out in the winter, before Christmas. I had not only promised dozens of Grandmasters and Masters that it would be out, but I also had many readers who have been anxiously awaiting the release of my new book series, *Secrets of the Martial Arts Masters*. I always keep my word if it is humanly possible. A man's word should be his bond and should be as strong as any contract. So I worked, even in the ICU, to make this series as good as I could make it, thinking of formatting issues, listing the things I needed to get done when they let me go home, and yes, writing more content.

Secrets of the Martial Arts Masters was all about gathering as much martial arts knowledge, wisdom, and motivation as I could. And, after 3½ decades as a martial artist (Wow, I can't be that old!), writing several bestselling books on martial arts philosophy, and studying many ancient and modern books on the arts, I thought there was not that much more I could learn. I was wrong!

There is so much amazing information in *Secrets of the Martial Arts Masters* that I actually had to read several of the chapters and sections, over and over, just to grasp the teachings. Some of them are that deep. The wisdom and teachings in this series are some of the best martial arts teachings I have read.

These will be some of the most eclectic martial arts books that you will ever read. We covered a vast array of topics, getting deep into each one. Once the topic was decided on, the author took that topic in the direction that he or she saw fit. Many times, the master and I would agree on a topic, and I thought that he would be going in a certain direction, but when I got his chapter, he had taken the topic in a totally different, unique direction. This is only one of the many things that makes this set of books so unique.

I can say with a fairly high degree of certainty, that, no matter how long you have been in the martial arts, you will learn a lot from these books. There will be things which you probably know, but have forgotten, or not thought about in years, and you will be reminded and motivated to integrate these teachings back into your life again. There are other teachings which you may have never heard before; I know that I hadn't.

You will find *Secrets of the Martial Arts Masters* motivating, inspiring, educational, and highly interesting. There are chapters which will inspire you to train harder and motivate you to continue your journey, no matter what obstacles you have to overcome. Others will bring tears to your eyes, educate you on topics you may not have ever thought about, enlighten you, shock you, entertain you, and even re-ignite the martial arts spirit in your heart.

I have been so honored by each and every martial arts master who has taken part in this enormous project. I am honored that each one thought highly enough of me, and/or this project, to be a part of this series. Each added a unique part to this series with his or her own distinctive knowledge, wisdom, stories, and secrets, which make *Secrets of the Martial Arts Masters* what it is – an amazing series of vast martial arts knowledge and wisdom.

I also want to point out that no one book is better or more important than the other two. I tried to make each of the books equal as far as the masters involved and the information presented. And I think when you see the table of contents and the masters included in each book, you will agree that each book can easily stand alone as a valuable resource, but taken together, they are an invaluable set. Hopefully, you obtained all three books in the series and not just one! If you only bought one or two, you are missing out on an abundance of knowledge and wisdom!

Also, the chapters are not presented in any certain order. The chapters can be read in the order they are presented or in any order you wish. Each chapter is able to stand alone, as each master's teachings are his or her individual teachings alone. And, I will add, that each chapter is well worth reading!

I also want to make it clear that each master is only responsible for the views expressed in his or her own chapter and may or may not agree with what is written in the other chapters in the book in which his or her work is included. And that goes for me as well. I wanted to allow each master his or her own voice and not edit it to fit my beliefs or anyone else's beliefs.

In addition, some of the masters in the book asked that their titles be used only in the biography section at the end of each chapter. In order to maintain a consistent appearance throughout the book, I elected to only use the masters' names and chapter titles at the beginning of each chapter. So you will definitely want to read each biography at the end of each chapter. The biographies will give you a sense of awe for the master or grandmaster whose teachings you just read, as well as their contact information, websites, etc.

Read each chapter with an open mind. Apply what resonates with your spirit, discard what doesn't. As you travel your martial arts journey, you may want to revisit these teachings at a later time. If you do, you will likely find that some of the teachings, which did not resonate with you when you first read them, will then be seen in a different light.

As we mature, grow, and learn, our minds open up and we can understand concepts and teachings which may not have clicked with us the first time we read them. I can tell you from personal experience, that when you go back and re-read the books later, you will find things which you missed during the first reading; and things which you didn't comprehend or didn't agree with the first time, may seem completely clear to you later.

The more you dig into each chapter, the more benefits you will receive from each of the teachings. Don't just read these amazing teachings, but apply them to your life. If you do, I can promise you that you will be a better martial artist because of your effort. As Johann Wolfgang von Goethe taught, "Knowing is not enough; we must apply. Willing is not enough; we must do." The only way that these teachings will help you is if you apply what you learn to your life!

I feel that these are books that you will refer back to time and time again and will be a vital part of your martial arts library. The vast martial arts knowledge in these books will be a valuable teaching tool for you, if you are a martial arts instructor; and some amazing knowledge for instructors and students alike. May these books bless your life and may you always live with honor!

Shihan Bohdi Sanders

Secrets of the Martial Arts Masters

Bushido

xxx

Life and Death – When Seconds Count
Casey McPartland

Imagine leaving a party having had too much to drink and suddenly finding yourself attacked by three individuals! It's a blitz attack in the dark, so you didn't see it coming and worse, the three people were "friends" you knew in high school. Suddenly you are being held and beaten in the dark. Literally held from behind and pummeled!

You can't believe this is happening and then, it gets worse. You're in the fog of being beaten by people you know, at the same time trying to clear your head, sober up, and figure out what to do. Right about then you're dropped to the ground and they're kicking you in the head and body, then repeatedly stomping your face and head. You're fighting to stay conscious, while still trying to make some sense out of what's happening, and then darkness!

At that point there are three alternatives available: 1) Give up and suffer whatever consequences may come, 2) Lay there in desperation and maybe someone will find you and help you out, or 3) Call upon that deepest of instincts and take action to survive. From deep in the limbic brain, the place where each of us still have pure "animal instinct," comes the will to blindly get up and take action, more a state of "no sanity" than insanity. The only action available to the warrior is #3, survive or die!

Even from a limited cognitive state, training and muscle memory take over, coupled with the animal that is in all of us. If no serious training has taken place, "whatever works" works or doesn't.

If the body has been trained through repetitive movement, the muscles and subconscious memory have stored the actions necessary to fight through the life-or-death situation. There are no guarantees, but the odds are better if training has been undertaken and "the desire to get home" is strong.

One of the three has left and suddenly the other two are walking away. Somehow through the darkness an awareness strikes, the "animal takes over," and as messed up as you are, you take action. Rushing the two from behind, your survival instinct comes into play and you attack.

You're not cognizant of exactly what you're doing, but "survival at all costs" is at play, and what ensues can only be termed "ugly." No concern for form or technique, just neutralizing your attackers – the retaliation is quick and dirty. All you are aware of is someone in the fog of the whole mess yelling, "Wait, we'll take you home!" You run off into the night, bloody, broken, and not able to think clearly.

While the previous account sounds like something out of a movie, it happens in reality, and for some reason the "victim" survives and may even emerges the victor. There are times in our lives when we must survive or ultimately face death in defeat, whether metaphorically or in fact.

These are times when inaction, or giving up, doesn't yield acceptable results. What drives someone to emerge out of the heat of conflict, broken and battered, to lick his wounds and carry on?

Not being an expert on the topic of survival, I can only offer my opinion, learning, and philosophical perspective on what sets up the circumstances around making the "right" decisions and taking relevant actions in those few seconds when life or death depends on it.

Most people in the western world today are unprepared for the actions they may need to take, given an unexpected assault, attack, or accident. Anyone can be taken totally by surprise by an event in the course of their daily life. This gives them no time to plan the actions necessary to survive; they are left only to do what's absolutely necessary to escape the circumstances they find themselves in, without being caught on the wrong side of life or death.

Certainly, first responders and military operators train for the unexpected on an almost daily basis, and many martial artists train their minds and bodies for such an event. However, martial artists are more likely to train in a "laboratory environment," whereas first responders and military personnel are more likely to be confronted with a life-or-death situation at almost any time.

So how does one prepare for making it through a life-or-death situation before it ever happens? Perhaps a more common question in today's world might be, why should one prepare himself for such a situation when the odds aren't very high for such a thing to happen?

The answer could be just to be ready for anything that could present itself. In the case of the military and first responders, whether or not they really expect a life-or-death situation to be lurking around every corner all-the-time, they must constantly prepare.

When are Life-or-Death Decisions Made?

Life-or-death decisions are certainly made on the spur of the moment, and fight-or-flight follows, but what moves that decision into action? We can spend hours, days, and even years training our bodies and minds to take action based on specific stimuli. We can mentally and physically choreograph the action we will take if or when a life-threatening event takes place, and know just what to do and how to do it, or so we think.

It is common knowledge among those who study disastrous events, whether it's a weather phenomenon or a blitz attack on the street, that things never go exactly as we've prepared for them to go. In reality, events go totally sideways and inside out, all of the elements are there, but none of the organization, and stuff just happens. It seems like, whether or not we spend a lot of time training or just let things happen as they will, we are totally at the mercy of the event. Here are a couple of facts about life threatening events:

3

- They happen randomly, making no sense (for example, they're not dependent on nice weather, light or dark, physical location, or who you are with.)

- You are likely to respond in one of three major ways, probably based on your personal mental and physical preparation:

    1) If you've trained, you may respond or react using elements of your training to take the actions necessary to survive, this is especially true if part of your mental preparation was to survive at all costs, so you will likely fall back on what your mind and body "know."

    2) If you have not trained, you simply lash out and do something, take any action, *maybe*, just maybe, you will get lucky.

    3) If you have not trained and you don't want to fight, you might curl up into the fetal position and hope you don't get killed. We might call this, "I'll surrender and maybe things will work out okay, because everything is based in goodness."

It seems like just doing anything, or hoping everything will work out okay, have their pitfalls. Even being well-trained and mentally prepared has its problems, but the risks are reduced by having a *clue* and the drive to survive.

Because of the instantaneous and unexpected nature of life-threatening events, decisions of fight-or-flight, or to assess and take action, are literally made in a split second, and with not a moment to spare!

That *moment* may seem to take minutes, but at the speed of the human brain, perhaps only microseconds pass – fight-or-flight decisions in the moment might better be termed life-or-death.

What Decides the Fight-or-Flight Decision?

Awareness plays an important part, even in that microsecond before action is taken. If we are trained, even in the dojo, there is a certain feeling, or set of feelings, that takes place when things are about to go awry. It might appear as anxiety, or the hair standing up on the back of our neck, or just a sense that everything is not okay.

We might have seen something we didn't consciously *know* we saw, something that puts us in a heightened state. It might be a glance, a gesture, or a movement that brings at least our subconscious to an alert state and triggers the action required to survive, whether through avoidance, evasion, or engagement.

However, as in the example given at the beginning of this chapter, you may not have the awareness to even know the danger that you face until it's in progress. That lack of awareness, that you have to conquer, might be caused by coming out of a deep sleep, self-induced by alcohol or drugs (legal or otherwise), a concussion or other injury, or illness that dulls the senses, or just trying to get a grip on what is happening to you.

The life-or-death decision starts a blinding flash of clarity, in a process that I term "getting a grip," which can change your state from the haze of confusion to survival at all costs! This change of state hopefully happens before it's too late. When the awareness takes place, action must follow!

As presented at the beginning of this chapter, a life-or-death situation can come at the most unexpected time, with no warning, and from sources that may not make sense.

It took pretty much the entire length of the beating for the victim of the assault to snap out of it and make the life-or-death decision. Possibly, in this case, the alcohol-induced daze may have played in the victim's favor, and maybe even in the attackers' favor.

Why would it have been in the attackers' favor? Think about what might have happened if the victim had not been so impaired? After all, the attackers chose to take on the victim as a group, and only when his defenses were down! One can only imagine why.

In this case, the life-or-death decision was made when seconds counted, and probably a little late. It wasn't just to survive and get away, but to retaliate in kind and then leave the scene, all the while, in a state which could easily be called blind rage, not cognitive reality. Given other circumstances, this would not have been the best choice of actions. This was a state in which the "animal within" leapt out of control and took the offensive and, thank all that is mighty, that no one was killed!

The result of a decision made when seconds count doesn't have to be some violent encounter. It may simply be gathering oneself and perhaps others and getting to safety, or presenting oneself as someone who shouldn't be taken lightly, with a subtle smile and an air of confidence, or walking away before things go south. Whatever the action, it should serve to end the situation, and it must take place quickly.

There is no perfect formula for making a conscious or subconscious decision, when life-or-death is in the balance. True enough, if we spend time training to respond to dangerous circumstances, or even just thinking about courses of action that might be taken, we are programming our responses to make a life-or-death action – when seconds count!

It's not easy for me to write about walking away from a situation that could have ended a lot worse than it did. It dredged up a lot of memories that I'd rather forget! I was home on leave in late 1964, when I went to that party and drank far too much alcohol, and walked out with "friends," or what we call friends when we're 19 or 20 years old.

It took four or five years of nightmares and bubbling fragments of memories to remember. I only really remember going to that house party, being picked up by a friendly police officer who I knew well, and driven home, a mangled mess.

He dropped me off in the driveway, so he wouldn't have to write a report that would have caused me problems with the military, all the while, making sure someone answered the door, and that I got safely in the house.

I remember going to the hospital in the middle of the night with Mom and Dad and hearing the emergency room doctor asking me if I'd been in a big fight, because two other guys were brought in earlier in pretty bad shape. Of course, I said "no," and that I wasn't sure what happened to me, and for those four or five years I really wasn't.

I won't go into a lot of detail about all the damage I suffered. Suffice to say that I had many stitches and some broken bones and certainly a major concussion. All these years later, some of those injuries still come to "visit" me. The next day I was at home in my bedroom and had occasion to see my image in the mirror, at least I thought it was my image, I couldn't really tell, it was like something out of a horror movie!

Over the next few years, I could only assume that I just got the hell beat out of me that night. One evening, I ran into an old friend in a restaurant in San Francisco. He had been at that party back in 1964 and was one of the people who came out as I was leaving on foot. He tried to get me to wait, but I was incoherent and disappeared into the night. He looked for me, but couldn't find me. He filled me in on what had happened, at least as much as he knew. After that chance meeting, I stopped having the nightmares, and my memory started to come back. Now the whole thing is just a vague nightmare.

I learned over time, through training and study, that all of us have that potential to take appropriate action when seconds count, and with maturity came the wisdom to never put myself in that kind of bad situation again.

You must be prepared for the unexpected. Train your spirit, mind, and body to know what to expect from the adrenaline rush that such a situation causes. This is where reality training comes in very handy. You must train to be able to handle yourself in a life-or-death situation.

Be prepared for anything on the streets and be aware of your surroundings. Being aware of your surroundings will prevent you from getting into these kinds of situations to start with, at least most of the time. You must be prepared to handle these life-or-death situations *before* they arise. That is one of the main reasons you train.

Never leave your life up to lady luck! Prepare yourself and be prepared at all times for the unexpected. Never leave your life to the mercy of those on the streets, as they have little mercy to give. When seconds count, you must be prepared ahead of time.

Sr. Grandmaster Casey McPartland is a martial artist with 40 plus years of training and teaching students martial arts from three basic directions: 1 – The Art and its beauty and form, 2 – Sport, with its timing and rules, and 3 – Self-defense in all its ugliness. Over the years, he studied aspects of many martial arts, both classical and contemporary, and now holds a 9th degree black belt and the title Grandmaster in the Gaylord Method Kajukenbo under Senior Grandmaster Pete Morales and the Golden Dragon Ohana.

He has been with Senior Grandmaster Morales for nearly 40 years as a student, head instructor, and chief instructor, and now as spokesman for the Ohana. During his business career he performed as a life and professional coach, and as a management and technical consultant in information technology building and managed large consulting organizations for over 45 years in the industry.

Grandmaster Casey McPartland

Wisdom

10

Loyalty, Integrity and the Grandmaster Pandemic
Al Dacascos and Bohdi Sanders

Loyalty is described in terms that are common across the board. It has the explicit meaning of allegiance, faithfulness, adherence, homage, devotion, steadfastness, staunchness, true heartedness, dependability, reliability, trustworthiness, commitment, and dedication toward those who you claim to be loyal to in life.

These words are stated clearly, leaving no room for confusion or doubt, and are very important in the martial arts world. Do we support one another or run and hide when the going gets tough?

The senior martial artists should be examples and lead the way when it comes to loyalty. They should stand tall, speak up, and be recognized as being loyal to their own instructors, their system, and their dedication to what is right.

What senior martial artists do, affects the future of their students' belief system and the future of the martial arts as a whole. When a senior martial arts master runs from controversies for which he should stand up and confront, that is a sign of poor leadership and cowardice.

Loyalty is not as simple as people think. It is easy to define, but it seems hard for some people to live up to. Our senior martial artists should make loyalty a part of their core beliefs. It is their responsibility to conduct themselves with loyalty and integrity at all time.

How can others respect you if you don't conduct yourself with integrity? Why would you expect others to be loyal to you, if you are not loyal to your instructors or to your students? Martial artists should be the most responsible, most honorable, and most loyal people on this planet. They should do things the right way and not lower their standards, as so many other people do in life.

11

Loyalty is a part of your honor as a man or woman of Budo. True loyalty cannot be bought, although many in today's martial arts world try to buy loyalty by offering belt rank or titles to those who have not earned them.

I am sure that many of you who are reading this have been betrayed by a trusted martial arts friend or instructor, or have been offered a bribe to buy your loyalty in the martial arts world. This should not happen in the martial arts!

In addition, there are others who are fence sitters. These individuals can't seem to decide who they are loyal to. They try to walk the middle of the road at all times, in a vain attempt to please everyone, but end up betraying those who they should be most loyal to.

In other words, they are like sleazy politicians who watch which way the polls are leaning before they decide what they "stand for." They will side with whoever they feel can do the most for them personally. They live for scoring brownie points and are always worried about what the most politically correct move may be. And, in that process, their loyalty blows with the wind, and their integrity is lost.

It only takes a small percentage of martial artists acting without honor, integrity, or loyalty, to give the entire martial arts community a bad name. Less than 10% of an organization can destroy the whole organization, if they are acting maliciously, without loyalty to the organization or integrity in their actions. Your members must have integrity!

Integrity is the quality of being honest and having strong moral principles. It is being morally upright, honest, of good character, ethical, fair, sincere, trustworthy, and genuine in your actions. It takes integrity to be loyal to your instructor or friends. Like honor, integrity must be maintained regularly; it is not something that you can put on and take off like you do your coat. You either conduct yourself with integrity or you don't.

In today's martial arts world, it seems that many have lost their integrity. There is a pandemic of martial artists who are gaining rank and titles by false means. I call this the grandmaster pandemic. It seems that integrity and loyalty have gone out the window for many martial artists.

I am sure that you are familiar with the saying that there are two sides to every coin. Just as there are two sides to every coin, there are also two sides to the martial arts world.

One side maintains itself with character, honor, loyalty, and integrity; the other side is the opposite side of the arts. It is full of greed, pride, deception, deceit, ego, and no loyalty to anyone other than yourself.

This is the dark side of the martial arts world, where martial artists cross promote each other to the title of Grandmaster, where they sell each other rank, where they support each other's lies so their house of cards will not come crashing down when the truth is told. These people are nothing more than paper tigers!

Paper tiger grandmasters promote others to paper tiger grandmasters, like the title alone makes them a great martial artist. This is all about ego. Where did the humility, honesty, and loyalty to our character, integrity, honor, and the martial arts, go? We used to never hear the term "grandmaster," but now it seems that there are grandmasters everywhere you look.

There is a pandemic of paper tiger grandmasters in the martial arts world today. Some people even pay thousands of dollars to obtain this title, instead of focusing on their training. If you buy your rank or title, you have nothing. Martial arts are not about your ego; the martial arts are about training – spirit, mind, and body.

If you are making shady deals for your rank or title, you are only hurting yourself, and deceiving your students and others in the martial arts world. You have disgraced yourself; and you have freely given away your honor.

You have burdened your mind with maintaining your own ego-driven lies. You have weakened your spirit by lowering your character and integrity. In fact, you have completely destroyed your integrity! What honor is there in lying? What honor is there in deceiving others about your martial arts skills or rank?

We both know many martial artists who have lowered their standards to obtain rank and titles in underhanded ways. We have both been personally attacked when we have told the truth about those who live this life of deception. There are so many of these paper tigers in the martial arts world, that it has absolutely become a pandemic.

This may be harsh, but we have news for those of you who traded, cross-promoted yourself, or just plain bought your martial arts title and/or rank – you haven't increased your skills one bit by doing so; all you have done is disgraced yourself and proven that you have no true honor. There are some things you can't buy or trade for; you have to earn them!

Martial arts rank and titles are not things that you are automatically entitled to simply because you want them. You have to put in the time, the effort, and the blood, sweat, and tears. You have to work through the pain and injuries.

The difference between a paper tiger and a real tiger is like night and day. You may think you have gotten away with your little deal, but in the end, you are only fooling yourself. Real martial artists can see right through you, and know that you are not only dishonest, but are, in truth, a joke.

When you get through school by cheating, the only person that you are hurting is yourself. Instead of getting an education, you have nothing but a meaningless grade. Where others learned, gained knowledge and wisdom, and have something that no one can take away from them, you walked away with nothing but meaningless grades and an empty diploma.

The same principle applies in the martial arts. With today's modern technology, and the lack of honor, loyalty, and integrity in the martial arts world, anyone can obtain a fake rank or title, just like any student can cheat in school and get a good grade.

But, just like the cheater in school, you have gained nothing for your effort. Where others have earned legitimate rank, title, and honors, you have nothing but a meaningless piece of paper. You have cheated yourself out of the essence of the martial arts. And not only that, but in the process, you have robbed yourself of your honor and integrity; you have lost your way and proven your disloyalty to the martial arts and to your instructors.

We see the strength of weapons grade steel as the equivalent of real integrity. It is divine and unbreakable, the type of blade that pierces to the bone and defeats your enemy without fail. Integrity is that unbreakable sword in life. It is your defense against the evil in this world and you should never be without it.

When you have loyalty and integrity, you won't lower yourself to the standards of those who are more interested in stroking their ego, than doing the right thing. You won't disgrace yourself by being disloyal to your instructor. You won't lower yourself to lie about your rank or manipulate the system in order to call yourself a grandmaster.

Part of martial arts training is developing your character. Gichin Funakoshi stated that the ultimate goal of martial arts is perfecting your character. He never said it was gaining more rank or manipulating the system in order to call yourself a grandmaster.

In fact, we have never seen anywhere where Master Funakoshi called himself a grandmaster. What arrogance some people have to consider themselves above even the founders of the martial arts systems when they haven't put in the time or the effort!

15

Without integrity, there is no loyalty; without loyalty, there is no integrity. You cannot buy loyalty; you can only buy the appearance of loyalty. If you think you have bought loyalty, see how long that loyalty lasts when you are no longer paying for it. And you certainly cannot buy integrity. Integrity must be developed and maintained; it can never be bought.

There are too many martial artists who are more concerned with appearances than with reality, with rank instead of skill, and with fake titles instead of real, honorable titles, given out of honor and respect. Many times, taking shortcuts only gets you lost. Many martial artists have lost their way. They have been deceived by their own egos and have left the straight and narrow road which leads to true honor, skills, and integrity.

True martial artists should ban together to fight this dishonor which has plagued the martial arts world. We must bring honor, loyalty, integrity, and character back to the martial arts. Don't call yourself a grandmaster, or even a master, if you have not earned the title.

Don't seek rank; seek the perfection of character. Don't seek titles; seek to perfect your martial arts skills. Rank will come when you have the character to earn it; titles will come when you have developed the skills and earned the respect of real martial arts masters.

Look inside yourself. Do you have the right motivation? Why are you training in the martial arts to start with? Are you conducting yourself with character, honor, integrity, loyalty, and respect?

Using Buddha's Noble Eightfold Path is a great way to keep yourself in check. Always strive to make sure you are following each of these eight teachings and you will not allow your ego, or unscrupulous martial artists, to cause you to lose your way. Buddha's Noble Eightfold Path teaches us to follow eight practices that will keep us on the right path. We have applied them to the martial arts here. They are:

1) The Right View: This means seeing things in the right perspective. You must see things as they truly are. Have the right view of the martial arts and what martial arts training is truly all about.

2) The Right Thought: Buddha taught that you are what you think. Your mind determines how you will act and what you will do. You must have the right intentions in order to have the right actions. If your thinking about the martial arts is not right, you will soon find yourself cutting corners and doing things that are not right. Maintain control of your mind!

3) The Right Speech: You should only speak the truth. Don't libel, slander, or gossip. Control your speech and think before you speak. Don't badmouth other martial artists. Don't participate in negative speech about your instructor or fellow students. Don't verbally attack other martial artists out of jealousy or envy. Focus on your own training and behavior.

4) The Right Action: Behave peacefully and stay in harmony with others. Don't be a part of fraudulent or deceitful practices. Do what's right! This means you won't take part in fraudulent practices such as faking your credentials, buying rank, or manipulating the system to obtain titles.

5) The Right Livelihood: Earn a living honestly without illegal or disreputable activities. If you are going to make a living as a martial artist, do so honorably. Don't lower your standards for money.

6) The Right Effort: Put your whole heart into everything you do. Always strive for excellence. Don't look for shortcuts in the martial arts. Obtain your goals by putting in the effort and the work required. Earn your rank!

7) The Right Mindfulness: Keep your emotions and thoughts controlled. Don't allow your mind to control you. If you keep your mind focused on the right things, you will not be controlled by greed, covertness, anger, jealousy, or ignorance.

This means you will not become jealous of other martial artists. You are only competing with yourself. Always keep in mind that you are only trying to be better than the person you were the day before.

8) The Right Concentration: Meditate in order to become what you want as a martial artist. Learn to maintain your focus. Concentrate on your goals and on becoming the kind of martial artist that you can be proud of being. Don't focus on awards and recognition; focus on being the best you can be. Focus on making yourself better, not on thinking you are better.

If you integrate each of the parts of the Noble Eightfold Path into your life, you won't have to worry about becoming a paper tiger; you will always walk in integrity and honor. You will not have to worry about being disloyal, as it will never cross your mind to be disloyal to those who you owe respect and loyalty to in the martial arts. You will not have to worry about letting your ego get the best of you and causing you to desire titles and honors which you have not earned.

Make your objective to perfect your character, not to cater to your ego, and you will become a true martial artist, a martial artist worthy of respect and honor. Never compromise your values or lower your standards.

Always maintain your character, honor, and integrity; stay loyal to those who have helped you along the way. If you do this, you will maintain your peace of mind in the martial arts world which is full of martial artists who have compromised their integrity and given away their honor.

Sifu Al Dacascos, a 9ᵗʰ degree black belt, lives on the island of Oahu, Hawaii. In 1965, he moved to Northern California where he started his first professional martial arts academy in San Leandro, California and there, started to innovate and develop his version of the Kajukenbo system which eventually came to

18

be known internationally as Wun Hop Kuen Do Kung fu. Al Dacascos has been featured on over 200 magazine covers and dozens of martial arts hall of fames.

With his innovation on this art, he has produced many international and national champions that have gone on to become internationally recognized on their own. One of them is his son Mark Dacascos, who became a martial arts action adventure movie star and recently was the nemesis to Keanu Reeves in the franchise movie called John Wick Chapter 3. After retiring from teaching full-time as a professional in 2002, Al Dacascos now lectures and teaches martial arts fight choreography. His book, Legacy: Through the Eyes of a Warrior, published in 2016, became #1 bestseller on Amazon and details his life's journey. Copies of LEGACY: Through the Eyes of the Warrior are available from Amazon at: https://tinyurl.com/LEGACY-Al-Dacascos. Those who would like signed copies of LEGACY can get them directly from Sifu Al Dacascos.

~

Sifu Al Dacascos

Dr. Bohdi Sanders is a multi-award winning and bestselling author of 15 books and 100's of articles, and is an 8-time Martial Arts Hall of Fame inductee. He started training in martial arts in 1984 under Bob and Nikki Allen and now holds the rank of 5th Dan in Shotokan Karate from Shihan William Jackson. Dr. Sanders was awarded the official title of Shihan by Soke Richard Hallman, along with Soke Stephen Barber, Soke-Dai Scot E. Philips, and Renshi Young Author Smith, III.

He has also been awarded the honorary title of Hanshi, (teacher of teachers) for his teachings and writings on the martial arts, by Sifu Al Dacascos, Col. Phil Torres, Grandmaster Eddie Mapula, Shihan Bill Holman, Soke Richard Hallman, Grandmaster Richard Hackworth, Grandmaster Joy Turberville, Grandmaster Terrence Shea, Shihan Dana Abbott, Grandmaster Dan Tosh, Grandmaster Harry Mok, Grandmaster Harry Greene, Grandmaster Dave Johnson, and Grandmaster Eric Lee.

Dr. Sanders has won multiple national book awards for his books. He has written three #1 Bestsellers, and six of his other books have climbed into the Top 10 on Amazon's Best Sellers List. His books have won 1st Place awards from the Indie Excellence Book Awards and the USA Book News Book Awards. In 2011, he was named Inspiration of the Year by the United States Martial Artist Association Hall of Fame. In 2018, Dr. Sanders became one of the first five Westerners elected to the World Martial Arts Congress in Beijing, China. He is also a member of the Golden Dragon Ohana, and the Independent Warriors Association.

He also holds national certifications as a Specialist in Martial Arts Conditioning and as a Certified Fitness Trainer. In addition, he is a Usui-Tibetan Reiki Master and a Master of Acupressure. He has a doctorate in Natural Health and Naturopathy, along with a BA in Sociology and a MA in Education. Dr. Sanders is also a columnist for Taekwondo Times Magazine and has written articles for several magazines and websites. In 2017, Dr. Sanders was inducted into the Elite

Black Belt Hall of Fame and also awarded a Lifetime Achievement Award for his contributions to the martial arts. Dr. Sanders is available for inspirational and motivational public talks and may be reached through his website, www.TheWisdomWarrior.com or through his social media pages.

Shihan Bohdi Sanders

Overcoming Fear on the Mat and in the Streets
Jino Kang

Fear is real! You can feel that sick feeling in your guts. The butterflies churning your stomach into knots. You can feel the moisture building in your palms. Your body and voice start shaking uncontrollably, and your eyes narrow into a tunnel vision. This happens to everyone. It's your body and mind telling you that something is wrong and giving you the "Fight-or-Flight syndrome."

This has happened to me a couple of times in my life, and it really scared me. I couldn't make sense of it. After all, I have trained in martial arts my whole life, since I was four years old.

The first time was in middle school. Our family emigrated from South Korea to the United States when I was ten years old and I didn't speak English at all. One day, out in the courtyard, I was playing ball with some friends and this big bully stole our ball and wouldn't give it back. When I tried to snatch the ball back, he just pushed me down with ease. The kid was hormonally imbalanced and way too big for twelve years old.

Once I was down, he threw the ball away and wanted to fight me. This event alerted the whole school and immediately, I was surrounded by bloodthirsty kids yelling, "Fight!" Kids can be very mean. Before I could react, the bully pushed me down again.

By this time, I felt this weakness overwhelm my entire body and I just wanted to crawl in a hole and let death consume me. But I managed to get up and threw a feeble front kick, which the kid caught and flipped me over.

I don't know what came over me, but I kept on with the weak kicks and the bully kept throwing me to the ground. Each time I was flipped over, the laughter grew, and then something really strange happened. My friends, or those I thought were my friends, were laughing too. Thanks guys! A furious rage erupted inside me and that fear and fright was gone. I was a raving lunatic and started to swing wildly. Luckily for the bully, a giant hand grabbed me from behind. It turned out to be the Dean of the school. I was thankful and ashamed at the same time.

I have reflected on that day many times, and what I have gleaned from that experience, besides knowing my friends weren't really true friends, was that I can summon courage when I need to, but I need to control the fury and not just behave like a wild beast in a fit of rage.

I spoke with my father, a grandmaster in Hapkido, Myung S. Kang, extensively about what transpired and how I felt that day, the fear and rage. He explained that with more control, you can master your body and mind. I asked, "How do I do that?"

He simply said, "Train, spar, and meditate, and you'll understand it someday." Now I do. You can learn the techniques needed to control your fear by training and then applying the techniques by sparring.

The sparring portion of any martial arts class is the closest aspect to real combat. Of course, during sparring session, we are not trying to kill each other, but rather learning from the experience.

In addition, meditation helped me to learn to calm my mind. It also allowed me to clear the doubts I had about my abilities as a martial artist, and gave me the courage to continue to pursue martial arts training to become a better martial artist.

Getting back to sparring, my first school in Concord, CA opened in 1982. We were a fighting school. From the moment we opened, we sparred every single day, several hours at a time. This is when I gained my true confidence against any opponent.

We also had many challenges and I took them all on. I had developed nerves of steel. I won most of the battles and I went searching for schools and opponents who had higher skills. And, if they beat me, I would drill myself on how to win and to defeat their skills, until I could; and then I proved it. There were many nights that I came home with bruises, black eyes, and sometimes, even broken bones. I'm not saying to go out looking for fights, but rather, I am saying to train yourself to be better at actual combat skills, because the confidence that you gain from the continued experience will carry you through your entire life.

Throughout my adult life, there were instances when I was also challenged on the streets. But because of my sheer confidence in my skills, the bullies would sense my abilities and they would back down when they experienced my exuding confidence. The bullies were nothing more than cowards who attempted to prey on the weak.

Real life training grounds vary. I found that the grocery store offered lots of opportunities to test my courage. My father owned a grocery store in San Francisco and I worked there.

There were numerous minor incidents that were almost daily occurrences. One incident that comes to mind was when three thugs were caught stealing merchandise by my father. My father asked me to kick them out. I had asked them to leave, but they were combative, verbally abusive, and non-compliant.

I came around the counter and faced them, and one of them reached out to grab me. I instinctively spun him around by his outstretched arm, took his back, and applied an Okuri-eri jime (sliding collar choke). I moved to the side, brought the captured thug outside, and the other two goons followed.

Now we were outside on the side walk, with plenty of room and where no property could get broken. By this time I could feel the thug was going limp from the choke hold. So I let him go and he slumped to the ground.

The second thug rushed in with a raised fist and cocked his arm back. I chambered my right leg for a side kick. Had the goon

25

continued to lurch forward, he would have felt the bottom of my shoe in his face, but he was quick enough to react, and slid under my leg, falling on his back.

He raised his hands in submission. When I saw the fear in his eyes, instead of stomping on his head, I let him get up. The third raised his hands to signal, "No-Mas." The two goons on the ground got up and the three stooges sprinted away.

Afterwards, I reflected on what had transpired. I had no fear. My action was totally instinctive; I had total control. I was not out of control or in a rage as before. I later asked my father about it and he said that it was "Ki," when your mind, body, and spirit become one.

There was no fear, just pure reaction, not thinking about doing this move or that move, all your reactions just happen without your brain interfering or hampering your movements because you think too much.

I notice when I spar, when I think about what move I'm going to do next, my opponent is already seeing what I'm going to do and will counter my moves. The best outcome in my sparring matches happened when I wasn't thinking, I just was – no thoughts, just being.

Growing up in the city, violence is just part of life. I had numerous, nefarious incidents where I was engaged in unwanted aggressions. There was this time I was in my twenties, I was driving down this street with two of my friends.

Sean and Don (names changed) were in the car when, all of sudden, beer bottles came crashing down on my car. I screeched to a halt and noticed that there were about twenty gang-bangers drinking beer, shouting obscenities, and trash cans were on fire. It was just like a movie scene from *Streets on Fire*.

There was a hoard of guys. I happened to carry a stick in my car for emergencies like this. So I grabbed it and jumped out on the road. Upon seeing me, about half of them split. My odds were improving. My friend, Sean, ran towards the park chasing a few guys. Two goons were charging me, so I ran towards them and landed a flying side kick on one of them and a round house to the gut on the other one.

I grabbed one of them and was about to interrogate him, as he was the only conscious one left. He said, "I didn't throw the bottles, man!" I was about to beat the truth out of him with the stick when my friend, Don, tapped me on my shoulder and pointed to the other side of the street. My friend was on the ground and one guy was beating him with a stick, while the other guy was standing over him with a knife.

I released the thug and sprinted over to my friend who was fighting for his life. Then a strange thing happened, everything seemed to be happening in slow motion. The thug with a knife slashed at me, as I flew into the air, narrowly evading evisceration.

My stick caught the thug squarely on the top of the head. He crashed to the pavement and was out like a light. I turned to the second thug, who looked like a deer caught in oncoming headlights. He dropped the stick, turned, and ran.

I was in the middle of street, and strangely, no cars were around except a rapidly approaching car with red and blue flashing lights on it. I looked over, and the other two goons were gone, and there was just the one guy that I hit, unconscious on the ground. I dropped the stick; and my friend and I dragged him on to the side walk.

A cop finally showed up and I explained what had happened. He said we should go and he would take care of it. The cop also said, "These guys are known as the "Nasty Boys" and they routinely hang out here in this park, causing terror in the neighborhood." The cops routinely chased them out, but they came right back like cockroaches. Several years later, I heard through a friend, that the gang never congregated in that park again.

Most of the time, I can stop a fight before it escalates into a combat situation with my sheer confidence. But that doesn't happen with just class practice alone. You must actively engage in regular sparring sessions. My training in sparring helped me with my confidence and self-assuredness.

Make sure to attend a school that incorporates sparring as a regular training tool. Sure, you'll have bruises and nose bleeds, but that's what makes you tough, and you'll be able to stand up to bullies, to injustices, and you will squash your own fears.

Another time, which I experienced controlling my fear in a real life situation, was after I was submitted by my own student. Of course, it wasn't stand up sparring, but rather Brazilian Jiu-jitsu sparring.

In 2003, I was a 6th Dan Hapkido Master and a black belt in Tae Kwon Do and Kyokoshin-kai Karate. I also studied Judo. One of my black belt students approached me and asked if I was interested in BJJ. I said yes and we sparred in a friendly match. Because of Judo ne-waza (ground techniques) training, I was somewhat familiar with the grappling game.

After a minute or two, I had to tap out, because I was caught in a Kimura (arm lock). Afterwards, my student told me he had been training in Gracie Jiu-jitsu for over a year and invited me to meet his teacher. I swallowed my pride and accepted.

On the day of the meeting, I felt that same uneasy sensation again, clammy hands and body trepidation. I had to stop whatever I was doing and meditate. I have found that you must overcome this fear, no matter what.

The only way to conquer this fear is to face it head on. I needed to take action. I needed to be proactive. Don't procrastinate – do it immediately! I meditated, saying to myself, "I am a badass."

This affirmation was repeated while I was controlling my breaths, slowly and methodically. Suddenly, I had my answer.

Upon meeting, we rolled and needless to say, I was humbled and became a student myself. I had tapped out every minute of the five minute round. After the training session, I had noticed my mind and body was calm and that annoying anxiety was gone.

However, it returned whenever I thought about it, but was gone again during, and after, the session. This repeated on a daily basis. I wrote down every move that was taught, and practiced it with my students. I bought numerous books on the subject and read and practiced what I learned.

I studied YouTube BJJ videos and also bought DVD's from renowned athletes. I was obsessed; I was all in. Little by little, day by day, the anxiety disappeared and by the sixth month, the fear subsided and I had my confidence back. The pecking order had changed! Instead of me being tapped out, I was tapping them out. Of course, it was the higher belts, mind you. In BJJ you truly earn your belt rank.

After several months, the teacher left and I sought out Master Charles Gracie in a nearby school in Daly City. He graciously took me in and I never looked back. Fifteen years later, I have an association and I am now a black belt Professor in BJJ.

Train, spar, meditate, and repeat on a daily basis. This will help you overcome your fear and build self-confidence. This is what I live and breathe by. Don't procrastinate! Do it now! You'll be rewarded with the gift that only true warriors possess. It will bring out the fearless warrior within you.

Jino Kang, is the son of Hapkido Grandmaster Myung S. Kang, and grew up in South Korea during the 1960's, a time when the influence of the Western world was just beginning to emerge.

Grandmaster Myung S. Kang trained under the founder of International Hapkido Federation, Jae Nam Myong. At the age of 4, Jino often found himself waking up on the mat, with his gi on, already dressed by his father. Jino would jump in the class with the black belts, and his father, before everyone went to work. Around this time, the founder, Jae Nam Myong and Myung S. Kang incorporated Aikido (soft and circular) into Hapkido (hard and linear) combining the best of each system into one.

The Kang family immigrated to San Francisco, California in 1971, immersing Jino in a new language and culture. Jino was taught Hapkido in the garage, personally by his father, until Jino was old enough to receive a black belt. While Jino adapted quickly to his new environment, he followed the traditions of his father. He opened his first Korean Martial Arts school in the 1980's. Today, Jino holds a seventh degree black belt in Hapkido and continues to teach at his school Hapkido USA in San Francisco. Jino Kang was inducted into Master's Hall of Fame in 2009.

Jino's quest for never-ending improvement didn't stop at Hapkido, Jino sought out other arts as well. His second achievement was Kyokoshin-Kai Karate with Master Don Buck, and Jino received a black belt only after four months of training. Jino continued to seek improvement in himself, and got his black belt in Tae Kwon Do by training with Master Lee Lawler. After that, he tackled Brazilian Jiu-Jitsu for 15 years with Charles Gracie and received his black belt Professor Degree. Jino continues to train in BJJ until this day and has incorporated BJJ into Hapkido and calling it Hapki-Jitsu. Jino's new challenge is now Judo and Eskrima/Kali.

During the late 1990's, Jino starred in, directed and produced his first feature film, Blade Warrior, shot in glorious 16mm. Blade Warrior was picked up right away and was distributed worldwide. To date, Jino has shot, produced, and acted in Fist 2 Fist, aka Hand 2 Hand. Fist 2 Fist won numerous awards and was critically acclaimed as, "Belongs in the top end of the scale

30

of Martial Arts films," and was released in the USA and Canada on November 15, 2011 and has been released in various parts of Europe and Asia. Jino's latest film, Fist 2: Weapon of Choice won "Action Film of the Year" at the Action on Film International Film Festival in Monrovia, CA in 2014. Weapon of Choice has been distributed in North America and worldwide and continues to thrive and enjoys garnering rave reviews and accolades from film critics throughout the world.

Master Jino Kang

Festival of the Naked in Japan
Bob Allen

In June of 1970, I was released from active duty in Iwakuni, Japan, from the United States Marine Corps. Usually, anyone wanting to live in Japan would have to go back to the United States and apply for the appropriate visa. But I was studying Karate at the Marine Corps Air Station in Iwakuni under Hitoshi Akiyama, who was the Chairman of the Japan Karate Association and was also a multi-millionaire.

When I went to the Japanese immigration board, I qualified for a visa for the following reasons: I had money in the bank, a job teaching English, recommendations from my officer in charge, and the Commanding Officer of the Marine Base, and a letter from Sensei Akiyama.

When the immigration officials saw Mr. Akiyama's financial statements, they were really impressed. Also, I had tested for my Shodan a few weeks earlier and had passed. At first, the immigration officials didn't know what type of visa to issue me, so they ended up giving me a special visa and I ended up living in Japan for five years.

Eventually, I went to live in Saidaiji, Japan, which is on the outskirts of the larger city of Okayama. The Karate club there was at a recreation facility connected to a temple. We worked out every Tuesday, Thursday, and Saturday from 7:00 p.m. to 8:30 p.m. The training was very hard and exhausting, with emphasis on basics and kata.

After I had been there for about four months, I was asked if I wanted to go to a festival. Most of the club, about a hundred students, were going to it. I had no idea of what was in store for me, as no one could really explain what the festival was about.

A few days later, a radio station came to my house to interview me. They asked me if I was excited to be a part of the festival called the Hadaka Matsuri, which, roughly translated, means the

33

"Naked Festival." The Hadaka Matsuri has been celebrated on the third Saturday in February at 10:00 p.m. for over 400 years. I would be the first foreigner to ever participate in this event.

The participants were required to wear "fundoshi," which is a long cloth that is wrapped around the groin area. It is much like what a sumo wrestler wears. It was very tight, and my butt cheeks were exposed. After a while, I got used to wearing it, although, I didn't know that I would be wearing it all day.

Over 5,000 participants paraded through the city on their way to the temple. After being "purified" with cold water thrown on them, the participants gathered in the Saidaiji temple where at 10:00 p.m., a Shinto priest would throw two sacred sticks, "shingi," and a hundred other lucky ones into the crowd of men. It is quite a sight to see, all these men wrestling with each other to get the sacred sticks. All this struggle was to catch good luck for the upcoming year.

Our Karate club was sponsored by a Chinese restaurant. We drank sake and shouted kunpai! Everyone had red tape wrapped around their wrists and ankles, so we could recognize who was in our group.

We lined up outside in the street five abreast. It was about a half mile to the temple and we shouted "washoi" as we came closer. As we came into the temple grounds, there were thousands of spectators cheering. Television cameras turned toward our group, and I found out later, they were filming me and mentioning that I was the first foreigner to participate in the festival.

As we came further into the temple, there was a group of yakuza gangsters. They had tattoos all over their bodies and were shouting obscenities towards our group. All of a sudden, they came rushing at us and started a fight. I think they must have been drunk, because we outnumbered them three to one. All of my club members circled around me because they knew that they were there to attack me.

Even with this protection, and my martial arts skills, I still caught a punch to the face. I fought back and hit one of them and he fell to the ground. My senpai, Kanai, had one yakuza in a headlock, and was punching him in the face.

Two policemen grabbed Kanai and I pushed them away. We got back in our group and quickly continued on into the temple grounds. We made our way to the main temple, and pushed through the mass of bodies. We finally arrived at the base of the temple and started up the large concrete staircase. There were two extremely large pillars holding up the porch ceiling.

Kanai told me to climb up into the rafters, and he came up after me. We were about fifteen feet above the heads of the other men. Kanai explained that when the sticks were thrown out, we would jump on the heads of the other participants to get close to the sticks.

I looked down on the heads of the other participants and realized that there was no way I was jumping down on their heads! I told Kanai that I wanted down, and was helped down by my other club members.

Even though there was snow on the ground, steam was coming off the bodies of the participants. Several of the men were very drunk and could hardly stand up. I stayed with my group because I was a little nervous by this time; no one had told me that it would be this crazy!

All of a sudden, the crowd started yelling and pressing forward to the temple. I saw several sticks flying through the air and about ten seconds later another two came out by themselves. I realized these were the "important" sticks.

I remember getting very close to the sticks because there was a strong aromatic smell emanating from them. One man had his hand wrapped around a stick, but several others had grabbed his arm and wrist so he couldn't let go. They were punching him in the face, but he couldn't let go even if he wanted to.

The crowd swayed back and forth, with me packed in the middle of them like a sardine. Then the crowd started moving quickly in all directions. Our group ran after them, and it was over almost as soon as it had started.

We gathered up our group and headed back to the restaurant, where we started drinking, and everybody had to tell, in his own words, what had happened. I told them that I was amazed, scared, and happy, all at the same time.

One of the students related the story about me saving Kanai from the police, and from that moment on, I was really accepted as a member of the club. We left the restaurant and headed home. Later, as I was soaking in my hot bath, I still couldn't believe what I had just experienced.

I went on a television program a few weeks later. They wanted to know how I felt during the festival. I told them that I was very excited and had never been through anything like that in my life. We had a mini re-enactment of the festival, and I had to wear the fundoshi again.

The experience of the Naked Festival reminded me of the Japanese kanji word "chikara," which was a component for man or male. Thus, strength and power was visualized as the legs of a man "putting his shoulder to the wheel" or straining to move something. This is the kanji that I use for the symbol of my club.

Strength
36

The Hadaka Matsuri was an example of chikara because the extreme number of men fighting and striving for two holy sticks was exemplified in the strength and power exerted in an effort to attain something higher than themselves.

The brotherhood of men striving under extreme pressure, and possible harm, brought out the vital strength of a man. All men, the world over, have chikara in their basic DNA. Not surprising, the kanji character for sword or katana is identical to chikara except for one small stroke on top.

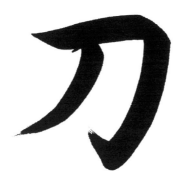

Sword

The reason for putting the kanji on my club's gi is to remind me and my students to become strong – mentally, physically, and spiritually. That is what every true martial artist should strive for in their training. May your martial arts skills be forged with the strength of the katana!

Shihan Bob Allen started Karate in 1966 during his duty in the U.S. Marine Corps, and practiced Shotokan Karate at different duty stations. He eventually moved to the Marine Air Station in Yuma, Arizona and joined a club in town, earning the rank of brown belt in two and a half years, before going to Chu Lai, Viet Nam.

Allen studied Tae Kwon Do with a South Korean 4th degree *black belt who was a staff sergeant named Byung Chul. In a year, he was promoted to red belt. In 1970, he was sent to the Marine Corps Air Station in Iwakuni, Japan and continued his study of Karate at the base until he was released from active duty. The instructor at the base was a 6th degree black belt named Hitoshi Akiyama. He was the Chairman of the Japan Karate Association. With his sponsorship, I was able to receive a Special Visa to remain in Japan.*

When he returned to New Orleans, Louisiana, he started training with Sensei Takayuki Mikami and trained there for twelve years, receiving his 4th degree black belt, and then moved to Monroe, Louisiana and opened his own club in 1975, where he has been teaching for the past 43 years. He also became the instructor and coach of the Northeast Louisiana University Karate Club and which eventually won eight Collegiate National Championships.

He later became Chief Referee for AAU Karate, and was also Chairman of Referees. Later, he became a World Referee with the World Karate Federation, and judged and refereed in several World events. Currently, he is a member and President of the Traditional Karate Federation. He received his 8th degree black belt in 2006. Bob was National Champion in Kumite several times and has taught over 400 national champions.

Shihan Bob Allen

Training to Win
Eddie Mapula

As a three-time world champion in both kickboxing and Karate, I can tell you a few things about training to win. It takes a lot of focus. You have to be very disciplined. Your training will not be on Tuesday and Thursday night. You will have to train every single day. You will also have to train with the mindset of winning.

If you know what you want, you have to go for it. If you just want to learn martial arts or self-defense, you can train every other day or 2-3 times a week. But to become a champion, to truly be great, you must train every day.

The warrior is always training to one extent or another. He takes his training seriously. It is not a chore, but becomes who he is deep down inside.

When you train to win, you must aim to master your skills inside and out. You must train your mind first and then your body. You must train to discipline and motivate yourself. I started training at a young age, but I had to learn to motivate myself, to discipline myself to work out every day. Competing helped me create the mindset of a winner.

It takes maturity to discipline yourself. Too many people in the martial arts are immature. They want to have the skills without working for them. It is like wanting to have the muscles of a bodybuilder without being willing to lift weights. It doesn't work that way. This is where discipline comes into play.

You will not always be motivated; you must learn to be disciplined. My motivation comes from my desire to be extraordinary in both my mind and body. I strive to achieve perfect health, strength, maturity, wisdom, and learning. Even now, I am constantly striving to improve myself. The attitude of winning is a lifestyle, not something you only do every now and then.

You must aim for developing the perfect attitude, keeping your mind focused. Discipline yourself! That is the most important thing when it comes to your training. Without the right attitude, you will fail before you even get started. With the right attitude, you can maintain your discipline and motivation to continue to formulate different combinations.

I have designed a formula for training by knowing from the beginning who I really am. You need to be present and aware. Know yourself and understand yourself, otherwise you will become like everyone else. You must develop the desire to be the best and maintain that desire throughout your training.

Your will is very important. You must have the will to continue and never give up. You always need to keep in mind what you are doing and why you are doing it. Be willing to work 10 times harder than everyone else. Strive to be smarter than all the other guys. Train smarter. Work harder. And keep a good attitude. Always be positive about what you are doing and why you are doing it. Maintaining a positive attitude is so powerful!

There is a big difference between training to win and just training like everyone else. You must be real. Don't lie to yourself. Don't take short cuts. Do the work for real. Always be real no matter what. Be honest with yourself about where you are and your skills. That is how you become a real champion.

When I was competing, I trained three times a day, for a total of six hours each day. I would run several miles in the morning. During the mid-day, I would work on my techniques and general exercises. In the afternoon or night, I would spar either in kickboxing or boxing. Training was always on my mind, as was winning. When you train to win, you must stay focused.

Life is being the very best you can be, both in the mind and body. You will find it both motivational and educational to help others improve themselves and be better. I find that it motivates me to help others create an extraordinary life, to teach them to be the best that they can be. The more you motivate others, the more you will motivate yourself.

If you want to become a professional fighter, you must train with the mindset of winning. You have to be mature, dedicated, disciplined, and totally committed. I would say do not use any drugs or alcohol. Find a good coach or instructor and listen to him, whether you think he is right or wrong. Listen! That is what you pay him for.

If you find that he is wrong, then leave and find someone else to train you. But do not stay with a coach and then refuse to listen to him. That is a recipe for failure. Find the right instructor and stay with him. When you follow the right instructor, that will lead to success.

I enrolled in a Karate studio affiliated with Chuck Norris Tang Soo Do. Mr. Norris started to pay attention to me when I was winning Karate tournaments. Soon I became a Karate champion, and later a grand champion. My team defeated Chuck Norris' undefeated team. I was the youngest captain ever for my team.

Later, in the 70's, Mr. Norris invited me to his home in Palos Alto, CA. We trained together working on kicks with focus pads. The training was very simple. You must perfect the basics. A good foundation will serve you well. I was very honored and content that Mr. Norris shared his time with me. It always helps to train with other champions. Working with the best instructors you can will help you fine tune your skills.

If you are serious about training to win, you must be serious about improving your diet as well. Good nutrition is a very important factor for both your body and your mind. You will find that you have a very hard time staying motivated if you are not feeding your mind and body good nutrition. The right diet gives you the energy and the strength that you need to continue with rigorous training. It also helps you maintain your mental focus, which is vital because without good mental focus, you will become undisciplined.

In addition, I would highly recommend that you incorporate meditation into your training. Relax, breathe, and ask for what you want and what you need. Focus on a positive, powerful mindset to overcome any obstacles. It will be difficult at first, but with practice it will become something you thoroughly enjoy. My meditation is so easy and clear now that it comes naturally.

Once you start training to win, you can easily transfer your training from the ring to self-defense. The mindset for me is the same. You hear people saying that training to fight in the streets is different than training for competition. That is because those people do not take the training for competition seriously. They do not train to win.

When you truly train to win, the mindset is the same, even when there are rules in the ring and not in the street. You must make it the same or you will confuse yourself. You just need to know how to connect your art with your mind. Once you do, it becomes the same.

Training to win means always working to improve yourself. Know the difference between right and wrong, be mature, be positive, and create a positive story for your life. That is my philosophy of life. You must live your life with honor, integrity, respect, loyalty, and a code of ethics.

If you do this, you will be a winner both inside and outside of the ring. You will be a competitor only for a short while, but when you train to win, you will be able to take those qualities with you in whatever you do with your life. Train to win and create your life as you should.

GM Eddie Mapula has been studying martial arts since he was a teenager, with John Robertson and Raul Hernandez. He is a

3-time World Kickboxing/Karate champion. He has trained with Pat Johnson, Chuck Norris, and Howard Jackson as well. He is the founder of the U.K.B.A.F., The United Kick Boxing Arts Federation and the United Boxing Arts Federation U.B.A.F. In addition, he is a 7-time martial arts hall of fame inductee in both the United States and Mexico.

Eddie created his formula with street fighting, Karate, boxing, Kickboxing, Muay Thai, and wrestling. He became the first founder of Black Belt Development in U.K.B.A.F. (United Kick Boxing Arts Federation,) and U.B.A.F. (United Boxing Arts Federation) in the world. Eddie is available for teaching, training, and fitness training in the San Diego area. Eddie can be reached at: <u>EddieMapula.com</u>.

Grandmaster Eddie Mapula

The Hidden Code of Martial Science
Rick Moneymaker and Michael Patrick

Since the earliest times of mankind's tumultuous existence, warriors have sought to increase the effectiveness of their combative arts. As advances in the culture's understanding of the human body increased, so too did their ability to attack its weaknesses.

With the discovery of Traditional Chinese Medicine and acupuncture, the correlation of attacking the same targets of the body matured into a martial science. Acupuncture is believed to have been discovered after warriors were wounded in battle and then seemingly, miraculously healed of long, chronic conditions after recovery.

Over time, it was discovered that the specific location of the injury, and the degree of injury, could be lessened until only a small needle prick was enough to a precise target to get the same result. Thus, the needle replaced the spear. In parallel, advances in the arts of acupressure were advanced allowing the practitioner to bring healing with only a touch.

As this medical knowledge was applied to healing, the antithesis was revealed as well. What heals can also inflict injury and even death! The same points that brought healing could be manipulated in such a manner as to render someone unconscious, to destroy limbs, and even render death. The overarching difference was in the type and level of stimulus, along with the application of other sciences, and defining the sequence of blows. Even a blunt strike could do the same.

Over the centuries, this knowledge was collected in secret warrior texts and further hidden in martial arts forms. With the passage of time, sadly, much of this knowledge was lost to antiquity, until a fortuitous visit by an Okinawan master to the United States changed all of that. His name was Taika Seiyu Oyata. The old arts were about to get new life!

Professors Tom Muncy and Rick Moneymaker happened upon a training session with Master Oyata and experienced firsthand his seemingly superhuman ability to render a person unconscious with merely a slight tap. This was unheard of in present day martial arts. But, how was he able to do this? How did it work?

Master Oyata was very forthright in explaining that he did not know how it worked and only knew the techniques he had learned from his family art. The science was missing to explain the techniques, which seriously hindered the ability to advance the art. A paradigm was needed, but none was in sight.

After developing a close and personal relationship with the master, Muncy and Moneymaker buried themselves in researching the "why it works" aspect of the martial arts. An answer must be found so they could apply the newfound knowledge to their arts and others. If this could be documented, more of the lost combative arts could be resurrected, picking up where ancient warriors left off.

They knew they must crack the hidden code of martial science which had been dormant for eons. To break such an old code required immersing themselves in the minds of their predecessors and becoming experts of the medical sciences of their day, Traditional Chinese Medicine. They would have to become expert laymen in acupuncture.

Acupuncture had spread from mainland China to other continents of the world and influenced, not only the medical sciences, but the martial arts as well. Japanese, Korean, Indian, and other people had benefited from its contributions. Many of these people were martial artists wanting to incorporate the teachings into their art forms.

After a few years of hard research into these lost arts, Professors Muncy and Moneymaker met up with Michael Patrick, who has continued their research along with the other DSI instructors. Professor Patrick immediately immersed himself into the

Eastern sciences and began the arduous task of documenting what had been discovered, online, in books, and videos. His technical and graphic arts backgrounds, along with a dedication to martial arts, was a perfect fit. Together, the men toured the world sharing the discovered martial science of Torite Jutsu.

The foundation of these sciences were the Five Elements and the Yin/Yang Theory which describe how energy, known as Qi (also known as Chi or Ki) flows through the body and how it can be manipulated for either improving one's health or to its harm. Qi is the combination of food, thought, breath, and blood that results in the energy used by the body to sustain activity. It is an invisible force that can only be felt and not seen.

We know that the body is fueled by bio-electrical energy. Since energy has both a negative and a positive polarity to its charge, this comprises the Yin and Yang. As it is energy, it can be manipulated. This is what systems such as acupuncture, shiatsu, reflexology, and even martial arts attempt to do. Any time the energy is blocked, weakened, super-charged, etc., illness, disability, and even death can occur.

The Yin and Yang Correspondences of the Body

Each of the organs and bowels (Zhang and Fu) of the body, are linked with either Yin or Yang. The Yin organs are the Heart, Pericardium, Lung, Liver, Kidney, and Spleen; the Yang bowels are the Small Intestine, Triple Burner, Large Intestine, Gallbladder, Bladder, and Stomach.

The energy flows through channels known as meridians. Meridians may be compared to blood vessels which route blood through the body. Likewise, meridians route energy. These meridians are interconnected and each is responsible for routing the Qi from its source organ or bowel and into the next meridian in a sequence.

The Qi that flows through each of the meridians provides the energy for its paired organ or bowel that allows it to function. If

49

this energy were to not flow properly, disease or death would be the result. This circuit is referred to as the Diurnal Cycle and is also known as the Horary Rhythm. The proper sequence of the Diurnal Cycle is: Lung → Large Intestine → Stomach → Spleen → Heart → Small Intestine → Bladder → Kidney → Pericardium → Triple Warmer → Gall Bladder → Liver → Lung (completing the cycle).

Once the energy exits the Liver meridian, it will return to the Lung meridian, and the process starts all over. This flow of energy will take 24 hours to complete. Please note that there is always energy flowing through each of the meridians, and not only at the specific times. The specified times are when the energy peaks in each of the respective meridians. The energy will be highest in each of the meridians for approximately two hours, at various times of the day.

Pressure Points on the Front of the Body

Meridians course throughout the body, and their depth varies greatly. In certain areas of the body, the meridian is superficial, while at other points, it is deeper. There are also eight extraordinary meridians. The two most common ones are the Conception Vessel and the Governing Vessel. These two run down the centerline of the body. As such, they are not bilateral as the other 12 meridians are.

The primary role of the extraordinary vessels is to regulate the flow of energy within the body. When a meridian is in excess, it is able to drain the excess off into one of the connected extraordinary vessels. Likewise, if a meridian is deficient, it may receive the necessary energy from one of the extraordinary vessels. In this sense, these may be likened to reservoirs of energy or reserves.

In addition to the two above cited extraordinary vessels, there are six others. These are the Yin Linking Vessel, Yang Linking Vessel, Yin Motility Vessel, Yang Motility Vessel, the Girdle Vessel, and Penetrating Vessel.

There are a lot of misconceptions and bad information out there about what a pressure point is and what it is not. Basically speaking, a pressure point is a region where the meridian comes close enough to the skin to be manipulated by a needle, pressure, or a strike.

This is the reason that you see depths given in acupuncture books relating how deep to insert the needle. Pressure points are most often not related to nerves, although at times, they do overlap. However, there is not ample information available to suggest that the effects of pressure point strikes can be explained via the nervous system.

To make identification of the points easier, the pressure points are named for the meridian on which they lie. The points are numbered from "1" being the first point, and so on, to the end of the meridian. There are varying numbers of points on each of the meridians.

Pressure points are located all over the body. There are over 700 points on the body. Most of these points are bilateral, appearing on both sides of the body, with the exception of the mid-line points along the Conception and Governing Vessels.

While there are all of these points available on the body, they are not all created equally, as related to the martial arts. We have found that some simply work better than others for fighting.

The points work best when struck at the proper angle and direction. The really good pressure point charts, such as those available from the Dragon Society International, show the proper angle of attack. It is important to note that the points will still respond at other angles, but this is the optimal angle to attack them.

Most points are struck at a 15°, 45° or 90° angle. Determining the direction from which to strike the point at the prescribed angle is more challenging. Basically, it depends on the anatomy of the region and whether you are trying to increase the energy within the meridian or decrease its flow.

Some points will naturally respond better to a rub, pressure, or a strike. Please note that the points will respond to any of the three. There are few, if any, points that will not respond to a strike, but there are points that will respond to only pressure or a rub.

To determine the direction of the flow of energy through the meridian, just look at the direction in which the numbers of the pressure points increase in number. That is the direction in which the energy is said to flow.

It is important, in the application of martial science, to have a fairly high degree of accuracy when manipulating the points. Fortunately, the striking surface we employ is often large enough to make up for the level of accuracy required.

For instance, a strike with the two knuckles of the fist will often overlay more than one point in a cluster of points. Even though this is true, it is still necessary to regularly practice the art to maintain the level of skill necessary to be an expert practitioner.

Each of the meridians are assigned to an element. The Heart, Pericardium, Small Intestine, and Triple Burner are associated with Fire, Lung and Large Intestine are Metal, Gall Bladder and Liver are Wood, Spleen and Stomach are Earth, and Kidney and Bladder are Water. This is important to understand, as there are systems to describe how each interacts with one another.

The points are often struck in particular sequences. The most common sequence utilized is known as the Destructive Cycle and describes how various elements have a controlling or adverse effect upon one another. The sequence is Fire burns Metal, Metal cuts Wood, Wood penetrates Earth, Earth contains Water, and Water extinguishes Fire. From there, the sequence begins again.

Five Element Theory Symbol showing the Constructive Cycle (outside circle) and the Destructive Cycle (inner circuit)

There is also a Constructive Cycle which describes how elements are able to nurture or strengthen one another. This is described as Wood creates Fire, Fire creates Earth, Earth creates Metal, Metal creates Water, and Water creates Wood. This cycle can be manipulated as well to produce harmful effects by creating an overabundance of energy in an organ or bowel or to back feed the system in advanced dim mak or "death touch" training.

Of course, this is only a brief introduction to the sciences taught by Dragon Society International, but it does give some insight into the underlying sciences. As time continued its perpetual march onward, however, many of these advances became lost to the newer generations.

Techniques were being taught without the explanations of where and why they were included in the forms. As a result, the

53

secrets were buried within the forms, waiting for someone to find them again. The continual degradation has continued into the modern era, with few martial arts practitioners even knowing the deeper aspects of their arts ever even existed!

Investing countless hours of deep and difficult research into TCM, Professors Muncy and Moneymaker, began to recognize the targets of the master's strikes. Furthermore, they even began to realize the sequencing of the blows were integral to their effectiveness. Finally, the code was beginning to be cracked, and a new era in martial arts about to begin! As the dust of antiquity began to release its grip, the arts took on new life.

With a renewed vigor for research empowering them onward, they began to identify more and more of the "why" the arts were designed as they were.

Not only that, but the effectiveness of the techniques soared to new levels as they applied their new findings! This was a new genesis in growth for, not only their arts, but all martial arts. Martial science was born!

While training with the old master as much as they were able, they continued to refine the basis of the techniques and perfect their system. Not only that, but they began to see patterns and subtle nuances in the techniques that made them really work.

These became known as "Players to the Game" for lack of a better term. These were identified across numerous systems from all over the globe, although many current practitioners do not even know of their existence or practice them today.

Now, with over three decades of traveling the world and forming their own martial arts organization to continue the research they started, the Dragon Society International is doing just that. The martial explosion they ignited has grown to levels no one ever expected all those years ago. Certified instructors continue to document and identify the martial science "Players to the Game" to levels previous generations never knew.

Imagine if the warriors of old time could see where things have evolved now! Over two hundred "Players" have been identified in the time since this research began, and it is nowhere near complete.

Much work remains to be done. While others are practicing the same techniques and forms over and over, devoid of the deeper understanding required to make their systems work, the DSI continues to lead the way just as it has always done. The rebirth of the martial sciences will continue as long as martial artists like the DSI continue to lead the research and share what they have discovered.

Grandmaster Rick Moneymaker has earned the "Man of the Year Award" presented by the World Martial Arts Hall of Fame, and has been recognized by the International Society of Headfounders/Headfamilies as a 9th degree black belt and Soke of Torite Jutsu, awarded the Golden Lifetime Achievement Award, and the Meijin Award presented by the directors of the International Shurite Yudansha-Kai. He has been inducted into the International Karate and Kickboxing Hall of Fame and inducted in Combat Magazines Hall of Fame.

Rick Moneymaker is also a high dan board member of the AKBBA and has appeared in five nationally published magazines and five international magazines. Grandmaster Moneymaker has taught on the international seminar circuit for over 30 years. During his competition career, he won 25 Black Belt Heavy Weight Championships and one Grand Championship. He has had the honor of instructing numerous members of the military, police and private security officers for over 30 years. Professor Moneymaker is available to teach seminars on a variety of martial arts topics and his Masters Series seminars are world-renown. You can contact him via the internet at www.DragonSociety.com.

Grandmaster Rick Moneymaker

Grandmaster Mike Patrick has a diverse background in both practical reality-based personal defense, firearms, law enforcement, and martial arts. He has taught internationally at seminars and conventions, taught online training, published books, and produced DVDs. He has been recognized by both the World Martial Arts Hall of Fame, as well as the United Karate Systems of America Hall of Fame for his accomplishments in the martial arts and was inducted as "Instructor of the Year."

He founded his own defensive tactics system called Personal Defense Tactics which he has taught to individuals of all ages and abilities. This system eventually evolved into a more robust system through his partnership with Rick Moneymaker. Together, they developed a new system, known as CombatiX™ which is the practical application of their many years of experience in testing what works in real world environments aided by his background in Law Enforcement. These techniques have been taught to and studied by individuals from a number of law enforcement agencies and military groups.

His videos and books have gone throughout the world and thousands of students have been enriched by his efforts. Mike Patrick is available for seminar instruction and is willing to travel anywhere in the world to share his expertise. He would love to speak with you and help you and/or your students or officers to continue your training and take it to a new level. You can contact him at www.DragonSociety.com.

Grandmaster Mike Patrick

Strategy versus Skill:
What Kata Teaches Us
David Hansen

There is a vast difference between strategy and skill. Strategy is how we will accomplish a particular task, directly or indirectly. Strategy is a skill in and of itself, but different from your actual martial arts skills. Strategy can be very simple or complex. Martial strategy can correlate to civilian problem solving. For example, if given no way out, this is the action of No Karate Sente Nashi, the first strike. Hesitation will get you killed.

How you perceive your surroundings will give you a basic strategy. I've never been one to wait. Hurry up and wait was part of being a Marine. I hated it, but it might have been one of my best lessons as a Marine. I'm never late, ever.

Tanden is a word that not many use anymore. Tanden, or hara (腹), is your center, located around two inches below your navel. If you take two lines, the intersection will be tanden. Your tanden will always be moving or flowing. Your centerline will be equal to your tanden going up and down the body.

If you look at a kihon, known as crescent stepping, you're starting the journey of strategy called body shifting. This type of movement, or crescent, will move your tanden off your centerline, left or right, depending which step you use. Even the slightest movement off centerline can have a dramatic effect.

How can you tell if the learner is performing this type movement correctly? Someone with experience will notice the movement of tanden. For those who get "kung-fused" on tanden, you can also watch the Obi knot for movement. This could be a huge advantage when strategy comes into play. You can't move in any direction without moving your Obi knot.

Secrets are information not shared openly. You just got one. Use it and master it. Share with those you deem worthy. I'm giving you good solid strategy that has taken me a lifetime to grasp. We are going deeper now into the realm of strategy.

Embusen is something that's rarely taught anymore, but is vital in strategy. Embusen (演武線) is a Japanese term used in Karate to refer to the spot where a kata begins, as well as its line of movement. Though it is not stressed in Okinawa, nearly all Japanese-influenced kata start and end on exactly the same embusen point (Kiten). Embusen is critical in proper distance and position. Without embusen, your correctness is not on the mark.

Distance and position will decide the outcome. If you're thinking, "That's some good information. How can I learn it?" There is something of a misconception about what I am going to teach you.

Remember your kata. Each kata has an embusen that will start and complete at the same spot. If you cannot finish very close to where you started, you must continue to practice the footwork until you do. Every kata you practice should finish within inches from where it started.

This proves proper distance and position, or strategy. It takes the guessing out of the equation, when you fully understand the conceptual learning of kata. In order to grasp the meaning within these templates, you must practice beyond solo practice. You must go back to the beginning, to two person drills.

Some of you may be wondering about fighting. Well, I'm not a fighter preparing for my next fight. I'm known as a practitioner. I practice the Big 3 – Kihon, Kata, and Kumite. Let's travel deeper into the strategy and conceptual learning. Most seasoned sensei do know that every kata has its own strategy, concepts, embusen, etc.

Long before me, the masters before me knew of this, because someone created it. How can we practice strategy and techniques that could result in maiming, or worse, without hurting anyone or being hurt? How can we practice our techniques without anyone seeing our strategy? The answer is by practicing kata, by practicing them in such a way that the actual meaning, or bunkai, is hidden.

Eventually, if practiced enough, you will see what others do not. Let me explain. With enough study and understanding, your knowledge of movement will expand. What some may see as a technique, you will see as multiple techniques with strategy, offline, tanden, distance, etc. This is a huge difference between a white belt and a black belt, depending on age and instruction, of course.

As you approach Yudansha, the rank of black belt, you understand that this is actually the beginning of true understanding. You are about to reach the mountain top. But as you look around from the top of the mountain, you see you've only climbed the *first* of many more to come. I view my daily life as one big kata. Always thinking on how to improve and becoming better than the day before.

In order for bunkai to become comprehendible, you must see and feel how these sequences correlate to one another. I have always preferred going to the outside, or offline. This gives me an advantage of superior position. The strategy found in each kata may have numerous templates. For each movement, you should have three variations. One bunkai leaves you highly limited; more than three will slow your thought process down.

Three has always been such a unique number within Okinawan culture. Your strategy should include transitional movements as well. It's what holds all the sequences together. Basic strategy can go a long way. A very silly bunkai is far better than none at all. As the sensei, it's up to you to guide your students, without actually explaining every step to them.

Here, I want to explain my definition of Karate. Yes, it does mean "Empty hand," however, the word "empty" can be viewed in different ways. I do not view "empty" as your hands "are empty with nothing in them." The word "empty," to me, means your hands are moving without conscious thought, as if they are empty.

Any martial strategy will attempt to gain an advantage of position. Your striking distance can only be as far as your weapons can reach. Strategy is pre-emptive, and, at times, will take form quickly without notice.

Skill, on the other hand, differs greatly from strategy. Skill cannot be bought; it must be earned or developed. There are some commonalities between strategy and skill. Skill puts your strategy into action, when needed. Knowledge gained through experience equals skill.

I'm going to share with you one of the most important skills – relaxation when under duress. It is easier said than done. While in the Marines, we did a lot of rehearsing on what your job will be during a particular mission. This rehearsing was done over and over again, until it became automatic.

Within Karate and Kobudo, the weapon systems of Okinawan martial arts, we have rehearsing as well. We take several sequences and put them all together to develop a kata. These kata will give you a skill set that is proportionate to your time spent learning.

Kumite is putting what you have learned into action against another practitioner. The more experience you have, the more confidence you have. This gives you the ability to relax and allow your knowledge and experience to surface.

Skill can be viewed as knowing what to do at the right time. If you have to think about how to react, you will become too slow or a step or two behind. Your actions, or reactions, must become instinctive, without conscious thought.

Can skill be taught? Of course, but it must be sharpened, and kept sharp. I prefer to use kata to keep my skill sets sharp. I use a complete system of both Karate and Kobudo. Each one has its own skill set. Each one different, with different sequences and/or scenarios. You should always go deeper within each kata.

I'm not a kata collector. The founders have already taken the guess work out of kata for us. In years past, some of the most experienced masters from Okinawa knew perhaps only three kata. They believed each kata was a system within itself.

Skill is not how many kumite matches you've won; skill is the knowledge and experience that have given you the tools for survival. Skill in the vast universe called life. It's not how many techniques you know, but how many you have mastered.

The ones that continue training throughout their lifetime, may have a large toolbox of skills, however, they may use but a couple of them, most of the time. Think about the tools you use most of the time, a flathead screwdriver, a Philips head screwdriver, and a hammer. Get it? My strategy is simple – to use my skills for protection of others and myself, within One Heart Way.

Kyoshi David Hansen started Karate at age 14 with Roger Carpenter Sensei. He joined the United States Marine Corps right out of high school and served as a combat engineer and 0352 TOW Gunner. He spent several years in Okinawa studying martial arts from various martial arts masters.

Later he trained under Steve Young Hanshi and served on the Executive Board for the AOKA. He is the head instructor at Hansen's House of Isshin-Ryu. He has taught seminars serious practitioners from Puerto Rico, the United States, and Canada. He is presently a lifetime member of the United States Isshin-Ryu Karate Association under the leadership of Phil Little Hanshi.

Kyoshi David Hansen

Simplifying Your Martial Arts
Bohdi Sanders

I no longer train to test for belt rank or to learn fancy, cool looking techniques. I train to keep my family, those around me, and myself safe. In short, I train for self-defense. Yes, I still respect traditional martial arts and I still do katas and train with traditional martial artists from time to time, but my main focus is on training for when the wolf attacks.

When you find yourself in a real life-or-death situation, all the high kicks, complicated techniques, and fancy, cool looking moves are pretty much worthless. If you have ever been in a serious fight, then you know exactly what I mean. At that time, everything boils down to your down and dirty self-defense training. This is why I am a big advocate for simplifying your martial arts.

One of my Shotokan instructors used to call out about eight different techniques, as fast as he could, using Japanese terms, for us to practice all at once. The vast majority of the people in the class could not get them right or could not remember what they were supposed to do after the third or fourth move. I always thought that this was kind of a silly exercise, but he was the sensei.

To me, this is a fairly worthless training method, especially for self-defense training. Don't get me wrong, practicing a prescribed set of techniques is not necessarily a bad thing for self-defense training – if they are practical and useful for a fight.

For example, if you kick a guy in the groin, we all know that there is an automatic reflex that we can expect from that guy. He is going to bend forward and grab his groin. You can see this autonomic reflex even if you simply feint a kick to the groin. It is a natural response, just like you will blink if a mosquito flies into your eye.

There are many examples like this. If you throw a kick into the side of someone's knee, you have a pretty good idea of how he is going to react. The same goes for breaking his collar bone, breaking his ankle, his elbow, striking him in the throat, the eyes, etc. We know how people will react to these kicks or strikes, thus we can develop a follow-up strike(s) or kick(s) for each of those.

This is not the same as simply practicing a bunch of random kicks and punches in class. Of course, practicing those kicks and punches do help us develop our "muscle memory" and ingrains them into our subconscious. That is why we practice kicks, punches, and blocks over and over again. But that is not the same as practicing a set of kicks and strikes in a specific, prescribed manner that we know we can expect in a fight.

Here is an example of this kind of training. If you throw a front kick to a man's groin, as I stated above, he will automatically bend over and grab his groin. There are several follow-up moves you can practice for the position he will then be in. You could follow up with a forearm strike across the back of the neck. Or you could throw a front kick or a knee to the face. Or, while he is bent over, you could break his ankle with a side kick, etc.

The variations of this kind of practicing are virtually endless. This is simplifying your martial arts for practical self-defense applications. Of course, I cannot go through each and every sequence with you in this short chapter, but you get the idea of what I am talking about. You can develop your own sequences that are customized for your own strengths and weaknesses.

The key is to focus on vulnerable targets when you are training in this way. You don't want to practice striking targets of no value. When you are in a serious fight, you want to end it as quickly as possible, with few or no injuries to yourself. Take some time to list the most vulnerable targets on the human body; there are many. The human body is very easy to break, injure, or destroy, if you know your anatomy.

66

List those targets, list the kicks and strikes which you would use on those targets, and then develop your own practice sequences. This can be done in solo practice, but, as with all self-defense practices, it is better if you have a partner.

I must caution you here; this kind of practice *must* be done very carefully, and in slow motion. We are targeting very fragile, easily broken targets, and serious injuries can occur if you are not controlled and careful. Practice these moves even slower than you would when you are practicing joint locks, at least until you have become very proficient at them.

You are practicing for a serious self-defense situation. This being said, use what you are comfortable using when you are setting up your sequences. Don't get fancy! This training is meant to end a fight quickly, period! You are breaking and destroying the attacker's body in order to put him out of commission and render him no longer a threat to you or those around you. Practice that way!

If you are not comfortable with a certain kick or punch, then don't use it when you are practicing your self-defense sequences, at least not until you get comfortable with it. You can look at this kind of practice as your bread and butter techniques.

Of course, you can continue to practice your traditional martial arts and all the fancy kicks and moves. You can continue to do katas, breaking, what have you. This is simply your down and dirty, destroy your attacker, practice. This is simplifying your martial arts down to just plain fight-ending, body destroying techniques, which will provide your attacker with a nice long vacation in the local hospital, or if necessary, a permanent stay in a custom made box.

Are these techniques brutal? Yes, they are. Fighting is a serious business. It is not playing around, pushing, and shoving, or sparring at some tournament. It is not a sport, and it is not to be taken lightly. Every time you get into a fight, there is a real possibility that someone is going to die. That is just a fact.

Even if you only throw one punch, which would not lead to any serious injury, the guy could fall down, hit his head on something and die. This has happened many times to people who found themselves in some stupid fight over nothing important. One guy lands a good punch, the other guy falls, hitting his neck on a turned over bar stool, a chair, a step, etc., and is paralyzed or dies from this freak accident. But the courts will not see it as an accident, but as manslaughter or something along those lines.

I cannot emphasize enough, the importance of never fighting unless you have no other option! Always try to de-escalate the situation. Walk away whenever you can. Don't let your ego cause you major hassles. We live in a time when our justice system looks down on violence, even if you are defending yourself. Never put your life in the hands of the justice system if you don't absolutely have to!

The techniques I am referring to here, and the sequences that I have urged you to practice, are for serious, life-threatening situations only. But, if you find yourself in such a situation, you must know how to respond and respond in a simple, but effective way. That is what simplifying your martial arts is all about.

Many of these techniques can be deadly; others are crippling. Too many times, martial arts instructors do not emphasize how deadly some of the techniques that they teach truly are. And, many instructors no longer teach these techniques, either because they never learned them or because they are afraid of getting sued.

Martial arts were never meant to be a sport or a hobby for kids. They were meant to teach people how to defend themselves from vicious, life-threatening attacks. The martial arts world has moved away from its core, from its true purpose. It has become more about money and sports than about teaching people how to save their own life, if they ever find themselves in that position.

When you are attacked in the street, in a bar, or wherever, your body produces a release of chemicals, hormones and adrenaline, which sends your body into the fight-or-flight response.

You must practice to learn to control yourself when this happens. In order to do this, you must practice a reality based martial art. This training helps you understand this response and what happens to your body during a brutal attack.

All of the training in the world will not save you if you panic during the attack. You must know your techniques well enough that you don't have to think about them. Trying to use complicated techniques will only make things worse for you. You must simplify your martial arts and have an arsenal of basic, fight-stopping techniques that you can use automatically.

Think about this. When you drive your car, after you have been driving for 20-30 years, you don't have to think about how to turn, put on your turn signal, when to brake, etc. It is natural because you have done all of that thousands and thousands of times.

The martial arts techniques that you use for self-defense must get to that point. When you get to that point, you will enter the state of Mushin during the fight, where you don't have to think about what to do.

You must practice these techniques and these sequences to the point that you no longer have to think about them. When you get to this point, if you throw a front kick to the groin, you will no longer have to think about how you will follow that kick up. Your next move will flow naturally, and the next, and the next. This is simplifying your martial arts for self-defense.

You can find posters and diagrams in many places which will

point out the vital targets of the body. Get one and design your self-defense targets. Then design your sequences. Know which targets will disable and which will kill. Know these targets and these techniques like the back of your hand.

Also, make sure that you don't get into the habit of only practicing for one specific sequence. This is very important. A fight doesn't happen according to any set pattern. The body's reaction to certain kicks or strikes is predictable, but not how a fight will happen. Each attack is uniquely different.

You must practice for all different situations. You may not be able to throw a kick to the groin. Then what? Make sure you mix your sequences and attacks up for different situations. Practice for different positions, multiple attackers, and for if you miss your first strike or kick, etc. Always be prepared for the unexpected!

Train your mind to see the open target. If the groin is not open for a front kick, you may have to start by breaking the ankle with a side kick, and then follow that specific sequence. Or you may have to start by breaking the elbow or the knee. Practice for many different variations.

Furthermore, you need to understand that, in order for many of the follow-up techniques to work, you will first need the initial injury. That initial strike or kick is vitally important. That is what starts the sequence. You may have to fake a strike or a kick to open up your first target, and then follow through with your sequence of kicks or strikes.

What if the guy has a gun? Or a knife? What if two or three guys attack you at once? You need to practice for all of these possibilities.

Simplifying your martial arts doesn't mean that you don't need to train, or that it will be easy. While injuring the body is easy, you still need to train for all the different possibilities.

The bottom line in simplifying your martial arts is to:

1) Know your vital targets by heart

2) Know how to attack each target

3) Understand how your attacker will respond to each strike or kick to each target

4) Develop many sequences according to how your attacker will respond to each previous strike or kick

5) End the threat as soon as possible

6) Stop injuring your attacker when he is no longer a threat

I want to give you one other piece of advice before I end this chapter. When you strike a target, whether it is by a strike or a kick, you should be trying to severely injure your attacker. For example, if you are throwing a front kick to the groin, your target is not his testicles; your target is the pubic symphysis. You objective is to break this in half. This is a fight-ending kick!

When you break the pubic symphysis in half, a man cannot stand. If a man can't stand, he can't fight. Each of your techniques for self-defense should be a fight-ending technique in and of itself.

You are not trying to hurt your attacker or cause him pain; you are trying to injure your attacker, end the threat, and leave safely! That is what this kind of training is for, period. Your targets should be targets which stop the fight. This is similar to the Karate saying, "One Punch – One Kill." But we don't want to kill anyone if we don't have to; we just want to stop the other guy from killing or injuring us. Each of your targets should be focused on this objective.

The follow-up targets are to ensure that he cannot continue to present a threat to us. Don't ever rely on only one strike or kick. Follow-up with several targets until you are completely sure he is no longer a threat!

I won't list all of these targets here. If you are a martial artist, you should know what targets will put a vicious attacker out of commission and which ones won't.

Choose your targets carefully and according to your own abilities and weaknesses. Then perfect your attacks on those targets, along with your follow up attacks. This is the basis of simplifying your martial arts for self-defense.

Dr. Bohdi Sanders is a multi-award winning and bestselling author of 15 books and 100's of articles, and is an 8-time Martial Arts Hall of Fame inductee. He started training in martial arts in 1984 under Bob and Nikki Allen and now holds the rank of 5th Dan in Shotokan Karate from Shihan William Jackson. Dr. Sanders was awarded the official title of Shihan by Soke Richard Hallman, along with Soke Stephen Barber, Soke-Dai Scot E. Philips, and Renshi Young Author Smith, III.

He has also been awarded the honorary title of Hanshi, (teacher of teachers) for his teachings and writings on the martial arts, by Sifu Al Dacascos, Col. Phil Torres, Grandmaster Eddie Mapula, Shihan Bill Holman, Soke Richard Hallman, Grandmaster Richard Hackworth, Grandmaster Joy Turberville, Grandmaster Terrence Shea, Shihan Dana Abbott, Grandmaster Dan Tosh, Grandmaster Harry Mok, Grandmaster Harry Greene, Grandmaster Dave Johnson, and Grandmaster Eric Lee.

Dr. Sanders has won multiple national book awards for his books. He has written three #1 Bestsellers, and six of his other books have climbed into the Top 10 on Amazon's Best Sellers List. His books have won 1st Place awards from the Indie

Excellence Book Awards and the USA Book News Book Awards. In 2011, he was named Inspiration of the Year by the United States Martial Artist Association Hall of Fame. In 2018, Dr. Sanders became one of the first five Westerners elected to the World Martial Arts Congress in Beijing, China. He is also a member of the Golden Dragon Ohana, and the Independent Warriors Association.

He also holds national certifications as a Specialist in Martial Arts Conditioning and as a Certified Fitness Trainer. In addition, he is a Usui-Tibetan Reiki Master and a Master of Acupressure. He has a doctorate in Natural Health and Naturopathy, along with a BA in Sociology and a MA in Education. Dr. Sanders is also a columnist for Taekwondo Times Magazine and has written articles for several magazines and websites. In 2017, Dr. Sanders was inducted into the Elite Black Belt Hall of Fame and also awarded a Lifetime Achievement Award for his contributions to the martial arts. Dr. Sanders is available for inspirational and motivational public talks and may be reached through his website, www.TheWisdomWarrior.com or through his social media pages.

Shihan Bohdi Sanders

20 Survival Secrets from an Undercover Drug Agent
John Duncan, Ph.D.

During my long career as an undercover drug agent, I learned many things that are useful in staying alive in potentially dangerous environments. I'm talking about things that work to minimize tactical danger, give you an advantage, and, when solidified into automatic habits, will make you a harder target for criminals.

This advice was learned the hard way, by me, or others who came before me, who paid a dear price for this knowledge. Many of them are not typical behaviors, so you must change the way you think about what is safe and what is not.

1) Light and Dark: Most people want to be in the light so that people can see them, and somehow this is supposed to protect them from an assault. Well, I guess that if you trust others to come to your defense, and don't mind not being able to see your attacker, then stay in the light. In contrast, I learned that it is safer to be in the darkness and keep potential attackers in the light. Use the darkness as a cloak. I am not afraid of the darkness because I am ready – I am the predator.

Even at home, I prefer to not turn on the porch lights before I go outside; instead, I do just the opposite. While the outside lights are most often on when I am inside, before I go outside, I turn them off. Also, I make sure that I am not silhouetted in the doorway, or other background, when I go through a door or pass by a window.

I always have a means of dominating the light. I carry a small, yet powerful flashlight in my pocket everywhere I go. Don't let others shine lights behind you, and make sure that you control the lighting when possible. The darkness is my friend, make it yours.

2) The Fatal Funnel: In the military, there are extensive studies of ambush and counter-ambush techniques. The basic principle is to set up something like an L-shape trap, in an area in which the enemy is restricted and cannot move or flee. In other words, you are first trapped, then killed. These "traps" are everywhere in our environment, yet I see people loitering in a "kill zone" all the time. Of course, we can't avoid these features of the world; however, we can know when not to stop and hang out.

Examples of fatal funnels are doorways, hallways, stairs, between cars in a parking lot, bathrooms, elevators, cul-de-sacs, windows, or any environmental feature that greatly limits your movement. In general, people are oblivious of the dangers from others, and totally unaware of these "kill zones" in their day to day world. We all have to use hallways, doors, and windows, but remember that these are areas of greater vulnerability and pass through them quickly.

Don't stand in a doorway looking to see what made the sound in your yard. If you are looking out of a window, stand back a little bit and make sure that you can't be seen. And be careful in parking lots, bathrooms, hallways, stairways, and other areas in which you can be ambushed. This is not being paranoid, but good habits soon become automatic behaviors. I don't consciously avoid these kinds of things, but I have developed automatic habits that help me stay alive in a dangerous world.

3) Looking at People: In some of the larger, more crowded cities, as well in some cultures, eye contact with people in your proximity should be strictly avoided. However, while they will tell you that they feel safer by avoiding eye contact, thus not allowing any personal awareness of the others, this is not the case. Just because you are not watching them, does not mean that they are not watching you.

For example, I scan every single person who walks close to me, just a natural habit. From having to know information that is important to my survival, I see their body language and pick up on their intentions from cues. Sticking your face into a smart phone is not smart, even when you are parked in a parking lot or stopped in a vehicle at a red light. The environment that can hurt you is here and now – be here and now!

4) Cover and Concealment: Wherever I am, I am aware of three things – the nearest cover, the nearest concealment, and the nearest exit(s). I don't actually think about this. It is just a passive awareness that has developed by living and working in dangerous situations.

Moreover, I also know how to get to each of those places in a single reactive movement. Some people call this muscle memory. In Tsunetomo Yamamoto's great, samurai manual, *The Hagakure*, there is a quote which reads, "Even if one's head were to be suddenly cut off, he should be able to do one more action with certainty."

A lifetime of both martial arts and living dangerously has conditioned me to be one reaction away from a deadly attack, taking cover, or going through an exit. This is just a directing of the "fight, freeze, or flee" instinct.

I am not sure I can tell you how to do it, but it comes from training to react in a certain manner to stimuli. It is like driving, when the light turns red, you don't have to do a bunch of thinking to automatically stop. Make your personal survival skills at least as common as your driving skills!

5) Spatial and Temporal Awareness: Be aware of space as danger in time. If someone is 10 yards away, the main danger comes from a pistol. Closer than that means they also can attack with blades, impact weapons, and physical force. Within arms-reach is even more dangerous; here they really gain the element of surprise and initial movement. Always remember that actions are faster than reactions.

If you are toting a pistol, realize that you must do some defensive movement *before* you can draw and shoot an attacker who is in physical contact, or is moving full force in close proximity. Drop back into a better balance, while you stiff arm his advance, shove him as you sidestep his bull rush, or attack into his attack. These should be included in your defensive tactics training. Stuff like this works better if you are a martial artist; however, it is best to be a martial artist *and* a fighter, *and* have solid gun fighting skills. As the legendary SAS commando, "Lofty" Wiseman, once taught, "Mindset is the key, followed by tactics, then skills, and last of all your kit," (the weapons and gear you have on you).

Mindset is a commitment to your survival. Tactics are general principles of how you respond to danger. Skills include your abilities developed through training, such as how to strike, shoot, or fight. And finally, "kit" is what you are carrying, such as a pistol or a knife.

Remember, at this level, there are no winners and losers, only survivors and funerals. The key to being a survivor is to manage the space around you and realize how proximity is the index of how fast things can go wrong.

6) Confrontations: Stay out of confrontations if you can, period. This is easy to say, but often difficult to do for two reasons: (1) sometimes you are not the one starting the confrontation, and (2) sometimes you are forced to initiate the confrontation. The first thing to do in a confrontation is to not let "tunnel vision" take over. Relax so that you can see the options; be calm, ready, and open to anything that happens.

Make sure that you control the relative position and WATCH YOUR BACK! It is common for one person to get your attention so another one, or others, can attack you from behind. Do not back down, because that gives the attacker total control, but try to de-escalate the situation if you can. If you can't, in my experience, it is better to get there *first with the most*. Don't jump into some Karate stance, make verbal threats, or otherwise betray your intentions. I avoid "stances" entirely in the street.

Instead, your initial attack into the opponent is your movement into a stronger body position or stance. Take a step to the left and, as the attacker starts to circle, attack him on his movement. Catch him following you. He is following your lead, so he is one step behind you in "tactical space." Keep it that way. However, it is better to avoid confrontations altogether. Even if you survive the confrontation, you may not survive the trial and incarceration that could follow.

7) Using Angles: If you stand directly facing the front of a person, and your weight is on your heels, you don't have much stability, and you are an easy target. Standing like that is just damn naive and too trusting! Instead, always have your weak side a little forward. This gives you more stability, and if you are armed, protects your weapon and allows easier access to it in the event you are "jumped."

Your choice of angle is designed to maximize your strengths while minimizing those of the other person(s). As a martial artist, I tend to dominate my personal space with angles. For the uninitiated, and for those who have lived a more sheltered life as a kid, one of the first lessons I learned is that, if I use my left hand to grab the right-side shoulder of another kid's jacket, and turn him away, he could not hit me back in a fight. I could beat the crap out of him! Angles work for attack *and*, more importantly to us here, for defense.

8) Camouflage and Fit In: Camo is most often associated with wilderness or desert patterns on clothing that is designed for military or hunting. However, urban camo is nothing but "ordinariness." Look ordinary. Don't wear "I'm a badass" clothing or logo items that give you away. I can tell you that I am not a "badass," but I will fight, die, or kill, if I need to, anytime it is required.

So, if you are in public, avoid sitting in places where you are surrounded 360 degrees by other tables, people, or open space. Use the edges, corners, potted plants, and natural obstacles as tools to help you control your environment while still fitting in. Wear the kind of clothes other people around you are wearing.

In other words, don't make yourself into a target by standing out. For civilians, the takeaway is to not be too flamboyant or show off. It is nice that you are rich, but if you are wearing a diamond bezel Rolex and a $30,000 diamond ring, face it, you're a good target and, most likely, easy prey!

9) Staging Your Weapon: This is important! Every millisecond counts in a life-or-death encounter. Every millisecond! So, make it a habit to already have your weapon in hand before the trouble starts. When I worked undercover, I would "stash" all kinds of things around in a motel room before a deal went down. I might have a pistol in a twelve-pack box of beer, a Fairbairn-Sikes dagger unsheathed in the fold of a newspaper, or a sawed-off 12 gauge attached by hangers to the bottom edge of the bed-frame. Little things, ready at hand!

Getting control of your weapon as early as possible is also important. An example is that you are sitting (generally a very vulnerable position) in a restaurant, when an armed robbery begins. If you have a pistol, this is a very good time to draw it and hide it in your hand under the napkin in your lap.

If you are walking to a dark parking lot at night and have OC pepper spray in your purse, put it in your hand, or, if you have a pistol in your purse, stick your hand inside the purse and grip the pistol until you get to a safer place.

Staging is used to address an emerging situation, or in the case of the parking lot, to give you a quicker reaction in a potentially dangerous environment. If you don't have a weapon, a gun, a knife, etc., figure out what is the closest object in your proximity which can be used as an improvised weapon.

For example, as Pat Hutton once said, "The three rules of a bar fight (other than leave before the fight) are as follows: (1) pick up something that is harder than the human head; (2) hit human heads with it; and, (3) get the hell out of there." A billiard ball is an example of an improvised weapon. So is the salt shaker on the table.

10) Focus, Tunnel Vision, and Peripheral Awareness:
Coolness is the ability to avoid sensory overload, tunnel vision, panic, or the paralysis that is often associated with the fight-or-flight response. Keep your cool. I do this by accepting my own death, which I did long ago.

It is out there in my future and I understand that it is present in every single moment of my life. I am not afraid to die here and now, not that I want to, but I understand that it is here. This mental game makes it easier for me to act with coolness in dangerous situations. If I am less startled, less flooded by adrenaline and cortisol, and keep my eyes open, I can act more quickly, better maintain my motor skills, and see what is happening.

Tunnel vision is dangerous. It happens as a stress response. We are creatures whose relaxed vision is designed for seeing things around us. As predators, this is for both protection and hunting. We also can focus or target a single thing amid the flow. That is also hunting and foraging. Both are necessary for survival.

If we are too aware of the surroundings, we miss the proximate danger; if we are too focused on the object, we are easy to sneak up on. Herbivores are more suitable for small object focus, nibbling on grass with their heads stuck down. Lions scan the horizon and pick their prey. The same is true of people. Those with their "herbivore nose" stuck up their "cell phone butt," are easy prey for predators like me.

11) Set Up and Sneak Attack: I mentioned this in the earlier part on confrontations, but it is worth further consideration. Setups can occur in any dimension. It means that you are being put into a position of vulnerability, so that something that you don't want to happen, can happen. For example, I was snitched off during a deep undercover assignment by a local law enforcement executive. When I showed up to a party, I did not know that there was talk going around of killing me. Fortunately for me, my informant gave me a "heads up," and I quickly left, never to return. That case was over!

Only years later did we catch the target with a wiretap. I had been set up. A sneak attack, on the other hand, usually comes in two ways: (1) a sucker punch or (2) an ambush. A sucker punch could also be a stabbing or shooting.

It usually comes from a single attacker; the point is to catch you unaware and then hurt you. An ambush is more sinister. It means that someone, or more likely several individuals, have decided, and perhaps devised a plan, to lure you into a place where they can kill or injure you.

For this reason, if I was doing an undercover drug deal, I always preferred to pick the location and time, avoid going inside someone's "turf" such as their home, and *never* leave and take a "road trip" to get the drugs. In civilian life, be aware when people start redefining your timeline, overstepping boundaries, or taking control of your mobility, and always be observant for signs that you are being set up.

12) Never Trust a Snitch: You'd think that undercover agents would be good at keeping things to themselves. But I have seen so many of them start working with an informant and before long, they've befriended that person and are chatting about official and personal business with them. This always comes back to hurt them somewhere down the line. There are several kinds of informants.

Example are good Samaritans, those seeking revenge, paid informants, and criminal informants that have gotten in trouble and are trying to get a break by snitching on their friends. Regardless of the type of snitch, they all are "telling on" someone to help themselves. In many ways, these folks are simultaneously telling you about themselves and their values.

A point to remember is, if they will snitch *to* you, they will snitch *on* you! So, if someone you know is always talking about someone else and what they do, be assured that they are talking about you to someone else in the same way. Keep your secrets to yourself!

13) Have Backup: When I went undercover, which was most often several times a week, I not only gathered information (intelligence) before the event, but I also made sure that I had some backup. Typically, if I was buying drugs, I had a few other drug agents "covering me," and listening to what was going on via a "body mic," i.e. a hidden transmitter. We had all sorts of code phrases that kept them informed and would signal things like, "Help now!"

I used, "You can't be too careful these days," as a bust signal, for example. We also had visual signals in case the body mic went out, things like taking off your cap, etc. In civilian life, the takeaway is to make sure that someone knows where you are going and what your timeline is. Make sure you have a plan in case things go wrong and you end up stranded somewhere or in case you come up missing. That way, we will know where to start looking for you and who to question first.

14) Watch Your Back: Most bad stuff that happens comes from behind. It is just easier for the bad guys to not have to fight. They'd much rather bushwhack you. I tend to not leave my back facing open areas. You can use your surroundings or rely on your friends to keep covered. The best thing is to not let things happen behind you, turn to face them, or better, block them by strategically using your environment.

This is also figurative in the sense that people who harm you at work, in social settings, or politically, mostly do it behind your back. In the past 20 years, I have been stabbed in the back by "friends" many times, by things such as snitches spreading bad rumors when I was up for a promotion. But in every case, at least for the past two decades, I had already "read" them correctly as a snitch and was not surprised, (or even offended), by their betrayal. I can sure spot a snitch! Always watch your back and know what is there.

15) Make Plans but Stay Flexible: All military and law enforcement people know that plans tend to fall apart. When we were doing an undercover deal, for example, we would come up with a plan to do the deal, and what to do in case things went "south." Problems arise when you go into a potentially dangerous situation with no plan; they also arise when you are inflexible and stick with the plan, even when you see it falling apart.

An example was the ATF raid on the Branch-Davidian Compound in Waco, Texas. Without going into great detail, the raid commander was using dynamic entry, which requires surprise, aggression, and speed to be effective. When a Davidian drove by the "jump off" point, saw the team setting up, and quickly drove back to the compound, followed by windows and doors being barricaded. The element of surprise was gone for the raid team.

Instead of recognizing that things were changing and that the method would no longer work, the stubborn commander drove on and caused many deaths from trying to make reality conform to his plan, instead of being flexible enough to find a workable solution.

This same kind of thing has led good pilots to crash their airplanes because they did not adapt to changing circumstances. The takeaway of this lesson is to make good and thorough plans, but be willing and ready to adapt to changing circumstances.

16) Watch Hands, Shifting of Weight, and Control Proximity: When you think that someone might pose a danger, there are several things to do. Of course, leaving is the first and best solution. That is not always possible, so watch for weapons and attacks. Weapons are mostly deployed by hand, so keep their hands within your awareness.

Clues to drawing a weapon are often raising the shoulder or the elbow coming up in back. Only the highly skilled can attack without preparation, most people have a "tell." They might shift their weight, make a fist, hide a hand, draw back to strike, step out with their front leg, change the level of their body or head, and other signs that they are not just talking with you. Learn to see these things and respond properly.

17) Listen to what People Say and Read Their Body Language: People talk too much. When I was undercover, we were taught to let them run their mouths. Many are convicted and sent to prison because they ran their mouth and they told on themselves. If you are sitting there thinking about what you are going to say, you may not be listening to what the other person is saying. Not only is that behavior bad manners, it is also depriving you of a great source of intelligence information. Let them talk – and listen! Encourage them to keep on talking!

Also, if they are shifting their eyes around, seem nervous, arms crossed, or have their body turned away from you, one thing is clear – they don't want to be there, they don't like being with you, and they may be up to something.

If their feet are pointing towards the door and they are restless, they want to leave; if their legs are "bouncing," they are symbolically "running" or "fleeing" from this place. Good listening skills and having a feel for body language go a long way to alerting you of impending danger. Don't miss out on this source of information.

18) Don't let anyone "Pat You Down" or Touch You: Don't let people put their hands on you if you don't want them to. During my undercover career, I had some high-level meetings with drug dealers. Sometimes I was buying a large quantity of cocaine.

The largest was 1,000 kilos. We were negotiating the deal in a hotel room, and nobody was frisked. They would not stand for it, nor would I. Even in low-level deals of smaller quantities, the rules are the same. Don't let anyone put their hands on you!

On TV and in the movies, undercover guys are always getting pat-down, checked for weapons, and being disarmed. I would never stand for that. I presuppose that they have a gun, and I know I do, (and expect that they suppose I have one as well). I did not respond politely to someone crossing the boundaries.

For example, on one deal, I was supposed to be the drug dealer, and the bad guy was negotiating to buy $1,000,000 worth of cocaine, which he thought I could bring up from Mexico (this is called a "reversal" and the bad guy is arrested for attempting to obtain or conspiracy). I forced a meeting with the prime investor named Bruce, who walked into the room and promptly demanded that I show him my ID.

So, I punched him in the face, pulled my pistol, and told the other suspect that this guy must be a cop or something, to talk like that. Think WWARBGD – "What Would a Real Bad Guy Do?" Never give up your weapon, never let people demand your ID, and never let them put their hands on you! This does not mean the police, if you are under arrest; in that case, do what the good people tell you to do, and be respectful.

19) Follow the Money: If you want to know who is in charge, why something happened, or even why a certain legislator voted for that totally screwed up bill – follow the money! Money talks! This was always true in the drug world. "Mr. Big" was at the end of a money trail. Everything we did was to work our way up that trail. This can be broadened to the question, "Who stands to gain the most here?"

Most relationships, except for the most intimate and personal, are instrumental in some way. People use other people. In these kinds of relationships, there is often a mutual benefit, but sometimes it is more of a one-way street. Since greed and self-gratification are the most common reasons people do things instrumentally, a great deal of motivation can be understood by just figuring out who is going to benefit the most. Figure out if you are being used and know where the benefit lies in these pernicious, but necessary evils.

20) Trust Your Gut Instinct: There is a biological reason you have "gut feelings." The human brain has approximately 100 billion neurons, and the human digestive system has another 100 billion. Most of our day-to-day awareness is subconscious. Through the automatic processors in our brain, we are passively aware of thousands of details which we could never hold in conscious focus all at once.

But we have a little "watchdog" in our brain called the amygdala. It is that part of our precognitive brain that scans every sensation for patterns of potential danger and automatically starts our defensive responses to it.

Of course, this all happens before we are ever conscious of anything directly. Instead, the amygdala tells the hypothalamus to send a signal to the pituitary gland to release hormones into the bloodstream, which then cause the adrenal glands to send adrenaline and cortisol – fight or flight chemicals – throughout the bloodstream.

This takes less than 10 heartbeats. One of the main functions of this flood of chemical messengers is to stop the digestive activities and redirect blood from the gut to the core of the body, for more energy to fight or run. We sense this as a little tightening and tingle in our guts. It occurs most often before we consciously perceive or think about the danger. As far as danger goes, our gut is already ahead of our head.

So, when you get that feeling in your gut, respect what it is saying. In the undercover drug world, agents could "fold the tent" anytime they had a gut feeling that something was wrong. Many have died because they ignored this "second brain" telling them that things just don't add up. Respect your gut instinct.

These are just a few of the hard-learned lessons, which I walked away with, from my career as an undercover drug agent. There are countless more, maybe I will write about them in a future article. Most of these lessons apply to everyday life, especially if you are concerned about personal safety or are in a hostile environment. When I speak about weapons, I do realize that there are many who do not carry them and, even for the ones who do, there may be times when weapons are not carried.

In truth, almost every object in your proximity is potentially a weapon, if you know how to use it. But the main, and best, weapon you have is your mind. Keep it active and you will be less likely to be the victim of a violent crime.

The difference between strategic thinking and tactical thinking is – strategic thinking tells me that it is dumb to go to the ATM at 2:00 a.m.; tactical thinking is what I must do after going to the ATM at 2:00 a.m. anyway, and now there is someone approaching with bad intent.

It is always better to avoid the problem in the first place, than to have to fight your way out of something. Most things don't just happen; there is a recognizable chain of events and decisions that led to this point. With your head in the game, you are more likely to see where these kinds of things are going and get out of there without the slightest problem.

Dr. John Duncan is an Associate Clinical Professor of Psychiatry at the University of Oklahoma Health Sciences Center, College of Medicine. John has been a full-time professor since September 2007, but worked as an Adjunct Professor since 1997. John retired after 27 years in law enforcement as Chief Agent with the Oklahoma State Bureau of Narcotics and Dangerous Drugs Control. Although he worked as an undercover agent for years, John was also a tactical trainer for the Bureau of Narcotics, teaching CQB and the use of weapons – handgun, submachinegun, carbine, and precision rifle. He also worked on combining hand-to-hand combat, with close quarter shooting skills. John commanded a tactical team that conducted military style counter-narcotics operations throughout the United States and was cross-designated as both a U.S. Customs and DEA agent.

John began training in Kodokan Judo in 1962 at age nine and earned a junior brown belt from Vince Tamura. He started taking Tae Kwon Do, at Allen Steen's Texas Karate Institute in East Dallas in 1967. Studying with Fred Wren, Charles Armstrong, Royce Young, Keith Yates, James Toney, Skipper Mullins, and Allen Steen, John was taught by, and exposed to, the old "blood and guts" Karate and to some of the finest fighters in the world, such as Chuck Norris, Joe Lewis, Jim Harrison, Ed Parker, and so many others who have become legends.

John earned his Shodan rank from Allen Steen in August of 1972. He worked for Steen's Texas Karate Institute for several years, as an instructor, and as head instructor, of the East Dallas School, until 1978, when he moved to Denton to attend college. John continued training in the martial arts during this time, studying kickboxing, boxing, and armed styles, such as escrima. He received belts in these styles and moved up in rank. His highest rank is 5th Dan in Hapkido, from Mansuk Kim in Norman, Oklahoma. John continues to train law enforcement officers in "integrated combatives" and is the Chief Instructor and Founder of Viper Combat Systems.

Master John Duncan

Tactical Firearm Training for the Martial Artist
Dave Johnson

Though I've always believed that perfecting one's body and mind to be the primary weapon for self-defense needs is best, I do recognize and encourage all practitioners to pursue ongoing and varied weapons training. Tactical firearm training is one example of varied training.

Before I continue, I must recognize several individuals that helped shape my life, supported my martial arts journey, and shared their skills, knowledge, and talents with me. Without these individuals, I would not be who I am and would not have the opportunity to share this knowledge with you. I am forever grateful to Officer Ralph Bareford, Officer Harland Walters, Don Cameron (Cameron Consulting), Bob Dugan (Executive Security International), Sheriff Bobby Whittington (Badlands Tactical Training), and Steve Collins (Foothill Training).

I am aware that the simple use of the word "firearm" can ignite a flurry of comments, both for and against, and in some cases, create very impassioned debate and even verbal attacks.

However, I have always adhered to the slogan or "moto" of the International SEIEIDO Federation, "Nunquam Non Paratus" (Never Unprepared). I have always felt that, as a professional martial arts instructor, it is my responsibility to teach my students everything possible that will improve their level of safety and decrease the likelihood of injury and death.

This would include avoidance, de-escalation skills, verbal judo, posturing, deflecting, defensive tactics, offensive tactics, ground fighting skills, weapon disarms, multiple opponent defense, and the defensive use of firearms.

Whether we are for or against the use of firearms, the fact remains that firearms exist. Therefore, we should not only be prepared for that potential type of threat, but we should train ourselves vigorously in the proper use of these deadly weapons.

91

As we all know, every type of weapon, including the human body, can be used improperly and in some cases maliciously. Unfortunately, this will always be the case.

Nevertheless, if we have been tasked with the responsibility, something I have always considered a privilege, of teaching others how to increase their level of safety and decrease the likelihood of injury or death, then we *must* include instruction in the safe and proper use of firearms. I do understand that much of what I write will not be applicable to specific countries and consider most of the content to be applicable mainly to the citizens of the United States.

Topics

In this chapter, I will be discussing the safe use and storage of firearms, the proper mindset, pros and cons to the different types of firearms, weapon retention, weapon disarms, shot accuracy, the importance of move/shoot training, advanced reloading skills, tips for carrying exposed and concealed, specifically designed "course of fire" scenarios, and multiple opponent scenarios.

Please understand that this information is but a very small part of the many important topics of safe, responsible, and effective firearm use that can be found from the many extremely competent instructors available throughout the world today. If you are serious about the use of firearms, please continue your research and never stop learning and practicing.

Safety and Storage

If you have made, or are going to make, the decision to possess a firearm, please do me, and all of us, especially our young children, a big favor; along with your purchase, make sure you have a way to absolutely keep these weapons secure in such a way that *you* must be involved in the access of it. I am so tired of seeing and hearing news reports of innocent children being killed, especially when the weapon is the property of a law enforcement officer. There is absolutely no excuse for this! I personally believe that everybody that wants to purchase a firearm must first prove how they are going to keep this weapon secure. If my weapon is not locked in a safe, it is always within my absolute control.

Please remember that these are deadly weapons. Absolutely train on a regular basis, i.e., site alignment, trigger management, accuracy, etc., but train just as much, if not more, on securing the weapon, whether on your person concealed, in your glove compartment, by your bed, etc., and *always* be aware of muzzle direction or what the gun is pointed at. If you're going to utilize a trigger lock, please think long and hard about where the key should be placed.

Please don't derive your training from police dramas in the movies. They are filled with deadly mistakes. Additionally, if married, I strongly recommend not sharing a firearm, but instead owning, and being totally responsible, for your own firearm at all times, even though both parties should be proficient with each other's firearm and know where it is at all times. Another suggestion, if possible, is to try to have the same, or very similar firearm, for each person, in case a situation arises where your life depends on the other person's weapon.

Another suggestion I would like to make, regarding the safe use of firearms, is to make sure the weapon is empty of ammo (always have another person double check). Also practice how you would go about a normal day, i.e., securing it in a safe, placing it near you at bedtime, while taking a shower, what you will do with it during the day, concealing it on your body, etc. This should be done extensively until all bad practices are eliminated. Again, always be aware of where the muzzle is facing.

The decision of whether to place a round in the chamber or not (semi autos), has a lot to do with your competence, the type of weapon, and what a particular situation dictates. If the weapon has a safety, *use it*, and be very competent in using it. For the most part, I would always recommend having a round in the chamber. After all, in a life-or-death situation, you will likely have only a fraction of a second to react. That said, if you are going to do this, please train properly and often enough to be competent.

If you have children, please spend some quality time familiarizing them with the weapons, properly train them in the correct use of a firearm, and instill in them how truly deadly they are. Don't do this to the point of fear and paranoia, but to the point of respect for the weapon and confident use if needed. I might also add that you really need to limit the number of people who know you have a firearm and where it's located.

Proper Mindset

This topic cannot be over emphasized. If you cannot honestly say, without hesitation, that you would use a firearm (deadly force) to defend your life, or the life of your loved ones, then you are not ready to possess a firearm.

To achieve this mindset might take some time, and some people may never be able to get to this point. I strongly believe that you must possess this state of mind if you are going to possess a firearm for self-defense. If not, you are likely to be more of a danger to yourself and loved ones than the criminal.

This topic must be settled before even considering the purchase of a firearm. It will take some serious soul-searching and mental role-playing, but it must be done. I have met many individuals that clearly should not possess a firearm. They are not mentally and psychologically prepared to make this split-second decision, nor are many of them safe in their handling of a firearm. This is very concerning to me.

Clearly none of us want to take a life or seriously injure someone, but this type of circumstance is always a possibility. That said, I've possessed a firearm and have carried it legally exposed and concealed, for more than 45 years and have never injured or killed anyone. Contrary to current media exposure, firearms don't kill people; people kill people.

Types of Firearms – Pros and Cons

This topic is not about what I like and dislike as it pertains to firearm types, but instead is about things you might want to consider when purchasing a firearm. You must decide if it's simply for home protection or will you be carrying it concealed.

Depending on if you are a man or woman, you will want to look at firearms that fit comfortably in your hands. You will also want to decide what caliber you want, and if you prefer a revolver or a semi-automatic.

Regarding this topic, you will want to consider ammunition capacity, ease of reloading, and the safety factor of a semi-auto vs. a revolver. Do not guess when purchasing a firearm. Try out various firearms, do your own research, talk to a firearms instructor, and ask a lot of questions before making a purchase.

Tip: Though I highly recommend everyone possess a firearm that will be comfortable to handle safely and one with which you will be confident using if needed, I strongly suggest a standard shotgun for home protection.

There are few deterrents as effective as the sound of a shotgun being racked. However, as I've mentioned before, please make sure you become proficient with the weapon and have established a safe and secure way of keeping it out of the wrong hands.

Semi-Auto

- Pro: Larger ammo capacity, usually fires more rounds quicker. Quick reload.
- Con: Ammo can jam.

Revolver

- Pro: Ease of use, unlikely to jam, normally less likelihood of accidental fire.
- Con: Smaller ammo capacity, slower and less rounds on target, slow reload.

Shotgun

- Pro: Covers larger area, less need for accuracy, great deterrent.
- Con: Large and bulky, not good for close quarters, limited rounds, hard reload.

Weapon Retention

This topic will be difficult to explain without live instruction, videos, or photos, but I'll do my best. I do encourage you to seek out professional instruction when it comes to the topic of weapon retention, weapon disarms, shot accuracy, the importance of move/shoot training, advanced reloading skills, tips for carrying exposed and concealed, and multiple opponent strategies.

When it comes to the basics of retention, we must consider a holstered weapon, a held weapon, a straight grab for the weapon, a front cross grab, a rear straight grab, and a rear cross grab.

With a hand-held weapon, it is best to grab the weapon with both hands and push forward, then up or down, or pull the weapon back and push up or down, being ever cognizant of trigger finger placement.

With a holstered or concealed weapon, it is also recommended that the weapon is first grabbed and secured with both hands, then depending upon how the weapon is grabbed, you will rotate your body approximately 90 degrees, or a quarter turn in the direction that will allow you to strike with your elbow, the attacker's locked out elbow, face or other vital target.

Remember, it is also recommended that kicks be utilized in conjunction with upper body techniques. Of course, these techniques should be practiced regularly and with safe training weapons.

Weapon Disarms

This happens to be one of my favorite skills to teach. However, we must always keep in mind that disarming techniques are last resort techniques, can cost us our lives, and must be practiced on an ongoing basis. *WARNING: There are many disarming videos on the internet that are being taught incorrectly and could cost you your life.*

Once again, my recommendation is to do your research and then practice regularly. Tip: There are a couple of very important things to look for in all disarming techniques: 1) The body must move out of the line of fire (don't just move the hands), 2) You must be sure a captured weapon is either ready to fire or disabled, 3) You must always retrieve the weapon and disable the attacker, and finally, 4) In practicing, you should *never* return the weapon to the attacker!

Shot Accuracy

Though this may seem like a no-brainer, in my experience, most firearm owners fall far short of being considered a decent shot. Please make sure you are taught proper site alignment. I'm referring to the correct way of aligning the back and front sites for shot accuracy. Please keep in mind that even with proper site alignment, you may find your shots not hitting the target accurately. This can be caused by poor trigger control or anticipation of the shot, among other things.

Proper breathing cannot be stressed enough. A slow, relaxed, steady exhale while pulling the trigger can do wonders when it comes to accuracy. Additionally, I highly recommend a slanted and somewhat relaxed stance when shooting. Don't lock your entire body and give the bad guy the biggest target possible.

Speaking of body position, I know a lot of instructors teach this stiff type of square stance. This may be fine for the brand-new beginner to just learn proper trigger pull, site alignment, and proper breathing, but if your objective is to be prepared to shoot in a high-stressed life and death situation, you better learn how to relax the body and be ready to move in any direction spontaneously *while shooting.*

Move/Shoot Training

As mentioned above, this type of shooting is imperative if you expect to be ready for reality. Granted, most firearm training facilities are indoors, but there are plenty of outdoor ranges that are definitely worth the search. Only by learning how to shoot competently, accurately, and safely while moving, will you truly be prepared for reality. It also prepares you for multiple attackers or shooters.

Additionally, with this type of shooting, you will learn to become proficient at "point" shooting. This is when you do not utilize your sites, but instead, train your body to perceive your firearm as an extension of your hand or arm.

Unfortunately, this topic is not discussed enough, but I am here to tell you that it is *very unlikely* that a life-or-death situation will have you standing still and focusing on your front and rear site before each shot. Please seek out this type of training.

Advanced Reloading Skills

Once again, if we are to train in such a way as to ready us for reality, we should be including a lot of "what if" scenarios into our course of fire curriculums. For example, what if you get shot in your dominant gun hand or your dominant reloading hand or arm? Skills such as dumping a magazine with a different part of your body or loading a full magazine with the use of your feet, must be included. This also applies to shotguns or AR type rifles. NOTE: This type of training can be very dangerous so take it slow at first. Highly experienced instructors are recommended.

Carrying Exposed and Concealed

If carrying exposed, make sure you are within the laws of your city, county, and state. Make sure there is nothing that could restrict the deployment of your firearm from its holster. Carefully consider the placement of other equipment on your duty belt so as not to interfere with the drawing of your firearm.

Additionally, with an _unloaded_ weapon, practice drawing your firearm, with and without, a jacket on. Practice removing everything else quickly from your duty belt to make sure there are no problems. You can't afford a problem under a stressful situation.

If carrying concealed, make sure you are within the laws of your city, county, and state to do so. Just as suggested above, practice retrieving and drawing your (unloaded) firearm with various types of clothing, and from the locations you will consistently conceal your firearm.

Be consistent in where you conceal your weapon. Practice for summer and winter, dress and casual, and coat and no coat. Additionally, make a firm decision regarding the use of the safety and whether there will be a round in the chamber, and _stick to that decision_.

Course of Fire Scenarios

Take some time to design specific "course of fire" scenarios. Some example are entering and exiting buildings, from a vehicle, while running, on your back, side, or belly, multiple opponents (targets), falling and rising while engaging targets, and the utilization of multiple weapon types.

I would also suggest developing scenarios that transition from hand-to-hand to firearm, and vice versa. Sadly, most firearm owners never consider this type of training and/or think it is unnecessary. Unfortunately, if they were to ever face a real life and death situation, they will have wished they did.

Multiple Opponent Scenarios

Multiple opponent training scenarios have been a crucial part of the "Seieido" martial art training system since 1984. To me it has always been a no brainer when it comes to training for reality. After all, more and more today, attacks are carried out by multiple individuals.

The same should apply to firearms training. If it's just one attacker, no problem. However, if there is more than one attacker, you will be ready. Remember the slogan or "moto" of the International SEIEIDO Federation, "Nunquam Non Paratus" (Never Unprepared).

In conclusion, as I mentioned in the beginning, this information is but a very small part of the many important topics of safe, responsible, and effective firearm use that can be found from the many extremely competent instructors available throughout the world today.

If you are serious about the use of firearms, please continue your research and never stop learning and practicing. Better yet, combine the proper and effective use of firearms with effective, efficient, and realistic martial arts training.

Dave Johnson, (Seieido – Shodai Soke), is a world recognized martial arts Grandmaster with 60 years in the arts, 30 years in law enforcement, and more than 25 years in executive protection. He graduated #1 in his class from Executive Security International in 1990, is a graduate of the Basic S.W.A.T. Academy, he founded the Hall of Masters Hall of

Fame, and holds an M.B.A. and M.P.A. degree, specializing in International Business and Public Administration. He teaches internationally and has schools in South America, Europe, and Asia.

Soke Johnson is available to answer questions you may have or to help you with your firearm training. He would be honored to help you increase your level of safety. You can contact Soke Johnson at: masterdavejohnson@gmail.com.

Soke Dave Johnson

The Dangers of Watered Down Martial Arts
Nicholas Moreno

It was a hot summer in 1995, when I had my very first experience with martial arts. My instructor turned my whole perception of what I *thought* I knew about fighting on its head. I grew up in Milwaukee, Wisconsin, experiencing difficult lessons on the street through the "school of hard knocks."

I was no stranger to violence. The kids I was associating with in Milwaukee had a habit of finding confrontations frequently; and I was usually the one to help solve the problem, after they had created it. I had a chip on my shoulder and a relentless desire to prove to myself that I could handle violent situations when they happened.

My instructors at this time were Kempo teachers. The only reference I had for physical confrontation was through seeing people get knocked out on the street. Naturally, I gravitated to the art that refined the practitioner's ability to throw multiple combinations of strikes to many targets. Little did I realize, I really had no conception of the depths of knowledge that surrounded Kempo Karate.

That day in the dojo, I demonstrated my "street ability" and poor judgment to my master instructor, who responded in kind by hitting me so hard that I ended upside down through two layers of drywall, desperately wondering what had happened. My whole world was shattered. My whole perception of my abilities, and the ego that belonged to it, was taken apart. Thank goodness!

This was my first experience with a proper teacher that wasn't teaching watered down martial arts. Behind every block, strike, movement, and breath, there was an explanation for the effort put forth. These weren't just outdated dance movements that made no sense. They were no-nonsense principles of kinesiology and kinematics that drastically increased the effectiveness of my instructor's movements.

There was no secrecy from my teachers. They were more than willing to provide answers and went on to explain that the movements I was learning were also subject to individual circumstances and scenarios.

They explained that a real life situation will never be exactly the same as training in the dojo, and that a proper instructor will show the difference between the lesson, or controlled environment, and dynamic stress training.

These instructors introduced me to the concept of developing sets of attributes and movements that would spontaneously come out during duress and dynamic training for the preparation of a true fight.

I was taught to look for success percentages during dynamic training sessions. During these dynamic sessions, my instructors pointed out which techniques I was very repetitive with, thus exposing the templates that I still needed to work on and "add to my game."

This learning curve created a baseline for me to evaluate my weak spots in any number of given scenarios. It was a scientific approach to improvement and training. These learning principles stuck with me over the course of a lifetime of training.

You see, in modern times, there are many motivations for a practitioner to study a martial art. Not everyone is looking to be a competitor, a tough guy, or has something to prove to themselves like I did. There is nothing wrong with that. Some practitioners are enrolling their children at early ages into martial arts schools in order to build a solid foundation of moral attitudes and codes of conduct that will shape how these children tackle adversity and treat people in real life situations.

There are other practitioners that use martial arts as a vehicle for rehabilitation and health. It is common place now to see people of an older age or who have received serious injuries taking part in martial arts classes to strengthen areas of the body that need rehabilitation. Others are present in class to get a good sweat, while increasing their daily activity regimen. I had to do this in order to rehabilitate my shoulder after surgery.

Another type of student that is arising more frequently in the martial arts world, is the practitioner that is enrolled in classes to learn a little self-defense. These types of students are looking to build their self-confidence and hopefully, to retain a life-saving skill or two in the process.

I bring up these different types of students to address a very serious issue that arises in the modern world, in regards to martial arts training. There is nothing wrong with the aforementioned motivations for training. However, it does present a problem that is becoming more apparent as the years go on within the community. What are the dangers of learning a watered down martial system? How do we evaluate what is a good system to study?

The dangers of learning a watered down system are simple. It won't work when you need it to. The movements will distract, and detract, your ability to save your life or the lives of the loved ones that you are hoping to protect. A clear distinction needs to be made in the mind of the prospective student when looking into the system of martial arts that they are studying.

The prospective student needs to evaluate their concise motivations for wanting to train. Is it for your family or health, or is it for self-defense and martial application? Is it the program for your kids? Is it for the community and social aspect for your family? Is it to increase your overall health, flexibility, strength, and confidence? Or is it because you want it to work when you need it? If the latter is the answer, then you need to be very careful of your choice of systems and instructors.

Learning a system of movements for self-defense purposes is arguably one of the hardest things to vet, and an even more complicated decision to make than one might think. For example, many people put forward that the art of Brazilian Jiu-jitsu is the most realistic and proven methodology to study for street fights. Yet, if you introduce multiple attackers or edged weapons into the scenario, you will realize that particular line of thought doesn't actually hold water.

I have seen many a man trust in plain old boxing as their "go to" for self-defense. In this more modern age of UFC fights, we also see a huge increase in the practice of various forms of American and Thai Kickboxing as well. Boxing and kickboxing, whatever the style or format, is a very reliable way for a practitioner to learn how to strike effectively and is proven to do so.

Even though this is the case, it is no secret that, with those skill sets alone, these practitioners are at an extreme disadvantage against a grappling man who does Judo, wrestling, or Brazilian Jiu-Jitsu.

Now, let's take a look into the perspective of active duty military personnel. They have no desire to engage in any type of fight or match. The only reason they are engaged in a confrontation of this description is because the enemy combatant has somehow gotten past their primary weapon system (a rifle), their secondary weapon system (a sidearm), and the edged weapon waiting in the sheath after that. Their only objective is to regain control of the situation and kill their enemy combatant.

In this case, virtually any of the competitive or sport applications of the martial arts which they are studying are useless. A Marine in combat wants to get to his weapon system as fast as possible to kill their respective enemy combatant not achieve points or a "double leg" so they can execute their arm bar.

With all of this knowledge being out there for evaluation, and readily available on the internet, it bluntly comes down to the individual practitioner, their motivation for learning, and their ability to research their teacher. The instructor, and system in question, should be vetted to make sure that they, not only are a part of a legitimate lineage in that particular style, but that they also possess the necessary, *tested,* physical experience in their field, to make them an expert at what they do.

It does no good to study from a combatives expert who hasn't been in combat himself or worked with those who have. It won't help very much to learn kickboxing or Muay Thai from instructors who have never sparred or gotten into the ring. The same can also be said of Brazilian Jiujitsu. Has your instructor had any competition experience? If they haven't, are they studying techniques from someone who has?

The concept of learning a watered down system is a very real concern. There are many Karate, Kenpo, Tae Kwon Do, and Kung Fu schools out there that are teaching the correct templates to their students, but have little to no knowledge of how to use their integrated structure, or generate force through these forms for devastating effect. These templates become dance movements!

There are many Brazilian Jiujitsu schools that teach the positions, transitions, and submissions of the grappling game, but are not covering a lot of the *hidden nuances* of body framing, correct weight projection, timing, and leverage that make the art such an effective machine for victory on the street. These schools are setting up their students for failure the moment they get in a serious situation.

There are many instructors in weapons based systems such as Kali, Escrima, Arnis, and Krabi Krabong, who are very concerned with acquiring their next set of drills for their students to clack their sticks to, all the while missing out on the true meaning of those drills as a bladed system of self-defense.

These attribute based drills become the focus of the training, versus the realization that these drills are simply a vehicle to learn. I have seen many an instructor of these various systems fold under pressure on base training with Marines once they are pressured in an uncontrolled environment. These are all examples of the watering down of the martial art systems and should be heavily weighed upon when researching your course of action.

To sum it up, you have to first be honest with yourself about what your true motivations are for getting involved in training. Chances are, there is a specific style and instructor who specializes in those needs and will be happy to accommodate you. Then realize that these motivations may change over time, and there is nothing wrong with changing directions in regards to style or a teacher to accommodate those changes.

Always do your research on the system, and especially the instructor. Don't be afraid to ask the "why" about a certain movement or set of drills. This is *your* training, no one else's; if you're not getting the answers to the questions you are asking, you should go to the school where you do. Search for teachers who aren't afraid of saying, "I don't know that." And make sure to hold on to the teachers that are willing to say, "Let me introduce you to a guy I know who does."

Nicholas Moreno has over 25 years of martial arts experience and specializes in the development and instruction of curricula with an emphasis on defense/control tactics, weapon of opportunity, Military Combative Blade and joint locks, and manipulation.

He is the current Director of Defense and Arrest Tactics for Naples Security Solutions in Naples, FL. These highly sought after custom training modalities are in high demand by law enforcement officers, military operators, private security providers, and civilians who want to learn a system that utilizes gross motor skills which are applicable in a variety of real world situations.

Prior to his relocation to Naples from San Diego, Nicholas taught as a subject matter expert to active duty military personnel at Camp Pendleton where he contributed over 1,600 hours of instruction to the Martial Arts Instructor (MAI) programs. During his tenure in California, Nicholas trained many elements of the military and law enforcement community including Marines, MARSOC, ATF, US Marshals, Navy SEAL SQT/Dev Gru, and NSW-ATC combatives staff.

Nicholas was promoted to Senior Sensei/Lineage Holder in Military Combative Blade in October of 2014 at WFTBN Edson Range (Weapons Field Training Battalion) Camp Pendleton by Ex SPF Green Beret, Grandmaster Harry Greene. In November of that same year, Sensei Moreno and Grandmaster Greene were invited to the Marine Corps Ball, where they received accolades and were honored for their contributions and commitment to active duty service personnel.

As Director of Defensive and Control Tactics for Naples Security Solutions, Nicholas brings a wealth of experience and credentials to serve his clients. Nicholas has held a 2nd degree Black Belt in Kempo since 1999, and has also been an avid practitioner and student under Rickson Gracie black belt Luiz Claudio of LCCT Combat Team since 1998.

Master Nicholas Moreno

Fighting Multiple Attackers:
The Jackal and the Wolf
Mike Mather

This is my expression, and opinion, on how to handle yourself and/or prepare yourself for a street fight against one or more people. First, let me start by saying that there is no perfect road map. My opinion is based on personal experience, continuous study, and understanding how the predators think, act, and prey on others.

There are two types of predators: the jackal and the wolf. The jackal preys upon the weak. A wolf will take on someone of equal or greater strength. Now imagine a pack of jackals or a pack of wolves. Understanding the demeanor of both packs, puts in perspective how you should train.

I think a person needs to be proficient in all five ranges: grappling, trapping, boxing, kicking, and projectile, with or without weapons. I've been fighting pretty much since I came out of the womb. I won't go into my whole background here, but I will say I wouldn't change a thing. I started out in wrestling at age six. Wrestling was a great attribute in developing my base, center, and, of course, explosiveness. Then I was boxing by age eight. Boxing helped me develop my footwork and hand speed.

My first lesson in kicking range was in Karate and Taekwondo. Those systems are considered a hard style. Karate and TKD taught me bone breaking power. By the age of 16, I held a black belt and started training with Sifu Al Dacascos. I had a great base. I was light on my feet, had fast hands, and had terrific power, but I was missing fluidity.

That's where the trapping range of Wun Hop Kuen Do came into play, while I was continually training in my bases. Eventually, I met Guro John Daniels and started my FMA training. So I am now covering all the different ranges. Again, that is only a brief explanation of how I started and what training helped me cover all five ranges.

I will start with body positioning. Regardless of the situation, understanding how to position yourself for any situation is 50% of the battle. I will tell you how I position myself in everyday life, so you get a better understanding of how I think 24/7.

When I go out to eat, or I am in any building where I will be sitting, I always sit where I can view any exit or entrance, especially the entrance. I do this so I can observe any person coming in. And, if I am with anyone, especially my wife, I always have her back. I also try to choose a seat where no one can sit behind me. A person might think this sounds like paranoia, but I can truly tell you, that is not the case.

I would just rather be prepared for a situation which is unexpected, than not prepared. When I walk down the street with my wife, or anyone for that matter, I always put myself between them and any other person coming from the other direction. This way, I'm in control of the range and can read any threat.

When being approached by a hostile person, my body position is at a 45 degree angle, hands up, palms facing them, as to say, "Stop!" without ever saying a word, and with a smile on my face so I appear harmless. If my bubble is breached, then I'm instantly standing on the balls of my feet, knees slightly bent, at a 45 degree angle, and hands ready to pass, parry, or strike within a split second. Since I'm on my balls of my feet, my calves are flexed, ready to spring into action in any direction. I call that the "Springs of Life."

My study has brought me to the conclusion that 95% of people strike first at the thing they hate the most – your face. Most of the people that you will come across, who are willing to do this, are usually untrained. Keep in mind that just because someone is not a so-called "martial artist," that doesn't mean they don't know how to fight.

I've met people, and have plenty of friends who have no training, that are tough street fighters and who would beat the shit out of most highly trained martial artists. Today, the criminals and villains are training just as much as the people going to martial arts schools, because you can find anything on YouTube, and most martial arts instructors will teach anyone with enough money to pay for classes.

So, how do you understand the jackal or the wolf? There is really no true way to understand them unless you hang around with, or "play" with, the predators. There is no book or instructional blueprint that helps you understand a person that says, "I CAN."

What I mean by this is that this person stands up for what he believes and will protect his brother at all costs, even if it means his life. The only other place you can find something close to this mentality is the military. My whole life, I've been attracted to those kind of people.

Almost every street fight I've been in has been against multiple attackers. Since most of my life has been around guys that have their brothers' back, I train to defend myself against those kinds of attacks.

Usually, if a group of guys approach you, there is always one guy who is the talker or the instigator. He is always standing next to the guy that he thinks is the biggest or baddest guy in the group.

My strategy is to first, put my back towards a place where no one can easily get behind me. Next, I take out the guy who is the quiet, intimidating guy standing next to the talker. When they see their toughest brother drop, it instantly deflates their confidence.

I am constantly changing elevation and direction, using triangular footwork, while striking in a new direction, as each target presents himself. The changing of elevation is done with my legs, like you would in a wrestling take-down or duck under.

If I ever have to turn to my blind side, I always cover my head with my hand which is on the side that I am turning into. I can't begin to tell you how many times I have witnessed fists flying over my head when doing this! Like I said before, the attacker's first natural instinct is to hit what they don't like, and of course, that is your face.

I also try and throw one of the guys towards his buddies. This puts an unconscious or dazed person between myself and the other attackers. When doing this, I have seen attackers accidently hit their own buddy.

There is a definite strategy in fighting multiple attackers. The most important strikes are the ones that affect their breathing, eye sight, or cripples them. If they can't breathe, they can't fight. If they can't see, they don't know where to hit. If they can't walk, they can't chase after you.

Always evaluate your perimeter. There might be an object you can slam your enemy into. This object can also be used as an obstacle, once the fight starts, for your enemy to have to maneuver around in order to get to you. This could allow you a second or two to reestablish your defense or attack.

You should also be aware of the ground you're standing on. Is it sand, concrete, dirt, gravel, ice, or grass? If it's sand, you have the perfect thing to blind your enemy by throwing it in their eyes; or if you end up on the ground, put it in their face. If it is concrete, use that hard surface to your advantage; make them land on it and then, use it like 20-grit sand paper across their face. Rake their face across it after you smash them into it!

If it's dirt, it has the same attributes as sand and is great for blinding or choking the attacker. If it's gravel, depending on the size of the gravel, it can be used as a long rage weapon. Small rocks, thrown hard enough, can hurt or knock a person out.

If it's ice, it is very hard and extremely slippery, so your moves should be evenly balanced in order to use this to your advantage. If it is grass, it could be slippery, muddy, and hard, so it has attributes you can use for blinding.

You can't always pick your perfect location or surface, so I choose to train my students outside any chance I get. So many schools forget the meaning of the term "martial." It basically means military or war. So why would you train on a padded floor in a gi; that is not reality. When is the last time you had a person threaten you with a gi on or on a padded floor? It's usually t-shirts, shorts, jeans, boots, etc., in my dojo.

Statistically, under tense situations, your brain remembers only a few instinctive moves. If you train for a person who isn't wearing a shirt, there isn't a sleeve to grab or a belt. You don't depend on grabbing a heavy gi, etc.

When you train this way, if they do have a jacket on, or a hoodie, this is just a bonus. Train as though your opponent has boots on, this way you are always expecting the unexpected. The key is train for reality. Train to fight against someone dressed as an attacker would most likely be dressed.

What if a weapon is pulled? Personally, I always carry a blade, or two, or three. Honestly, I usually carry three blades. One for my brother, one to throw away, and one to use. Remember, anything can be a weapon. Maybe you only have your car keys; well, the keys fit nicely between your fingers. I personally always have a weapon on my key ring. A deer horn is on one set, a blade on another set, and a travel wrench on another set.

Also, be aware of surroundings. Use your environment! You might be able to grab a bottle, a rock, a chair, etc. Using a projectile object can also be used as an ABC attack. Attack by combination, throwing an object at one guy, while striking another, or throwing something at an attacker, followed by a strike.

What if you are approached by multiple attackers while with your wife? How do you protect your wife, while, at the same time, defending yourself? This must also be talked about and trained for. Always put yourself between the threat and your wife or significant other. You should also educate your wife that she needs to get somewhere safe when the fight starts, especially if she is not trained to fight. My wife, of course, is trained and has been in a few situations like that with me.

This is one example of many. The year was 2007. My wife, the Big Indian, and I entered a lounge in Warrenton, OR, a big tourist spot on the Oregon coast. We had just ordered our drinks and sat down, and it was karaoke night. My friend, the Big Indian, David Brandon, loves to have fun and sing when he is drinking. Someone was singing his favorite song and he went out on the floor and started to sing with the guy. They were both having a blast.

Then, the Big Indian jumped up and stomped on the floor to the beat of music. Well, David is over 300 pounds, and when he stomped on the floor, the CD skipped and the song stopped. The other guy was fine; they gave each other high fives and David came over and sat down. The other guy was with a group of 12 and had a girlfriend who was in a leg cast. You could tell they had all been drinking for a while.

I overheard the girlfriend saying to him, "Are you gonna let some fucker fuck your song up?" She kept egging him on until he finally came over to our table and said something. David immediately jumped up, said he was sorry, and offered to buy him a drink. The guy said, "Cool," but immediately came back and said, "No, you need to buy all of us a drink!"

I then stepped up and told him in no uncertain terms, that this would not be happening. I told my wife and David to go pay our bill. I could sense trouble was brewing and wanted to get both of them out of a possible dangerous situation. While they were paying, I walked over to the group and confronted the guy and said, "Look, we are leaving. Have a good night." Of course, I was facing him at a 45 degree angle, hands up, palms facing him.

His response was, "You owe us all drinks!" Now, I could see it was going to be a problem. I responded with a stern warning, while moving my left hand down slightly, and showing him my chin. I knew he would swing, which he did. Where I approached him, was next to a pool table, so my sides were covered, as well as my backside.

He swung with his right fist. I passed the punch, grabbed him by the ears, and head butted him in the bridge of his nose about 10 times. Then I smashed his face on the edge of the pool table. I then changed directions, covering my head while turning. While in motion, I could see a fist fly over my head from the opposite direction. I put a side kick into the knee of the first person I saw while turning, breaking it as it folded backwards.

I immediately turned back and punched another guy in the throat. Now I had three down. I elbowed a fourth person with a right elbow to the jaw as he was approaching me from the behind. I followed that with a left cross to the same jaw. He was out. That was now four down. This all happened very fast! By this time, the bouncers stepped in to break it up. Three people took an ambulance ride!

I train for a situation in the way I would react myself. What I mean is, if I was with a friend and someone approached him in a negative manner, how fast would I react to aid him, whether it means controlling the approaching person or knocking him out. That's what I think about when I'm being approached by multiple people. I assume that everyone has the same process, so in a sense I'm fighting myself.

The question has been asked, how many street fights have I been in? The most honest answer is too many to count. I would say that 95% of all the fights I've been in were against two or more assailants. I can't think of any of them being similar to each other. There really isn't a perfect answer or a road map to success when fighting multiple attackers. The only thing you can do is prepare for the unexpected.

Try to add statistics to the equation of your training. Fighting one person, as opposed to fighting multiple attackers, is like comparing night to day. When dealing with one person, that person is in front of you and is your only focus.

When dealing with multiple attackers, the "what if" factor is in play – the unexpected, the unforeseen, the blind spot, the multiples of fist or weapons coming at you from all angles.

Fighting one person, to me, is like a regular sparring class. It is a walk in the park. Fighting multiple people is more like playing Russian roulette. The odds are against you from the start. The most dangerous part about fighting multiple people is what you *can't* see. Remember, if he can touch you, he can kill you.

Personally, I believe there are very few instructors that are qualified to teach students how to defend against one assailant, even fewer who are qualified to teach a student self-defense against multiple attackers or assailants.

Most instructors have never been in the position of defending themselves in a life-or-death situation. Everything you've been taught must become second nature, habit, instinctive, a split second reaction that causes the most pain with as little exposure as possible, while always being ready for what's next.

Some of my experience dealing with wolves on a professional level has been doing security work for the Hell's Angels. The reason I say wolves, is because they are a group of guys who not only have each other's backs, but will never back down or quit unless they are all dead, period.

Doing security for this type of group attracts other groups of a like nature, so you have to understand how they think, act, and move. I won't give any events or times, just understand I wouldn't have been put in that situation if I didn't earn their respect and trust. Things were handled accordingly, without prejudice, and very efficiently.

I've been asked, why I carry any weapons at all, considering the skill set I have. My answer is that I would rather have them and not need them, than to need them and not have them. A weapon is only as good as the person who is wielding it; so training every day is a must.

Reaction time is everything. Being proficient and precise is a must, because you only have that split second to gain the upper hand, before the second, third, and fourth person, etc., makes his move to take you out.

Understand the wolf and the jackal both attack with the intent to inflict extreme pain. It is not like the movies; they don't attack one at a time, *ever*! They attack all at once, and as fast as they can.

Look at it from this perspective, if you were with your friend, and a guy, or a group of guys, approaches him with a negative demeanor, how fast would you move to have his back? Now multiply that by 10 times, because these guys do this all the time. This is how you have to train to deal with multiple attackers.

I've been asked many times about going to the ground in a street fight. My opinion is, stay off the ground at all costs! I trained very religiously in grappling, so I can avoid going to the ground by defending against a grappling technique.

If you take the fight to the ground, I can guarantee you that the friend of your opponent will curb stomp your head. Staying on your feet is the only option for surviving on the street!

How does a person train to stay off the ground? I feel a person needs to be proficient in wrestling or BJJ. But that is not enough, a person also has to be proficient in boxing,

119

kickboxing, Karate, Kung fu, or the best, all-around martial art – Wun Hop Kuen Do.

Also, train as though your opponent has knives in his hands and on his feet. Understanding range is very important. You must be very quick and evasive. Learn to stick and move, and be light on your toes, using the "Springs of Life." Never give your attacker and easy target.

If there is one thing I can add for additional advice, it is if you're ever involved in any situation in which you are left with no choice but to use deadly force, hesitation is not an option! You must act fast and have the heart and willingness to see it through. THERE IS NO HALF WAY!

Sifu Mike Mather is an extreme martial arts stylist. He started training at age six in wrestling, boxing at age eight, where he received his coaching under the direct supervision of the #1 contender in the world, Sweet Richard Sue. He began studying Kung Fu at age 11 and Tae Kwon Do at age 13 with Master Marty Maye. Sifu Mather received his first black belt at age 16 under Grandmaster Wade Lewis. Mather is a 5th degree Master in Kyushu Jujitsu Karate under GM George Dillman, a 5th degree Master in Tae Kwon Do, and a Master in Shaolin Kung fu under GM Eric Lee.

He holds a 3rd degree black belt under Guro John Daniels, a full instructor under the great Danny Inosanto in the Filipino combative martial arts, which includes Jeet Kune Do, Kali Southern Filipino bladed art, Arnis (Northern Filipino stick art), and Eskrido stick and knife arts. Sifu Mather also holds a 6th degree black belt in Wun Hop Kuen Do under GM Al Dacascos and Mano y Mano hand-to-hand combat. He holds a 3rd degree black belt under Sr. GM Cacoy Canete in the Doce Pares System. He is a World Champion, full-contact fighter, holding over 30 national grand titles.

With over 40 years of experience in the martial arts, he has developed a unique blend of combative martial arts that delivers real striking power and force under extreme conditions. He has worked with the military and various other groups, on controlled force and defense against weapons tactics. Sifu Mather is the sole founder of Mather Martial Arts Academy, founded in 1988. He currently teaches traditional martial arts, mixed martial arts, and wrestling, and holds seminars worldwide.

His constant statement remains the same, "I owe all my training, dedication, devotion, loyalty, honor, integrity, and, most importantly, heart, to the most inspirational person in my life – my dad. Without my dad's superior job as a role model and a father, none of this would be. This is my love, my passion, and my life – always has been and always will be."

Sifu Mike Mather

16-Year-Old Black Belts
Don Newbill

Commercial martial arts dojos give belts to kids when they can perform certain katas, when they complete their contract, or in some cases, when they have been at the school for a certain amount of time. A black belt means you are a responsible, understanding, fearless, confident, tough, and mature practitioner of a certain martial art.

Realistically, kids cannot meet these requirements. In full contact arts, you have to survive some very difficult fights. These types of fights can be very damaging for children. Being a black belt means that the child, according to the grading system and requirements of that school, has achieved a certain level of proficiency and understanding of the art; nothing more and nothing less.

Some schools have diluted the spirit of the art by placing a high importance on achievement like getting a certain ranking or winning tournaments. You may see some schools marketing, "Get your black belt in one year with our super-duper-fast-track training program!" Luckily, these schools are the exception and not the rule. Currently, however, it seems the rule is swinging in the opposite direction. The problem is everyone is not created equal.

There are many examples of 16-year olds getting their black belt, while half a dozen of their classmates, who have put in their "time" do not get the rank. This puts instructors and schools in a very difficult position. You cannot keep failing them, or they will go somewhere else to train.

This puts instructors into a catch-22 situation. If they stick to their integrity, those students will go somewhere else, and the instructor will lose money. But, if the instructor caves in, he will lose his or her integrity by giving an unqualified student a black belt.

In Brazilian Jiu-jitsu, black belts must be at least 19 years old and recommends the student spend at least one year ranked as a brown belt to be eligible for the black belt. To me, the black belt is a rank of expertise, reserved for mature individuals at least 16 and older. Some people even think that age should be at least 18 years old before being awarded a black belt.

Each Dan level (1st degree, 2nd degree, 3rd degree, etc.) requires a minimum number of years in active training. The "Poom" is a junior black belt, represented by a half black and half red belt, which may be issued to anyone under the age of 16 who has met the skill and knowledge requirements of a black belt, but who is not old enough to be considered mature enough in life.

It is widely accepted that a child under the age of five cannot fully comprehend what they are taught. A child must be training as a color belt for at least 3-5 years to be considered for a legitimate Poom. To reach that level, a sixteen-year-old must start training around the age of eleven.

In the art of Taekwondo, official ranks must meet the requirements of the World Taekwondo Federation headquartered in Seoul, Korea. However, organizations, federations, and independent schools issue their own certificates, bypassing these requirements.

In many countries, children are permitted to wear black belts because their instructors are compromising the integrity of their art and caving in to the pressure of parents who want their child to have the coveted black belt. A lot of times, the schools use the child black belt as an advertising ploy as the, "Youngest Black Belt in the Area."

The United States Judo Association restricts promotions to juniors and seniors. The maximum age for junior ranking is 16 and the minimum age for senior ranking is 17. It would be impossible for a 16-year-old to earn a black belt in the USJA.

Having said all of this, what is a black belt? What does *being* a black belt mean? Let's go back to the beginning. A black belt was one of the community leaders. They were professionals such as priests and doctors.

Because of their intense training, they learned not only how to attack and destroy the body, but they also learned how to help heal the body. They were also, for a lack of a better term, *policemen* who protected their villages. It was not uncommon for the Master to use his students in the protection of the village.

Masters were often asked to mediate in civil disputes because of their calm manner and ability to make fair and balanced decisions. Masters were always courted by governments to train their soldiers.

Many black belts had occupations such as farming, art, carpentry, etc., and passed on their skills to others in the village. The black belt has always been known to fill many roles for the betterment of their communities. This is not something a child or a minor can do.

So, what type of goals do we set for black belts in modern times? Black belts should hold themselves to a higher standard. They should have confidence in their ability to reach any goal no matter the obstacles. They should have razor sharp focus and concentration. They are secure in their abilities and should not brag or show off.

The black belt should always be courteous and respectful. They are leaders, but also learners. He or she should believe in learning and growing every day of their life. We hold black belts to higher standards and expect much more from them than the junior ranks. Black belts should have a different standard in terms of mental capacity, healing arts, and pressure points.

There are those who believe that a 16-year old can be a 1st degree black belt simply because he or she has met all the requirements except for age. They learn how to run classes in the school. The 3rd degree black belt is expected to be able to open his or her own school, based on the advanced training provided.

However, a 16-year-old could not go out on their own, start and run a successful school. They are not mature enough to handle all the responsibilities including the financial aspects, legal challenges, marketing, and parents. While a 16-year-old may be able to defend himself against another 16-year-old, he probably would not be able to defend himself, or another person, against an adult bent on destruction.

I would not want to call the police for help and have a 16-year-old police officer as the one responding. They have not experienced life enough to make the type of split decisions (including life and death) needed and expected of a black belt. Back in the day, students were expected to train every day for up to five years just to be eligible for the Poom!

Today, students whine about having to train once a week, yet they expect the same rewards earned by those who have trained five to seven days a week for many years.

The Supreme Court heard oral arguments in Roper v. Simmons, in which scientific evidence highlighting the differences between adolescent and adult brains play a decisive role. Part of the argument was older adolescents may not yet have the ability to exercise adult impulse control, because their brains have not fully matured.

The prefrontal cortex is the last to be "remodelled." The brain develops from back to front. Remember, the prefrontal cortex is the decision-making part of the brain, often referred to as *executive decision making*. It is responsible for the adolescent's ability to plan and think about the consequences of his actions, sustaining attention, solving problems, and controlling impulses.

As the adolescent grows older, the myelin increases, improving the nerve cells ability to conduct electrical signals and function more efficiently. This study also used another argument, advanced by the AMA, which stated that adolescents rely more heavily on the amygdala, an evolutionary older area of the brain, associated with primitive impulses of aggression, anger, and fear, than adults do.

The prefrontal cortex, which interacts with, and in effect reins in, the amygdala, to temper impulsiveness and gut reactions with reasoning, does not fully develop until the early 20's.

Moral development is defined as an individual's ability to make principled choices and how to treat one another. Young adolescents often pose broad, unanswerable questions and refuse to accept responses from adults.

They tend to begin to view moral issues in shades of grey, rather than only in black and white, and tend to be unprepared to cope with them. Consequently, they struggle with making sound moral and ethical choices. (Kellough and Kellough 2008)

As you can see, a 16-year-old is not physically or psychologically developed enough for the responsibility that goes with a black belt. The black belt should symbolize the mastery of techniques required to reach the black belt level, but it should also symbolize maturity, mental and physical strength, humility, and respect.

You cannot compare the martial arts in the West with the martial arts in the East. The martial artists in the East train 3-4 hours, five days a week, and then additional time outside the dojo on their own. That is about 15-20 hours a week. In some schools the minimum amount of training time is 300 class hours and 36 months of continuous training to reach the level of black belt. There are few 16-year olds in Western martial arts that can boast of that kind of class time.

Also, they have not been battle tested by life. In addition, they are unable to show true compassion, as an adult can, and mentor students through the gateway of excellence. Remember, the black belt is the beginning of the journey, not the end. A 16-year-old may not understand that concept.

Keeping all of these concepts in mind, I do not think that it is appropriate to award anyone sixteen and under the rank of a black belt. For the black belt to truly continue to mean something, instructors must continue to have integrity in holding people to a high standard in order to earn this rank. They must not cave in to the temptation to lower their standards in order to compete with McDojos.

We must keep our standards high or else the black belt will not continue to hold any meaning at all. Make your training tough and keep your standards high. Don't give up your integrity for the almighty dollar!

Grandmaster Don Newbill started studying martial arts in 1964 at the age of 11 in Judo, along with what was then called Korean Karate. He was instructed by Sensei Les Fazakes in his garage in South Amherst, Ohio once a week. He won his first Junior Championship in 1967 and was mentioned in Black Belt Magazine in 1968. In 1969, he began studying a system called Ed Parker Kenpo Karate. He entered the military in 1972. He spent a short time in the jungle of South Vietnam, while stationed at Dak To, and studied a style they call Muay Lao, better known today as Muay Thai. In 1989, he became a police officer and taught martial arts on the weekends.

While teaching self-defense to prospective police officers at the Ohio Police Officers Academy, he met Sifu John Custer and began training in Hung Loy Kung fu. In 2002, he was awarded his Black Sash, 5th degree black belt, by Sifu Custer. In 2003, he was admitted to the Legion of Honor, a part of the World Hung Loy organization which was a sub group called the Poison Lotus Society. He took control of the Poison Lotus Society after being promoted to Lead Instructor (8th Degree Black) by Sifu Custer and instructed to make it his own. He is also a certified

Master of the Arts (9th degree black belt) Instructor with the International Kenpo Karate Academies. In 2005, he was inducted into the American Freestyle Karate Association Hall of Fame with a Lifetime Achievement Award.

Grandmaster Don Newbill

The Psychology of Self-Defense
Richard Hackworth

*"One of the most overlooked areas of training in
the martial arts is the psychology of self-defense.
Learning the psychology of self-defense could give
you an advantage when facing a violent attacker."*
Dr. Ronald Stone
*HaeMuKwan Hapkido Master, Martial Arts,
Sports and Injury Expert Witness*

When it comes to real world situations of self-defense where
you must survive a violent encounter, there are five stages of
psychological escalation that occur. The first stage is that of
unawareness. The second stage is awareness. The third stage of
escalation is being proactively aware. The fourth stage is that of
being physically and psychologically prepared. The fifth stage
is to be psychologically prepared to use the self-preservation
reflex.

Before elaborating on the stages of self-defense, it might be
wise to first define the concept. The dictionary defines self-
defense as a countermeasure that involves defending one's
health and well-being from harm.

The use of self-defense, as a legal right that can justify the use
of force in times of danger, is available in many jurisdictions,
but the precise interpretation varies widely. Furthermore, self-
defense can be broken down into the following categories:
physical, mental, and other forms.

Physical Self-Defense

This categorization can be further broken down into armed or
unarmed reactions to a physical threat. The chances of success
against such a physical threat depend on a large number of
parameters related to the severity of the threat on one hand, but
also on the mental and physical preparedness of the defender.
Control of fear, awareness, knowledge of techniques and

applications and practice become important factors in a successful defense.

Unarmed Defense

Unarmed defense against a physical attack is the hallmark of most martial arts styles and obviously relies on the use of one's body as a defense. Counter punching, grappling, kicking, joint locks, and counter chokes would pertain to this definition when applied in response to an attack or a recognized threat.

While combat techniques can and do occasionally apply, the applications of these techniques might not stand up well under legal scrutiny. In other words, rushing an opponent and purposely breaking his neck with a military combat technique might not be as acceptable legally as say a martial arts counter into a headlock. You must always think about the legal consequences of self-defense, as well as making sure you stop your attacker.

Armed Defense

Armed defense against an attack is defined by the use of weapons. A wide variety of weapons can be used for self-defense. The most suitable depends on the threat presented, the victim or victims, and the experience of the defender.

In many cases there are also legal restrictions, the primary one being the use of excessive force. In other words, a frail senior citizen in fear of his life from a much larger, stronger, younger attacker, (even one who is unarmed), might be legally allowed to use a cane as a weapon for self-defense.

Conversely, a person of equal size and strength as the attacker might not receive the same legal forgiveness. For example, using a machine gun against a civilian, who is merely threatening bodily harm to someone of equal size, would most certainly be considered excessive force.

While in some jurisdictions, firearms may be carried openly or concealed, expressly for this purpose, many jurisdictions have tight restrictions on who can own firearms and what type of firearms they can own. Knives, batons, defensive sprays, and personal stun guns are regulated much differently from state to state.

Everyday objects such as flashlights, tennis rackets, bats, rolled up newspapers or magazines, keys, utensils, and other tools, may also be used as improvised weapons for self-defense and are usually safe choices. On the other hand, items that are purposely built as weapons would leave the user highly vulnerable to legal prosecution, if used in a real world situation.

For example, a simple hook type cane would be viewed as an improvised defensive tool of opportunity, whereas, a cane advertised and sold with carved indentations, a sharp point, or one that has been filled with metal, certainly would be considered a weapon and not an improvised tool.

This is especially true if it has been marketed widely and sold as a martial art or combative weapon. The same would be true of pen knives, the kubotan (short stick) weapon, police batons, sword canes, switchblades, and modified metal reinforced martial arts umbrellas

Mental Self-Defense

Mental self-defense is the ability to get into the proper mindset for executing a physical self-defense technique. It is a truism that, if you are skilled in the physical aspects of a defensive technique but lack the mental preparation (expectation), toughness, self-control, and tenacity to execute it, you will not be able to perform the technique, especially under duress. Controlled environments cannot easily mimic the stress and adrenaline rush that occurs during an actual attack.

There is a very real need to be able to mentally enter the proper warrior mindset if one is to have a realistic chance of surviving a deadly encounter. This state of mind is the ability to focus purely on the successful outcome of a situation, without becoming concerned with the consequences, even if they prove personally injurious or fatal to an opponent during pursuit of the desired outcome.

The ability to get past any obstacle or attack is the essence of this never quit mindset. As mentioned previously, when trying to survive a potentially lethal encounter, there are five stages of psychological escalation that occur.

During *Stage One*, the defender is essentially unaware of any potential threats and has taken no steps to prevent any attack against themselves. They are not even situationally aware of their surroundings. An example might be a person walking around with a cell phone while concentrating on texting. At this point, they have little or no awareness of their surrounding environment.

In *Stage Two* of psychological escalation, we first become aware of a potential hazard, or several hazards. For example, in this stage, one might be casually enjoying a leisurely walk while enjoying nature but is only vaguely aware of any potential threats in the surrounding area. No previous study or preparation for defense has occurred. In this stage, the person is still not fully focused on the potential hazards that are present.

In *Stage Three* of the psychological escalation, we have taken a proactive approach by looking around for potential hazards and have mentally developed possible scenarios, or have considered potentially dangerous situations, in order to hopefully avoid them. At this stage, one has become focused on the surrounding environment. A conscious effort is being made to recognize surrounding environmental hazards and to identify people that might represent a potential danger to one's health and well-being.

The *Fourth Stage* of psychological escalation is that of being mentally prepared to defend ourselves or others, should the need arise. At this point, through study and practice, dangers, hazards, and appropriate responses are embedded in one's memory and can be recalled when necessary.

The **_Fifth Stage_** of psychological escalation is to be prepared and willing to trigger the self-preservation reflex. This means that we understand that we might be forced to take the life of another in order to preserve our own life or the life of someone that we are protecting. A commitment has been made to defend oneself.

At this stage, we must remain in control by not allowing the fight-or-flight instinctive response to take over. Religious or philosophical objections that might trigger any hesitation must be previously studied and thought through before putting oneself at risk. To hesitate is to fail!

Remember, the time to prepare for an emergency is _before_, not during, one. Although such a dangerous situation might be, or better yet, probably will be, instantaneous, we must train our minds to focus on the aggression and react as we have been trained. In other words, through practice we can learn to overcome fear.

It has been shown throughout the centuries of combat that not all soldiers start out as strong, brave warriors. Many are instinctively hesitant, shy, fearful, or too easily distracted. These behaviors are fatal in a life-threatening situation. It is for this reason that armies drill and practice combat scenarios.

It is also for this reason that the martial arts were developed. Through proper education and training, the flight reflex and other fearful behaviors are overcome. With practice and realistic repetition, a person can learn to react to attacks and recognize threats more easily. Proper self-defense or martial arts courses (not sports-based arts), should be marketed explicitly as being oriented towards effectiveness and directed towards situations as they occur in the real world, not in a ring with a controlled environment and a referee.

Once students have been properly drilled, they will have a much better chance of surviving an attack. Mental control, in addition to physical technique, is essential to such training, since people do not fear that which they have become accustomed to. There are also other forms of self-defense.

Avoidance

Being aware of and avoiding potentially dangerous situations is certainly a valuable technique for self-defense, as is learning how to make oneself less obvious. In other words, it is a sort of living camouflage. Obviously, it would be the loud, flashy, rich-looking pedestrian who is more likely to be mugged, than one who simply blends into the crowd. This might even be considered a form of modern day evasion techniques.

Recognizing likely scenarios and settings for ambush, as well as understanding the mindset of potential attackers, is essential if we are to avoid or escape a potentially life-threatening situation. Finally, when avoidance is impossible, one often has a better chance of survival by fighting to escape. Such escape methods have been referred to as *break away techniques* and are a mainstay for entry-level instruction in several arts such as Hapkido.

De-Escalation

This can be defined as using words, gestures, facial expressions, and body language to prevent, de-escalate, or end a potential assault. These verbal techniques include encouraging conversation, since the more an opponent continues to talk, the less likely he is to physically attack you.

Demonstrating empathy, offering a compromise or suggesting alternatives to violence, the use of multiple questions that require an answer, smiling, and strategically placing a barrier such as a desk, a counter, or a car door between you and the attackers, can also defuse a dangerous situation.

Finally, pointing out the fallacy of having a successful outcome to violence, such as having the opponent see you dial 911 or calling for backup from staff or strangers, may also have the same effect. In other words, de-escalation is a form of mental and verbal conflict management.

Alarms and Personal Barriers

The last category under this heading includes the use of such things as whistles, personal sirens, screaming, flashing lights etc., to deter attackers. A loud noise will sometimes draw the attention of others. In addition, such things such as large briefcases or purses can often be used to block an aggressor or to establish personal boundaries. Today they even manufacture such cases, purses, and luggage with built in Kevlar to deflect a knife or small caliber bullet.

On a final note, it is wise to remember the old adage that a successful defense is the one that works, regardless of how accidental, sloppy, or exaggerated it appears. After all, the goal is to arrive home alive, and anything that works to make that happen is a successful strategy or technique.

Grandmaster Richard Hackworth was born into a famous American military family; the military arts are in his blood. Hackworth is a highly sought after professional martial arts teacher, life coach, and business mentor. His martial arts career began as an exchange student in Japan. After graduation, he returned home and joined the U.S. Army. Stationed in Korea, he trained with the first generation of masters after the Japanese occupation.

KwanJangNim Hackworth was one of the first of what is now called a "Multi-Arts Grandmaster" having achieved Grandmaster level ranks in Taekwondo, Hapkido, Yudo, and TaeGukKwan. Hackworth's knowledge of Hapkido evolved into a new Hapkido form in itself. HaeMuKwan Hapkido, which became an official Kwan of the Korea Hapkido Federation in November of 2000. Hackworth has won international acclaim as a mentor and life coach to martial arts school owners. Combining his thorough research, motivational strategies, humor, wisdom, and international perspective, he inspires students and masters alike. He became the first non-Korean to be allowed membership into the prestigious Korean Martial Arts Instructors Association. He has earned seven martial arts Hall of Fame inductions in Korea and China.

In 2018, Hackworth become the first Westerner elected to the World Martial Arts Congress in Beijing, China where he owns a Taekwondo and Culture school, which provides Taekwondo instructors to local public and private elementary and middle schools.

Hackworth is the publisher of World Martial Arts Media Leadership Magazine, Producer of the World Martial Arts Radio Show, and Director of the World Martial Arts TV Show. The majority of his time is dedicated to helping traditional school owners grow their schools through the recourses that he provides at www.WorldMartialArtsMarketing.com.

Now making his home in Florida, Hackworth operates one of the world's most successful Korean martial arts schools. The American Dragon Martial Arts Academies is a chain of six schools dedicated to the preservation and promotion of traditional Korean Martial Arts. Richard Hackworth can be reached by e-mail at RichardHackworth@hotmail.com.

Grandmaster Richard Hackworth

Long-Term Effects of Hard Core Conditioning
Vincent Marchetti

I have been in the martial arts for 68 years. I boxed as a boy in Jersey City, N.J., but I don't count that. During that time, I have watched the training methods change drastically.

When you get old, your body tells you what things were a little too much. I have always trained to the limit. I took my training to the limit, as I always strived to make my instructors proud of me.

I was promoted to Grandmaster by the three greatest pioneers in all of the martial arts. These great men taught me to push my limits, and we were all close friends as well. My instructors were GM Peter Urban, GM Doug Nagle, and GM Michael De Pasquale, Sr. GM De Pasquale was a few years older than me and I loved him dearly; GM Urban and GM Nagle were my age.

I tried to gain the speed of GM Nagle by using rolls of quarters in my hands when I punched sand bags and speed bags. To honor GM Urban, I would punch a patio block 50 times every day with my right hand in order to toughen up my knuckles. I also practiced laying on the floor in a souchin position and having someone jump on my stomach.

In judo, while practicing a judo throw, I would do the entry to the throw 50 times and then make the full throw 50 times, and then do so with a partner (yow, JudoKa). Then my partner would do the same to me. Getting slammed to the mat 50 times every day takes its toll on your back! Too many years of that and I'm sure you would be dealing with some major health issues.

When learning joint locks, I would have my instructor put the lock on me to the max before I would tap out, so I could keep searching for the counters. We did the same thing with a choke hold; we would hold it until I would pass out. Michael "D" Serion was an example of how this kind of training can damage the body. He is now plagued with arthritis cramps in his hands and joints, just as I now have. Martial artists don't train like that now and that is probably a good thing!

So much of the hard core training from the old days was taken to the extreme. It is only when you get to be in your 60's, 70's, and older that you start to feel the negative consequences of such training. I actually have two fingers that will only move as one because of my hard core training. Two of my knuckles have fused together.

When you train in that manner, you don't consider the long-term consequences for your body. Many martial artists are riddled with arthritis, joint pain, joint problems, nerve damage, permanent loss of range of motion, shortening of the muscles, calcium deposits in muscle tissue leading to chronic aches and pains, as well as poor circulation and calcium deposits in bone tissue which leads to disfigurement and also loss of movement.

In addition, you can damage nerve pathways, encounter spinal problems, and develop weakened internal organs or heart problems from such training. If we are doing that much damage to our body, we are not practicing self-defense as it should be practiced. You can't defend yourself if you are too injured to fight back.

We should train hard, but also train smart. There is a right way and a wrong way to train. Be smart in your training, which means that you also take care of your muscles, nerves, joints, and internal organs. Don't do things now that will come back to hurt you later.

Hard core training is not the only thing which has changed over the years. Another thing that has changed a lot since the old days of martial arts is, when you were a black belt back then, you were something special. You were a person to be feared and respected. But you were also gentle, compassionate, and helpful to others. There was no such thing as five-year-old black belts or getting a black belt in one year.

It is silly to think that a five-year-old, or even a 10-year-old should be a black belt. Can these kids defend themselves from an attack from a vicious predator? Could they even defend themselves from an attack from a teenage bully? Not at that age! A black belt should mean something. It is not simply a participation trophy!

In my school, it still takes 7-8 years before someone can earn their black belt, but those who make it are *real black belts*. We don't take shortcuts! There are no real shortcuts in the martial arts. When someone tries to cheat in the martial arts world, he is only cheating himself and giving himself false confidence in his abilities.

Another problem that has been growing has to do with the black belt itself. Both teens and adults are now bleaching, sanding, and even dragging it behind a car to make it look older. The belt that is truly worn by years of use, wears only in the knot area and it is never supposed to be washed.

When you see a belt that is ripped to shreds, it shows me, and other real martial artists, that the person wearing it is trying to look more experienced than they really are.

Now there are companies selling these weathered, worn, and bleached belts. How phony is that! How is that any different from lying about your background?

I really find it funny, or actually, pathetic, when the age of the belt looks older than the person wearing it. This is not the martial way! A major part of Budo is the development of your character. How is deceiving people and lying about your background considered upstanding character?

We should get back to the old ways of martial arts and martial art training, but we should be smart about it. We need to bring back character and earning your belt, not buying them. We should get back to teaching character, honor, and the ways of

Budo to our students. We should make being a black belt meaningful again.

In closing, I would like to ask all my brothers and sisters in the arts to think about donating your talents to your community, your state, and our military. The police only get a one-time training with hand-to-hand close combat.

The military is the same, except for the Special Forces, which I teach. I also teach Military M.P. and SWAT divisions, Rapid Response Teams, and Special Reaction Teams on a regular basis. I have now taught each of these for 26 years, for free. They pay all expenses – hotel, air, and dinners. If you are capable, you can do the same for the great country we live in.

This is the greatest country in the world, fly that flag proudly and honor and support all uniform personnel. On a lighter note, lower ranks can also do free classes for organizations such as the Dare Programs, Boys and Girls Clubs, and the blind and handicap organizations such as HIP Foundation, which have no money to pay out. I have done hundreds of these in my 76 years in the arts. You will feel great and they will love you for what you give them.

Note: Grandmaster Marchetti passed away on September 5, 2018, just as the final edits to Secrets of the Martial Arts Masters were being made. During his last days, GM Marchetti said, "Life is about how to win." And that is exactly what he taught his students, the police, and the military.

We had several conversations after our introduction. I was finally able to convince him to write this chapter on the dangers of hard core conditioning. I would ask him to write me a chapter and GM Marchetti would respond, "I am not writer." But, in the end, he sent me this chapter, handwritten in what is fast becoming a lost art of cursive handwriting. The whole article was handwritten and mailed to me, along with several photos signed to me and thanking me for my teachings.

In my last conversation with GM Marchetti, I had just sent him the initial edits for his chapter for his approval. In his humble manner, he thanked me for, "Making him sound smart." And told me how honored he was by me allowing him to be a part of this book. He was too humble to understand that the honor was all mine. You will be missed my friend. Rei ~ Bohdi Sanders

~

Grandmaster Vincent Marchetti, a 10th Dan, not only taught the traditional Japanese martial arts, but also the history pertaining to its origin, and the ways of the Samurai. He was the founder of Michi Budo Ryu, which means the "Best of the Street Warriors." His system was a combination of the most realistic techniques of Judo, Jujitsu, and Karate. During his time, he participated in more than 1,000 shows and seminars throughout the United States. A plaque in his school read: "If a student fails to learn, a teacher fails to teach," and Sensei never failed his students!

Vincent entered the US Army in 1962 where he represented the US in Europe on the American Boxing and Wrestling teams. Since that time, as a certified police instructor, he had instructed continuous classes for police, military, SWAT, and US Marshals Rapid Response Team, and Counter-terrorism Units all over the country. His instruction brought him medals and awards from the Army, Navy SEALs, and Green Berets for teaching their Advanced Close Combat instructors, as well as awards from many state and federal agencies for teaching officers and agents.

Vincent Marchetti began studying Judo when he was 12 years. He had already earned his black belt in Judo when he began studying Karate with men like Don Nagle and Peter Urban, who eventually signed his Grandmaster certificate, along, with Michael De DePasquale, Sr. Vincent Marchetti accepted the title of Grandmaster out of respect for the men giving it, but was one of the most humble martial artists I have had the pleasure of knowing. He considered himself to be a teacher and his obligation was to pull his students up with him, leading by example and allowing them to continue to grow even beyond his

145

teaching. He never wanted quality students in any art to quit, and believed it was his job, and every instructors job, to help them continue training, especially when they lost their own instructor.

Vincent Marchetti owned Kearny Martial Arts in New Jersey for over 48 years and the school was considered to be the oldest of its kind in America. He also trained law enforcement and, as an Army veteran, was extremely dedicated to training the military, training our Navy SEALs, Green Berets, White House security officers, the U.S. Capitol police, U.S. Air Marshals, and the Department of Defense (DOD) Swift Reaction Team, and HE DID IT FOR FREE, as his contribution to our great country.

Vincent Marchetti believed in honor, respect and dignity; honesty and truthfulness meant everything to him. His handshake was his word, and he kept his word, and he taught his students to do the same. When a student asked him why he taught his students to fight so well, and yet told them not to fight," he explained that it is all based on respect. "When you respect someone you do not hurt that person. If someone disrespects you and wants to hurt you or your family, you teach them respect by being a great fighter. The last thing you want to do is fight, but you still have to have the ability to control yourself and to protect yourself and others when necessary."

GM Marchetti did not use some of the old school techniques in training his students, like toughening the knuckles by punching cinder block walls etc., because these training techniques are not healthy and would cause a loss of the hand dexterity necessary in today's world of technology, as his chapter stated.

In one of our conversations, he told me how he did this in the old days and that he now had two fingers in which the knuckles had fused together and only moved as one. He was wondering what he should write about at the time. I said, "THAT is your chapter! Martial artists need to know the dangers of doing such training." And from that came the chapter you just read.

Grandmaster Vincent Marchetti

Dragon

148

Martial Arts as a Path to Empowerment
Richard Van Donk

Is being a great martial artist more than just knowing how to kick someone's ass? For me, the answer is an emphatic, YES! Martial arts are so much more. 50 years in the arts, training, and teaching worldwide to thousands of students, has given me great insights that I would love to share with you. I was very fortunate to study with so many really great masters.

My thirst and quest to learn was deep and led me to make over 50 trips to Japan, India, and China to achieve top level Shihan or Grandmaster levels in three systems. I am telling you this not to impress you, but to let you know that I have traveled the distance and walked the walk, so that perhaps this may inspire you to do the same, or even to go even deeper into the arts, to embrace something more than just being a good fighter.

In the process of studying the arts, the training becomes a way of life and gives you many hidden qualities. Let me share with you my short list of what I like to see in my students in their reaching a black belt level. But first let me say that there is no greater feeling as a martial artist, or as a person really, than knowing that you can own a room. And that, whether they know it or not, everyone present is a little safer because you are there. That state of being alone gives you a human quality that is very rare. Everyone will respect you for your abilities and achievement in the arts.

Here are the qualities you will learn on your journey to becoming a martial arts black belt:

- Self-Assuredness
- Willingness to Learn
- Perseverance
- Focused Mind
- Strength in Body, Mind, and Emotions
- Mental Concentration
- Courage to Act Powerfully

149

- Overcome Inner Fears
- Dependability – Dedication – Determination
- Personal Discipline
- Commitment to Action
- Health Conditioning
- Enhanced Confidence
- Ability to Think a Few Steps Ahead
- Self-Defense Skills
- Increased Awareness
- Flexibility
- Ability to Stay More Balanced and Centered
- Self-Motivation
- Leadership Skills
- Ability to Deal with everyday Problems from a New Perspective

I know that is quite a list. Every moment that you train will be enhancing who you are. Every technique will bring new qualities to how you handle life. It is a natural byproduct of studying martial arts and of you taking the journey on the warrior's path. It will not always be easy, but the results are well worth your effort.

What would it be worth to you to have all these qualities in your life if you could just buy them? $50,000? $100,000? $1,000,000? I think they are priceless. In fact, for years, I asked black belts all around the world, while I was teaching seminars, if they would trade their black belt, and all the value they had gained on their journey to black belt, for $50,000, for $100,000, or for $1,000,000.

Everyone said an emphatic NO! Well, except a young 23-year-old who said, respectfully, that he would take $1,000,000 because he was young and he would just start over traveling around the world training with the money. That says it all. So, remember this when you are faced with dojo fees. Know that the training is an investment in yourself and who you are.

Having studied and taught the martial arts for half a century, I already had my own ideas about why people study martial arts, but I wanted to know from others, the deep internal reasons that actually drive people to the arts and keep them training.

So recently, I did a survey of several hundred martial artists of all rank levels to see what got them involved in martial arts in the first place. The survey statistics are very interesting and some of the percentages even surprised me.

I found out that people may start training for one very conscious reason, that turns out to be a cover story for fulfilling some deep inner need that is not so conscious to them. But people continue in the arts because training gives them so much more than what got them started in the first place.

It is most likely that one of those top 20 enhanced qualities you gain in training to become a black belt, which I mentioned earlier, are a heavy hidden influence that keeps you in the arts. I also find that friends and training partners are often the best encouragement to keep you going and showing up regularly for training. Do your best to get a training buddy!

Martial arts, for most of us, becomes a way of life – it kind of gets in our blood if you will. For me, now it is just plain fun and I love being very creative and going deep. I love to learn and I am constantly learning something new. Budo is in my blood. Do you ever feel that?

The Survey Results

34% of the students surveyed said they started martial arts because they wanted more self-confidence in order to feel stronger or to feel more empowered.

Self-confidence is about being more connected to who you are and accepting that. Being spiritual is about being fully connected. Also, nearly 100% of those surveyed confirmed that martial arts training empowered them in so many ways.

21% said it was the aspect of a spiritual path that drew them to the arts. This percentage was actually surprising to me, even though it was one of the main reasons that I sought out a dojo when I first started.

Most of them clearly stated that they were not seeking a religious path, but a spiritual one, with many of them wanting that spiritual path to also be compatible with their current religion.

It is interesting, if you look at the word *Budo* – Bu means martial and Do is the way or path. The Japanese Do, in this context, is the same word as Tao in Chinese. So, Budo can also be a spiritual path that is not defined by a specific religion. It is a study of nature, your nature, and the path of life you embrace. More on that later.

17% said that it was inspiration from a movie that got them to sign up to train. Now, who isn't inspired by Bruce Lee, Jackie Chan, Jet Li, Ninja movies, or a Marvel super hero? Who doesn't want to be able to do all those cool fight moves, right?

We've all come out of one of these movies wanting to Kung Fu something or someone. Fess up now, and raise your hand on that one. If not, it is back to basket weaving or yoga for you!

15% said it was because they were either bullied or lost a fight and did not want to be picked on, pushed around, or lose another fight again. I really think that this need for being able to defend yourself is, in reality, a deeper core than what is represented in this number. Who wants to be weak and helpless? No one! I can tell you from personal experience, it is a great feeling to know that you can own the room.

11% said they wanted to be able to defend their family. I think far too many people rely on having a gun to do this. 90% of all incidences will be in places where one may not have a gun, nor would it be advisable to use one. It is great to know that, wherever I am, people are a little safer because I am there.

A small 2% said that it was a friend that got them involved, but that still doesn't tell us the personal reason or the personal gain they received from starting the arts.

I personally think, at the core, martial arts builds self-worth by overcoming inner weakness and truly empowers us. People train because it makes them stronger in so many ways – physically, mentally, and emotionally, as well as spiritually.

Martial arts builds personal presence. In time, it will transform your ego and help you overcome all inner battles. At one point or another, the training will force you to look deep, and that is the real goal of stripping away all illusions of any injustice or battle within you – to reach peace and harmony. When you can live that and be an example of that, you are a true role model.

Martial arts begins and ends with respect. That should start with you and extend to the art itself, then your instructor, and then to everyone that you train with. Respect is honoring the core of yourself, a humbleness to the Source within you. Some systems would call that the Tao (道). In Japan, the same term is Do (道), meaning path or way.

Budo (武道) is a Japanese term for martial arts. Bu meaning martial and Do (道) meaning Way. We are studying the warrior's path – martial way. We study in a dojo (道場), meaning the place of the way – your place of practicing and experiencing the Way. We practice in a DoGi (道着) – which means the uniform of the Way. Dogi is commonly shortened to gi. The Tao is all encompassing.

Temple Arts
India – Tibet – China – Japan

Martial arts are temple arts. Historically, a dojo was a room in a spiritual or religious temple. Culture influences your religion and beliefs, which influence the way that you view the world. In India, the arts like Kalaripyat have a Hindu influence. In China, it is Taoism and Buddhism. In Japan, Shinto or Zen Buddhism have their influence.

In Japan, dojo training was done in a special room in a part of a temple complex. The training room was specifically built to create a sacred space where one could study oneself, as he or she practiced inner arts like meditation, as well as martial techniques.

The entire training was about personal evolution. Everything in the dojo space had a meaning and a purpose for empowering the space and the people training there.

The dojo is divided into four seats of power, distinct sides, and the direction orientations in the following order:

1) ***Kamiza*** – Upper side – South Seat of spirit or God (Kami - 神)

2) *Joseki* – East side wall

3) **Shimoseki** – West side wall – window to let in sunlight on shrine

4) *Shimoza* – Lower sidewall – North – students enter here, at the inferior seat, into the mat space.

The *Kamiza* (上座), being the superior seat of the dojo space, is the place of honor and is usually decorated with the sacred shelf known as the *kamidana*, (meaning spirit shelf). The *kamidana* can be as simple as a small wooden shrine or an elaborate shelf with many shrines, candles, incense, plants, *ofuda* (blessing plate), calligraphy, pictures of a master (living or past), swords, or other symbols of the school on it.

When bowing in the class, the *Sensei* (先生), one who has gone before, sits himself directly in the center of the space facing the *kamidama* (seat of power), about one-third distance of the dojo back from the *kamiza*. Sitting at this position, the Sensei will receive the light of the sun off of the mirror that is reflected from the window of the *Shimoseki* wall, so that they will be a mirror of light for the student as they say a prayer blessing, clap, and a bow them in to the *Tao/Do* or "Way."

This is one of the reasons why the highest-ranking students sit closest to the teacher. They have earned their way to be closest to the seat of power. Never would one sit in front of the teacher.

One day by the grace of the spirit and master, they will sit in that same position and bow their students in. I will never forget my first time bowing in about 100 students for Grandmaster Hatsumi's class, in his hombu dojo. (*To clarify, he was running a bit late and asked me to do this*).

Rei, or bowing, is entering "zero" and paying respect to the art, the space, and to those that have gone before you, including the sensei (one who goes before).

Did you know that in India the bowing of the head to the master was for the master to check the crown chakra of the student to measure their progression and allow him or her to feel deeply into the student's energy system to measure where they were at in training and in life? This gives the master knowledge by which to teach the student.

In my Dynamic DeCuerdas Eskrima system, it is customary for the head master to lay his hand on top of a perspective student's head to see if they have a hot head (checking the crown chakra and energy system). If their energy is too fiery they will not be taught the arts, or we will only selectively share with them.

A teacher is always responsible for what he teaches others. Monks in China do this through measuring the body's energy and learning the energy systems of the body. The Shaolin will overcome unbalanced energy by channeling it into body exercises and extreme conditioning, harnessing the power, and mastering it.

155

Martial arts masters of India, China, and Japan, have, since the beginning, tempered the power that they taught students with meditation. Ninja Grandmaster, Soke Hatsumi, once recommended that I train only with women for 6 months to balance my hard style Karate energy, as I needed the feminine balance. It did wonders for me on so many levels and changed my martial arts forever.

Stretching exercises open up the energy flows in the body to free any blockages in the body-mind-spirit system. This yoga method comes from the Nath Yogis that used stretching the body to open the nerve channels so that they could meditate longer.

Even in religious pictures, the Archangels are shown with swords or weapons. Saint Peter cut off an ear in front of Jesus. Arjuna fought for Krishna. Mohammad led armies. All this is a rise against injustice. That is the greatest reason for martial arts – to overcome injustice in all its forms.

In learning Marital Arts, what are we really protecting?

The longer you train, the more that you really realize that the toughest battles that you ever have to face are between your own two ears. Even if you can beat 100 trained men in battle, if your anger is always out of control, making you and your life suffer, then you are no better off as a warrior, as you are constantly defeating yourself.

Martial arts are also about personal empowerment. Again, the Do in Budo is the same as the Tao, meaning way or path. Learning to still your mind or focus your thoughts is important in life and imperative in a life-threatening situation.

The masters of these ancient Do teachings use them to develop incredible physical and nonphysical strength, with great inner powers. They use them to evolve their lives and become healers. They use them to become in tune to God and nature. They use them to do what others would call superhuman feats.

They use them in battle for survival. They use them for inner peace. The teachings of the Way have been in place for thousands of years. Some teachers mark this path well for their students, and others do not. One must realize that instructors are in their own various stages on the path.

At one time, the arts were only taught as a complete holistic way, not just in parts and pieces as it is today. When you were accepted to train at the temple, you would be working on refining your own inner self first and establishing great body conditioning even before you started learning the martial portions of the art.

It was imperative to have a pure, peaceful heart that was worthy of defending. In reality, the martial arts are meant to be taught integrated in this way, as one whole way of life, even if that's not what has been taught to you. People can only teach what they know.

There is no right or wrong in this it is just a matter of what your own desire is in Budo, and how far you want to go on the path. I personally feel that personal enlightenment can only come about through total immersion in the martial arts tradition as a way of living.

This enlightenment is characterized by the development of the benevolent heart. Stronger than love itself, the benevolent heart is capable of encompassing all that constitutes universal justice and all that finds expression in the unfolding of the universal scheme. Because you must connect with other people to learn, what we do is actually a study of humanness. So, through your training, you will actually come to understand your own humanity.

In the Bujinkan Ninjutsu arts, we have a term "Shidoshi," one who removes ignorance and shows the Way, for a fully licensed teacher, which is only given at 5th degree black belt after taking a test referred to as the "Sakki" or killing intent test. For this test, the student sits in front of a senior DaiShihan in seiza, with their back to the administrator of the test. The student sits silently in seiza and waits for an undetermined time until the sword cut strikes at their head. The student must not only feel that sword strike, but move completely out of the way without being struck.

Done properly, this test is much deeper than what it appears to be. A connection to the teacher is important. A student must trust that the art will take care of them.

The teacher first internally connects to the student, feeling to feeling, and sends energy through the spine of the student to reset their humanity, helping them achieve the state of zero.

When a student truly tunes in, they are moved by this downward strike, instead of moving themselves. It is an unforgettable feeling. I still remember my fifth dan test in 1987. I was one of the first to be given this test by Soke Masaaki Hatsumi and to pass on the first attempt, and also one of the first to give this test outside of Japan, on the Soke's behalf.

Before the 5th Dan, we study the *Omote,* or the outer side of the art, the more physical aspects. At the 5th Dan level, we begin to study the *Ur*a, or the inner side of the arts. We begin to learn more about the yin and yang of the arts, and about *Kyojitsu*, the art of knowing the difference between truth and falsehood. We study this in the world by first mastering it in ourselves.

There is a lifetime of travel on the journey of self-discovery. The further you travel, the more you learn that there are no mistakes, no real surprises, and there is no separation. This is why the Chinese have a saying about the Way which goes, "The Tao that can be told is not the true Tao."

For a better understanding of where you may be on the path, I have carefully marked the Five Tori Entry Gates on the journey. I've divided the progression along the way into several different stages, which I will call Tori Gates.

158

The Stages along the Warriors Path – the 5 Gates are:

Tori 1 – Practitioner
Tori 2 – Teacher
Tori 3 – Scholar
Tori 4 – Healer
Tori 5 – Shihan/Sage

I am giving just a brief summation as an overview here. If you are interested in this in greater depth, please see my work, *The Shidoshi Teachers Training Course.*

In training in the martial arts, you've already gone through the first Torii gate, that of a practitioner. In time, you'll begin to share the art with others, and you will develop into a teacher, going through the second Torii gate. Being a teacher naturally creates a desire to learn more details of the art so you can share them with others, which brings you to the scholar, the third Torii gate.

The more you understand about the past and its teachings, the more you begin to heal the inner and outer aspects of yourself. Others will witness your new abilities and the change in you, and will want your help and guidance for issues in their own lives.

Students will bring you their troubles, and they will trust your judgment, as you have already traveled this path yourself. This will bring you to the Healer stage on your path, the fourth Torii gate. You may even learn some healing arts. Soke Masaaki Hatsumi clearly states that medicine and Budo are the same.

Very few will continue far enough on the path in the martial arts to reach the 5th Torii gate, Sage or Shihan, as a life practice is required. But, if you do, after many years, you will have mastered your art as a practitioner, you will have taught many students to high Dan levels and you will be very respected as a teacher, and you will have helped many students and people in your community with physical, mental, or spiritual healing, to a level that you will be referred to as a role model, or Shihan. This level is also the level of the sage.

The Japanese word, some refer to as "master," really means role model. The Chinese word for this would be translated as priest or sage, and sometimes as Sifu or Daoshi. At this point, the wisdom that you have gained on the path to achieving the level of Sage will be received by others more as a transmission of who you are, than any technique ever will.

Your presence in the room changes the room and the way that people feel. All the highest teachings are really nonverbal; "Presence of Being" speaks volumes. Your martial skills will also now embody this. This infinite Budo path unveils an evolution of human potential that is unlimited. Living the Way fulfills my destiny and enriches my soul. I am sure that it will for you as well.

I personally use the term Doshi. Since the "Do" equals the Way and "Shi" is to show. So Doshi is a "Shower of the Way" or a "Way Shower." In Budo, that is exactly what I am. I do my best to do that as a role model by being everything that I am. It goes much farther than the techniques that I teach. Of course, it shows up in my martial ability. But then again, I always remember that I am on a journey of my own self-perfection. Every student is my mirror and everything is my teacher.

Again, if you would like a more in-depth view of these Five Gates, see my work, *The Shidoshi Teachers Training Course*.

How far should this level of personal perfection really go? When we surrender to who we really are, we transcend ourselves don't we? We then enter a spiritual realm. Our path is to be pure as the Tao. This is the ultimate harmony. To do this, we must learn and know our own nature.

I dove deep into my own nature and into the arts on this journey. I loved training and exploring it so much that it was all that I wanted to do day or night. So much so, that I figured out ways that everything that I did could relate somehow to some aspect of the training. I would even go around the house picking up stuff with my hanbo (short wooden staff). Over time it became my way of living. It can become yours too, if it is not already.

I mean this from the standpoint that everything in life can be training. The true way of learning is to grow in awareness. Although we study information, the teachings are not really in the information itself.

Information comes and goes out of your brain, but when you gain awareness on more levels, knowledge is automatically obtained without conscious thought. Once knowledge is incorporated as a part of you, it becomes natural and no thinking is required. This is why Ninjutsu Master, Soke Hatsumi, is always reminding students, "Don't think, *feel*."

Martial Arts is a Feeling Art – So is Life.

Your life will never change if you do not change your attitude towards life. In my honest opinion, life is what you make it and how you respond to it. Indeed, no one is better than anyone else, that is for sure. Some people see life as lemons and others will just add a little sugar to it and make lemonade. I do hope you find the life you truly want. And yes, peace can exist, even in chaos.

So own yourself fully. Be empowered. Will you be white belt level empowered or will you be black belt level empowered? Or will you be Master Sage level empowered? It really is your choice. But remember, in reality, you will be graded more by others, and their experience of you, than by yourself.

By studying our own nature, we are studying our own flow in life. It is not just about studying the martial part of the art; it is about what you become in the process. Will these great arts, and this path of a warrior, simply build your ego, or will it strip away all the false illusions of who you are and lead you to a pure heart? Much Respect ~ See You On The Mat!

Grandmaster Richard J. Van Donk was born in Stockton, Calif. on July 15th, 1950. Warrior names: Kofukuryu (Happy Dragon), Mr. Happy by Soke Hatsumi. Spiritual Name: Satchitananda (Satji for short) meaning is Sat (Truth) Chit (Consciousness) Ananda (Bliss)

Richard considers himself to be a perpetual student of life, always questing the Divine within everything and everyone. This journey of self-discovery has brought Richard all over the world to discover everlasting Truth, Consciousness and Bliss. On his path to wisdom and spiritual growth, he went to every holy, sacred site he could and found the wisest teacher, guru, mystic, priest, priestess, or shaman to share with him their knowledge.

Richard spent time visiting such sacred places and people as the Pyramids and Nile temples in Egypt, Machu Picchu in Peru, Satgurus and Temples all over India, the Dali Lama, the holy lands of Israel, Stonehenge, Glastonbury, and Avebury in England, Ephesus, Delphi, and Istanbul in Turkey, Mt. Shasta, Ca., American Indian holy sites, Mikkyo Temples in Japan, Hunas of Hawaii, Central American ancient civilizations of Palenque, Teotihuacan, and several others deep in the jungles of Mexico, etc., searching and studying aspects of spirituality. Richard is now studying Mikkyo (and kuji kiri) with a master teacher in Japan and Hamsa Kriya Yoga from a Himalayan Nath Yogi (now at Acharya teacher level). His core teachings are embodied in Uni-DynamicsTM "The Science of being One."

Richard Van Donk started formal martial arts training at the age of 17, informal at age 11. Grandmaster Richard Van Donk is the Founder and Director of Bushindo University and the International Bujinkan Dojo Association (Ninjutsu) operating worldwide in over 120 countries with its International Dojo Headquarters in Middletown, (Northern) California, U.S.A.

Richard is one of the highest ranking Bujinkan Ninjutsu Shidoshi (Instructors) outside of Japan (10th Dan in Ninjutsu/15th Dan in Budo Taijutsu from Grandmaster Masaaki Hatsumi) and an internationally acclaimed Eskrima Grandmaster (personal student and inheriting Grandmaster of the late DeCuerdas Grandmaster, Gilbert Tenio). Also he has been awarded black belt levels or above in Karate, Jujitsu, Tae Kwon Do, Muso Tenshin Ryu Iaijutsu (yondan), Aikido, and Enshin Ryu Iaido, and Batto Jutsu (from Grandmaster Kenshinsai Machida). In 1996 and 1997 the World Head of Family Sokeship Council awarded Master Van Donk with its most prestigious award of Grandmaster of the Year for his contributions to martial arts. He has been inducted into many Master and Grandmaster councils. You can reach Richard through the following sites: www.ninjutsu.com or www.bushindo.com. For online courses and teachings go to www.BushindoUniversity.com.

Grandmaster Richard Van Donk

Maai – Distancing
Carol Womack

Maai is a Japanese term in martial arts referring to the distance, timing, and rhythm between opponents. The art of Maai relates, and communicates, within constructed space-time intervals which people interact (Hall, 1989). Maai, in the martial arts, is the concept of the space between two opponents in combat that incorporates the span of engagement, as well as the time it takes to cross the distance to strike the opponent.

There exist several good examples of distancing in everyday life, such as the boundary of personal space, which is often referred to as the bubble or sphere that causes the individual to feel intruded upon. However, martial arts practitioners utilize distancing based on the strategy of timing and rhythm.

In Karate, Maai is taught in various degrees among different styles. Students gain an intuitive understanding of Maai through Kumite (sparring), Kihon Drills (basic drills), and basic self-defense techniques. To utilize these techniques, one must be able to close the distance using timing and rhythm.

Optimal Maai, or the critical distance, is to strike without being struck. Therefore, this is the maximum effective range, one inch further away and the technique would miss. If one intends to move forward, an action must take place. The maximum range at every point of the body includes motions of the body using a kick, punch, or weapon.

It is the surface around which the fighter can attack. If one is within the range of attack, he has to guard or move away from the immediate danger. By using Maai, the distance can be manipulated to control the actions of another without an actual attack.

In combat training, there is a cadence for each movement or technique. Distance, timing, and rhythm flow in variation, rather than a consistently, uniform manner. Defensive techniques used, such as blocking, dodging, or attacking, each has moments of rhythm and timing to create distance.

In Okinawa, many senseis teach that a lack of Maai is to move as water, without tempo or rhythm. Maai training is best understood and perfected by working with an actual opponent. However, supplemental training includes the makiwara, heavy bag, sparring techniques, and kata.

Miyamoto Musashi's *Book of Five Rings* describes the use of Maai as, "Daisho chisoku hyoshi no naka ni mo, ataru hyoshi wo shiri, ma no hyoshi wo shiri, somuku hyoshi wo shiru koto." William Scott Wilson translates this passage as, "Within the rhythm of large and small, fast and slow, you should understand the rhythm of striking, the rhythm between actions, and the use of counter rhythms."

Fighters must be able to discern distance. The timing considerations are slow and fast, whichever is relevant to the situation. Knowing the opponents timing will create unexpected opportunities to attack.

Optimal Maai is defined as the critical distance. Optimal Maai is the range in which the strikes will be superior and the opponent's least effective. It is the ability to make contact without receiving contact. The definition of critical distance, taught in all styles of martial arts, varies somewhat from style to style. Each style of martial arts teaches the concept of controlling distance within the fighter's range to win the fight.

Critical distance is an individual determination. Each attack will have its optimal distance based on the skill sets and style among fighters. This concept is what contributes to the overall concept of a fighter's critical distance.

Taller fighters are often taught it is more effective to fight on the outside, whereas, shorter fighters are taught to fight on the inside for superior penetration of space.

However, critical distance is determined by the skill set, as well as the style of the fighter. Every attack is unique and has its ideal distance. This ideal range is based on where the fighter can initiate his most effective attack without the opponent's use of his or her weapons. It is essential for martial artists to have a good understanding of range. The best fighters will have superior control of critical distance. These fighters will have an acute understanding of their range concerning their opponent.

Combat or attacks can occur from different ranges and quickly shift from one range to another. Understanding of distancing, works together with proper technique. Long-range, mid-range, and short-range confrontations all are based on different types of technique. A fighter cannot elbow someone from long-range unless the distance changes. It is also a challenge to front kick the opponent if in close range.

Many martial arts develop the transition from long-range to mid-range or short-range, to manipulate the distance and for counter attacks. In weapon styles, the ability to change the distance between the ranges is important since the weapon increases the distance. This includes the bo staff, sai, nunchaku of Okinawa Kobudo, or the long or short blade, using the katana and wakizashi or, as in the Filipino Arts of Arnis, the Espada Daga (sword and dagger).

It is significant to remember that each strike has its ideal distance. Long range is outside of leg reach, or just at the edge of arm's reach, medium range is within arm's reach, and close range is grappling contact. The most versatile examples of fighting ranges are out of range, long range, medium range, and close range.

Body shifting is a tool used in Maai. In Japanese, body shifting, or body movement, is referred to as Tai Sabaki (body movement), or Ashi Sabaki (foot or leg movement), and Tenshin (shifting). These are examples of how martial arts practitioners shift their stance or posture to evade an attack. One does not have to block an attack if one is not in its path. In

167

kumite, fighters often move forward and back to shift in and out of range. However, there are other types of maneuvering in the martial arts which are beneficial in all types of fighting, whether it be sport or actual self-defense.

Types of Maai (Distancing)

Out of Range

Being out of range means the distance from the opponent is too far to enable either fighter to make contact. Being out of range means that there is no immediate threat to either opponent.

Long Range

Examples of long range distance would include striking range attacks, found in the boxer's jab and cross, as well as a Karate fighter's roundhouse and spinning back kick. Long range is often a preferred choice for taller fighters that prefer to stay on the outside of a smaller opponent. Okinawan Shorinji Ryu was founded by Joen Nakazato, who based it directly on the teachings of Chotoku Kyan, and preserves the original Shuri-te. According to Nakazato, Kyan was a small man who had difficulty fighting taller opponents.

His strategy was the use of a vertical punch, which increased the distance to reach the face. Other examples would be the bo, also known as the long staff, the Okinawa eku, as well as the long sword. These weapons are best suited for fighting in long range to middle range distance. Examples of long range techniques and weapons are:

- Kicking Range
- Punching Range
- Bo Staff
- Eku
- Katana
- Wakizashi

Middle Range

The middle range may be defined as the distance from the arm's length extended, or where an uppercut or back fist would land. This is the danger zone for many fighters. Techniques that occur from the mid-range are power strikes. There is a short and explosive move from long range to middle range.

- Elbow
- Knee Range
- Uppercut
- Tuiefa
- Kama
- Nunchaku
- Angle Kicks

Short Range

Short range distance is intended to utilize the fighter's power. Short range boxing may also be known as "infighting" and is a learned skill. Many boxers can work quite happily at long and mid-range, but short-range work provides higher risks and is generally more physically and mentally tiring. Techniques delivered at close range are intended to deliver maximum power.

- Elbows
- Knees
- Palm Heels
- Judo
- Grappling
- Short Weapons

Timing

To hit the enemy "In One Timing." This statement means the fighter has closed the distance with the attacker to hit them as quickly and directly as possible. The timing involves attacking the enemy before they withdraw, move, or throw a technique, this is "In One Timing." One must train to achieve this timing, to be able to hit in the timing of an instant.

> *"You win in battles with the timing in the Void born of the timing of cunning by knowing the enemies' timing, and this using a timing which the enemy does not expect."*
> Miyamoto Musashi

To move a specific distance, from which he or she feels the most comfortable when engaging in conflict with an opponent, requires timing as well as rhythm. This timing is developed based on several elements such as body type, attitude, and type of martial arts styles.

The martial artist has to develop the ability to instantly identify the strengths and weakness of their opponent and move in quickly to deliver techniques which can overpower those strengths. Modifying the timing of techniques, or taking the opponent out of his range, are the key principles in Maai.

Altering Maai can force a reaction by the opponent. By adjusting Maai, one can ensure that he or she can react to the threat. The instant a fighter fails to adapt to Maai, there is a gap, and an opportunity, for the opponent to move into this space to strike.

Rhythm

Rhythm is connected to Maai, and is needed to control fighting range. Controlling the pace establishes the distance needed to execute techniques. Close range to the opponent will require more energy.

While out of range, both fighters circle each other until the distance changes through control of footwork to establish optimal fighting distance. The in-and-out of footwork is most intense at a distance of three feet.

170

At close range, it becomes a grappling situation, which not all martial arts prepare for, so many will move from close range to middle range, to readjust their footwork. In combat, the distance one covers with movement is something needed to calculate precisely to know when to execute the technique.

Get the pacing wrong, and one will end up missing the target and taking a hit. Understanding rhythm in martial arts is vital in both combat and self-defense. It should be taught at beginning levels of training from basic kihon, kata, and kumite.

In a traditional martial arts environment, the student first learns basic kihon drills. These drills introduce to the student Maai, rhythm, and timing. Fundamental training instills correct form into both the subconscious mind and muscle memory. Through correct body mechanics, martial artists' rhythm and timing are developed for hand-to-hand combat to react in an actual confrontation.

Developing Maai

Maai can be developed with the practice of kihon drills, kata, and kumite techniques. These are the standard practices found in most martial arts schools and dojos. Martial artists can develop stronger techniques by incorporating heavy bags, footwork, and shadow sparring in solo training. However, the best training situation is that which involves a partner.

Kihon combination drills (basic kicks and punches) with a partner develop Maai by repetition of drills that are based on attack and defend in a controlled environment. This develops an understanding of the distance required to block and delivery of techniques in motion. Kihon drills develop and refine individual techniques and body mechanics working with partners of different sizes and body types.

Kata was originally meant to record self-defense techniques and combat movements; it is the beauty of combat. Most important is the understanding of bunkai (application). This understanding

171

is expressed through rhythm and timing of technique. There is a relationship between the combined techniques, represented by pauses or natural transitions, between movements found in combat.

Kumite teaches distance and timing of striking spontaneously. This form of training is closer to a real-life situation than any other form of Maai practice. Having a strong understanding of distance, timing, and quick reflexes, allows one to prepare for various scenarios and create an understanding of the distance required to defend and attack, as well as when to retreat.

Kumite will develop an understanding of the best opportunities to hit the target, and how to move safely out of reach. Kumite is performed under controlled circumstances and is usually done with protective equipment, but the problem is that it is often predictable. However, one can benefit from kumite training by understanding how to change the distance to manipulate and develop optimal Maai.

In martial arts, the range of a fighter can initiate his or her most effective attacks. It is important to have an understanding of Maai and the various distance ranges to be a competent fighter. It is critical to know that every strike has its unique ideal distance. Through critical distance, the application of Maai concepts can be applied to actual combat situations through traditional training methods and dedicated practice.

Dr. Carol Womack has studied Karate and Kodudo for 36 years. She is an 8th degree black belt in Isshinryu Karate. Carol is a 7th degree black belt in Tokushinryu Karate under Tokumura Kensho Sensei, 9th Dan of Okinawa for 22 years. She is a 5th Dan in Ryukon Kai Kobudo under Iha Kotaro Sensei of Okinawa, 10th Dan.

Carol travels extensively to Okinawa, Japan to train in Karate and Kobudo in order to bring the history and culture of

Okinawa martial arts to Karate students in the USA. Carol holds a MA and MFA in Fine Arts, with an emphasis on Painting. She has a Doctorate in Higher and Post-Secondary Education.

Master Carol Womack

174

The Internal Warrior Spirit
Bohdi Sanders

My books have been sparking a debate for years over the definition of a warrior. Many people seem to take issue with my idea of what a warrior actually is. These people are usually very closed-minded and can't see past the strict, primary dictionary definition of a warrior. The first definition in most dictionaries is that a warrior is someone who has participated in a war. This is very short-sighted, and to be honest, just plain wrong.

There have been many people who have participated in a war who are not warriors; there have been many people who have never been to war, or even in the military, who are warriors through and through. Being a warrior is not about your profession or wearing a uniform. It has nothing to do with what you do for a living, whether or not you have been in the military, or even whether or not you are an expert fighter. Being a warrior is something that comes from the inside of a person – his or her internal warrior spirit.

There are warriors in all walks of life. I know that this statement irritates some guys, but it is true nonetheless. I have met many military guys who were not even close to being warriors. Some of them are cowards, some are just scumbags, and some are totally psychotic. These are not character traits of a true warrior. These guys may have been in the military, but they are a long way from having a true warrior spirit.

After I started writing about the warrior lifestyle, I had several guys ask me what my definition of a warrior was. One day, I sat down and gave it some thought and wrote my definition of a warrior. The following is what I came up with.

A true warrior is someone who has the ability and will to fight to protect himself, his friends, his family, and his ideals, and at the same time, seeks the perfection of his own character through a life lived with honor, integrity, and an unflinching dedication to what is right, according to his own code of ethics. The ability to fight is only a small part of this definition. The true warrior has to develop more than his martial arts skills; the qualities of the true warrior go much deeper than that.

Warriors should exhibit the best qualities among men. The true warrior makes a firm decision to try to perfect his character and to live by a strict code of ethics. His word is his honor. His duty stays fresh on his mind.

He lives life a little more seriously than most, but at the same time lives life to its fullest. He sees through the veil of appearances covering most parts of this world, but does so without looking down on those who are less perceptive.

Family and friends are important to him, and they know that they can always count on him for protection and help in their times of need. He bases his decisions on his code of ethics, and he instinctively knows right from wrong, and chooses right. He knows that, at times, there is a difference between what is right and what is legal, and what is wrong and what is illegal. As Lao Tzu taught, "Highly evolved people have their own conscience as pure law."

The true warrior is able to hold his head high with honor because he knows that he lives his life to the best of his ability, with honor and integrity. His code is ingrained in his spirit and is a part of his being. Warriors walk alone much of the time, as they prefer solitude to the company of lesser men.

The warrior is a man who shoots for excellence in everything he does. These are the things which make someone a true warrior; and the development of these traits leads to the warrior lifestyle. As you can see, there is more to being a warrior than joining the military and being involved in a war.

Others claim that being a warrior means working in a "warrior profession" such as the military, law enforcement, or maybe a firefighter. Again, this is a very short-sighted view. The warrior spirit is not automatically developed because you get a job as a law enforcement officer, a fireman, or because you join the military. I have met many people from each of those professions who were the furthest thing from a true warrior that I can imagine.

Let me make one thing clear here, I am not saying that military guys, law enforcement officers, or firemen are not warriors; I am simply saying that *not all of them are warriors*, and that simply signing up for these jobs does not automatically make one a warrior. Any clear thinking person will realize this as fact. We have all seen bad cops and military guys who were less than honorable.

The warrior spirit is something that is internal, not external. What you do for a living, going to war, and learning to fight, are all external things. They are things you do, not who you are. *Being a warrior is who you are, not what you do.* Although, once you develop your internal warrior spirit, your actions, and how you conduct yourself, will fall in line with who you are.

This leads to the question of whether one is born a warrior or if the warrior spirit developed. This also seems to be a point of contention among military guys, martial artists, and others. Although no scientific studies have been done on this, that I know of, I do have my own personal opinion on this subject.

Buddha taught that human beings are so malleable, that what one thinks, one becomes. If that is true, then anyone can develop the warrior spirit. My opinion is that each person is born with certain traits from both his father and his mother, but he is born with traits that are passed down from his ancestors as well. He may be born with musical talent, but if he never develops that talent, it is lost. Someone may be born with leanings toward being a warrior, but whether it develops or not depends on how he is raised and the decisions that he or she makes in life.

That said, I believe that the warrior spirit is a combination of being born with a tendency towards warriorship, how you were brought up as a child, and the decisions that one makes throughout his or her life. If someone was born with the spirit of a warrior, but was not taught the ways of the warrior, he may end up as a street thug. He has the fighting spirit, but he was never taught when or how it should be used, nor was he taught the character traits that should accompany the warrior spirit.

On the other hand, if someone was not born with warrior tendencies, but was raised to live the warrior lifestyle, this person may not be a natural fighter, but he may have more courage than the vast majority of men. His warrior spirit is developed, and he may be willing to stand against evil more than those who were born with natural fighting talents.

Whether someone is born to be a warrior or not, the bottom line is that being a warrior is something that comes from inside you; it has very little to do with what you do for a living or whether you work in some "warrior profession."

The well-loved teacher, Carlos Castaneda, taught, "Nobody is born a warrior, just like nobody is born an average man. We make ourselves into one or the other." God gives each man and woman on this earth a free will to choose how he or she will live their life. It is up to YOU!

Of course, some people have an easier beginning than others, but each person is given the free will to become who and what they will. The warrior spirit comes from the inside; and each person controls whether they cultivate the warrior spirit or other things in their spirit and mind.

Miyamoto Musashi is known as the greatest swordsman in Japan. He killed many men until he had a change of heart in his later years. Once he turned his mind toward philosophy and reflection on the ways of the warrior, he taught, "The truth is that strength lies in the interior of the warrior; in his heart, his mind, and his spirit." Miyamoto Musashi knew that being a true warrior comes from what's inside a man; it is not an external trait.

The warrior spirit has more to do with justice and someone's willingness to stand for what's right, and stand against what's wrong, than it does with actual fighting. Taira Shigesuke, author of *Bushido Shoshinshu*, better known as *The Code of the Samurai*, stated that, "As long as it is realized and accepted that warriors must comprehend right and wrong, and strive to do right and avoid wrong, then the way of the warrior is alive."

The true warrior must always take into account what is right and what is wrong. You may be an expert fighter, trained in combat, but if your character is not right, you don't truly have the warrior spirit. There is a difference between a warrior and a killer. Anybody can learn to fight or to kill. Even dogs and roosters can be taught to fight, that doesn't make them warriors. There is much more to the warrior spirit than knowing how to fight!

The internal warrior spirit is concerned with much more than learning how to fight or defend yourself. It is the spirit of living by a code of right and wrong, helping others, and defending those who cannot defend themselves, such as the young and the elderly. The warrior spirit is the spirit of living by a specific code of honor.

Thankfully, the warrior spirit can be taught and cultivated. Unlike what many people think, it is not something that you are either born with or not; it can be taught and developed.

There have been many people who were not raised properly and strayed off the path of the warrior, only to have found a true teacher and changed their ways. Nothing in this world is static; everything is flowing. If you have been on the wrong path, you can always leave that path and change directions.

The warrior spirit can be developed in anyone, but, as with most other things in life, it has to be continually trained and refined. Many times in the past, I have used the analogy of gardening to illustrate the warrior spirit.

If you plant seeds in fertile ground, those seeds will grow. But you still have to cultivate them. You have to continually water them and take care of them so that they will develop strong roots, grow, and bear fruit. But there will always be weeds which will pop up overnight. If you allow those weeds to continue to grow, they will overtake your garden and your plants will not be able to mature and bear fruit.

The same principle applies to your warrior spirit. You can have the warrior spirit inside you, whether it came from your parents, an instructor, or wherever, but if you don't cultivate it and allow it to grow, it will bear no fruit in your life.

The "weeds" of life will overtake your spirit. Those "weeds" can be most anything – hatred, anger, envy, jealousy, laziness, cowardice, focusing on the wrong things, not taking time for your training and meditation, etc.

I teach that life is fluid; nothing is static. You are either moving forward or you are regressing. If you are not developing your internal warrior spirit, and cultivating it, it will start to regress and you will begin gradually losing it.

Your warrior spirit must be fed and kept strong! Train, study, meditate, maintain your focus, and discipline your mind. Train to keep your body strong and your martial arts skills sharp. Study wisdom, warrior character traits, and writings which motivate you.

Make sure your focus is on the right things in life, *things which remind you of who and what you truly are*. Discipline your mind to weed out negative thoughts and keep your thoughts on things worthy of your warrior spirit.

Anyone can develop the internal warrior spirit, but it does take time and effort. Develop it, cultivate it, and train it, and it will be there when the time comes that it is called upon to stand up and do the right thing. And, if you have continued to hone your martial arts skills, they will also be there if they are required when you stand up to do the right thing.

You can be a martial artist without actually having the internal warrior spirit. Many people do martial arts for fun or for sport. They aren't necessarily warriors. Many do martial arts because they are into the ancient art aspects of the arts. Again, these people are not necessarily warriors. Martial arts and warriorhood are not synonymous, just like being in the military or in law enforcement does not necessarily mean that you are a warrior.

Always remember, being a true warrior comes from the inside, your warrior spirit. As I have taught for many years, it is not what you do; it's what you are. You can have a warrior spirit and be a teacher, a baker, a real estate agent, a singer, a cowboy, or whatever. Those are professions that you do to make money; they are not who or what you truly are.

The warrior spirit is integrated with your soul. It becomes a part of you, if you develop it and cultivate it. It is not a separate part of you or something you do during your spare time. It is an integral, inseparable part of what makes you, you.

Think of it this way. If you are making a sauce for your dinner, and you combine 10 different ingredients into the sauce, you can't separate each of those ingredients on your plate and pick and choose which ones you include in the sauce. Each ingredient has become a part of the whole – the sauce.

You can't separate the oregano from the salt, or the butter from the tomato paste. They are no longer individual substances, but rather, they have merged together to become a totally new substance. This is what happens when you integrate the warrior spirit into your spirit, mind, and body – they become one.

Your internal warrior spirit may be overshadowed by external "weeds" if you aren't careful about taking care of your "garden," (your spirit, mind and body), but it is always there. Once it is developed, it cannot be removed from your spirit. It has become a part of you – who you really are at your core. Even if you carelessly allow "weeds" to choke your warrior spirit down, it is still there if you have developed strong roots. It is there just waiting for its chance to grow and to bear fruit.

Remember, warriors are not always the fastest or the strongest men. Warriors are those who choose to stand between their enemy and those that they love or hold sacred.

You don't have to be especially talented in martial arts, or the best fighter around, to develop the courage to stand and protect those you love or those in need. Even Miyamoto Musashi said, "Even if a man has no natural ability, he can be a warrior."

Take the time to develop your internal warrior spirit. Keep your focus on the ways of the warrior. Buddha taught, "We are what we think. All that we are arises with our thoughts. With our thoughts, we make our world."

Discipline your mind and thoughts, and keep yourself focused on what you really are. Of course, it takes more than thinking about warriorhood to develop the warrior spirit, but the more you keep your thoughts focused on developing your internal warrior spirit, the more you will develop it.

People everywhere seem to go to great lengths to be unique and try to stand out from the crowd. If you truly want to be different, exceptional, and extraordinary, develop your internal warrior spirit and live the warrior lifestyle. Nothing sets you apart more than living with honor, respect, and integrity, especially in today's world where these traits have become extremely rare.

Your internal warrior spirit is sacred. Don't dishonor it by allowing yourself to lower your standards or live in a dishonorable way. Only *you* can dishonor your warrior spirit. Be courageous and walk the path of the warrior.

I will end this chapter with these words from Miyamoto Musashi, "There is nothing outside of yourself that can ever enable you to get better, stronger, richer, quicker, or smarter. Everything is within…Seek nothing outside yourself…Perceive that which cannot be seen with the eye… Never stray from the Way."

Dr. Bohdi Sanders is a multi-award winning and bestselling author of 15 books and 100's of articles, and is an 8-time Martial Arts Hall of Fame inductee. He started training in martial arts in 1984 under Bob and Nikki Allen and now holds the rank of 5th Dan in Shotokan Karate from Shihan William Jackson. Dr. Sanders was awarded the official title of Shihan by Soke Richard Hallman, along with Soke Stephen Barber, Soke-Dai Scot E. Philips, and Renshi Young Author Smith, III.

He has also been awarded the honorary title of Hanshi, (teacher of teachers) for his teachings and writings on the martial arts, by Sifu Al Dacascos, Col. Phil Torres, Grandmaster Eddie Mapula, Shihan Bill Holman, Soke Richard Hallman, Grandmaster Richard Hackworth, Grandmaster Joy Turberville, Grandmaster Terrence Shea, Shihan Dana Abbott, Grandmaster Dan Tosh, Grandmaster Harry Mok, Grandmaster Harry Greene, Grandmaster Dave Johnson, and Grandmaster Eric Lee.

Dr. Sanders has won multiple national book awards for his books. He has written three #1 Bestsellers, and six of his other books have climbed into the Top 10 on Amazon's Best Sellers

List. His books have won 1st Place awards from the Indie Excellence Book Awards and the USA Book News Book Awards. In 2011, he was named Inspiration of the Year by the United States Martial Artist Association Hall of Fame. In 2018, Dr. Sanders became one of the first five Westerners elected to the World Martial Arts Congress in Beijing, China. He is also a member of the Golden Dragon Ohana, and the Independent Warriors Association.

He also holds national certifications as a Specialist in Martial Arts Conditioning and as a Certified Fitness Trainer. In addition, he is a Usui-Tibetan Reiki Master and a Master of Acupressure. He has a doctorate in Natural Health and Naturopathy, along with a BA in Sociology and a MA in Education. Dr. Sanders is also a columnist for Taekwondo Times Magazine and has written articles for several magazines and websites. In 2017, Dr. Sanders was inducted into the Elite Black Belt Hall of Fame and also awarded a Lifetime Achievement Award for his contributions to the martial arts. Dr. Sanders is available for inspirational and motivational public talks and may be reached through his website, www.TheWisdomWarrior.com or through his social media pages.

Shihan Bohdi Sanders

Balance: Unifying Mind and Heart
Tak Wah Eng

Growing up in Hong Kong, I learned to enjoy the beauty of the sunrise. It was a time of great struggle for me and my family. My mom would wake me up early to watch the sunrise and teach me great gratitude. I learned that with each day, I receive a new day – a gift of life itself. Each new day brings all new possibilities. At sunrise, I take the time to meditate by focusing on letting go of everything. I constantly think about breathing in, inhaling, in through my nose and deeply letting go, exhaling out through my mouth.

I really try to rid myself of all bad, by cleansing myself through the breath. As my mind needs to travel, my mind goes off in different directions. I simply take it back to the breath. As I get more focused, every breath brings strength with release. I learn that I get greater strength the more I release, the more I let go. The art of letting go begins and ends in every breath.

This mindfulness of breathing gives me a sense of being home. A feeling of confidence in myself that creates positive vibrations. The energy is a barrier against any anxiety or anger that I experience. Through my discipline of simply breathing every morning, I have cultivated peace in my soul. This inner love is the way to bring out the best in myself and in others. It taught me to relax and see more clearly. I have learned to use common sense as my best defense. Standing for humanity and social justice is always present in my consciousness.

Seeing injustice only makes me work harder to make our world a better place for everyone. It starts within me and finds a path to reach many. In my meditation, whether I'm sitting still or moving in one of my katas, I focus on my breath and the light from inside my heart. I constantly challenge myself to unify my breath with my movement. I focus my breathing as if it were a stream of running water flowing with new energy that's refreshing. If I'm in a kata, proper balance is required to have speed, power, and stability.

Imbalance teaches me to go more patiently. To remain calm is vitally important. The mind sparks new ideas as the breath is the engine of our energy that holds our spirit. The spirit will awaken when the mind concentrates on a specific thought. The process is unlimited by the connection of the mind-breath-body unification. The power of the three united can create harmony when in balance as an everlasting process.

That's why I need Kung Fu to be a way for me to play and create, not just physical power, but to stimulate my brain, my heart, my guts, and my passions in, and for, life. My idea of changing the world toward greater love and understanding is possible. I realize cynicism cannot be a way of life; it cannot sustain life. Only optimism can sustain life.

Martial arts are based on a sacred devotion to the past even though the traditions slowly change with modern times. This process has kept many beautiful and useful elements to the Arts. There are some things better left in the past, but I've also learned to erase the chalkboard each new day, just like my teachers did in school.

I erase yesterday and begin new each day. This formula has brought me great success because it allows me to be very flexible to uniquely design a new lesson from an old book. The same kata becomes different although it's made from the same material.

Martial arts are a great way for me to create spectacular character katas of the dragon, snake, tiger, leopard, crane, or mantis. It has taken me over 50 years to realize the importance of simplicity. After decades of training hard and fast, I realized soft and slow is important to build sensitivity.

This allowed me to respond more quickly and more efficiently. My focus is to find the right balance between hard and soft, and fast and slow (yin and yang). To this day, I will find I am focusing too much on my physical being and not enough on my mindfulness.

When in the proper mindset, balance happens and my spirit awakens. This awakening can be very dynamic and unique to each person. It fills me with such good energy that it creates positive vibrations. The vibrations have a ripple effect and make everyone around me feel good.

I believe it is so important to feel good on a daily basis. Too often we train so seriously that we are hurting ourselves. It is important to feel the good positive energy that we create from training. It is important to be mindful of the positive energy, especially when you are surrounded by negative energy.

It's important to be able to view yourself with all positive energy. I will remind myself to listen to my heartbeat. When I hear it, I remember how awesome it is. I remember to feel and to listen. I am reminded of all the awesomeness that my heartbeat contains. The miracle of life is contained in the sound of my heart beating. To be mindful of this heartbeat creates a great sense of gratitude. Gratitude is my best attitude. Gratitude gives me the grace that I need to endure the burdens of life.

Another important ingredient to my training is my imagination. Our imaginations are a great tool that many people do not use. I love being creative and have found my imagination to be a great way in connecting my mind and body. Over the years, I've had many students with special needs, and my imagination allowed me to find a way to develop exercise routines that could help numerous people who wished to learn.

As different problems arose in the training, I found myself finding the answers to my problems in art. I have always loved the way artists like painters and sculptors could use simple ingredients to create beautiful works of art. Images of color expanded my mindset and taught me to break free from some of the traditions of my past. Ideas of teaching movement in color became a way to expand. Not allowing people's limitations to stop them from becoming one with their martial art. All my thoughts became interconnected as one.

This transformation was the way to find love and purpose in my life. The simple ideas of punching and kicking have taught me to be martial and at the same time, to be very artistic. Often the martial side has been overriding the artistic side, especially when I was younger.

As a young man, having great strength was the first goal for me to achieve. A feeling of accomplishment was never better than when winning a boxing match. It built great confidence; and it was a solid basis for my life as a martial artist.

But it wasn't enough for me to just be a tough guy. My mind was unable to rest at night, even though I had worked hard during my days. It was driving me crazy, my wandering thoughts kept me up all night long.

My thoughts brought on anxiety and at times depression. In time, I realized mastering myself would require me to break free from myself. I had to learn to allow myself to freely express myself. I had become restrained and wanted to be more creative.

Becoming an artist freed my mind. It helped me dream a different dream. I could combine more color into my movements. I also started to actually paint in my studio where I combined my movements of Kung fu with my abstract designs.

Painting helped me break free of what I felt was locked up inside. It's not easily explained. All I know is that when I am painting, I'm able to find my inner peace through the creativity of my boundless heart.

My art is explosive and is the opposite of my reserved nature. It is the opposing energy to my formal training in martial arts, as well as growing up Chinese. The way to my unification of my martial art is like everything in my life. I have tremendous respect for the past with all attention on the hopeful future. I stay present, in the here and now, enjoying everything in life as a precious gift.

As I said earlier, just being alive and being able to understand and appreciate all the good in life is such a blessing. It gets me through the tough times and makes me make the best of the time that we have. To be with family and friends is a great blessing, but I'm just as happy to be with complete strangers.

Most of the time I am surrounded by a lot of people, but there have been times when I've been all alone and have felt despair and loneliness. In such times, sometimes, I have met strangers who saved me. Strangers that showed me great kindness, love, and concern, that have forever touched me. Acts of kindness are amazingly beautiful.

Most often, it was an elder, a woman that has come through for me at my worst of times, with simple acts of kindness, which have been life-saving. Remembering their acts of compassion, and their words of wisdom, has empowered me throughout my life. Training one's heart's unity is absolutely necessary in the process of striving towards goals in life, as is keeping your mind from changing too often on too many thoughts.

I've learned to focus on my goals with one mind and one heart. It's hard enough to accomplish anything with one mind or heart. This is why we must have one mind unity. This unity will manifest our dreams into reality. Without our mind and heart in proper balance, glory cannot be attained even in victory. When our mind and heart are in proper balance, one can endure every defeat with grace.

Love is the greatest power to bring success and fulfillment. All of our physical desires are balanced when we humble ourselves to being loved, as well as to love. Learning to be humble and gentle is a great gift. Our human needs are both yin and yang. The beauty of love resonates such powerful energy that it can heal all that is present. Love should be most respected, like the sun itself, for if one is not careful, one shall be burned.

Any energy is in need of mindfulness so one does not destroy oneself by it. Love can heal and save, but it can also hurt and make you suffer. I had to learn to think with my mind and heart in a way that was unlimited, selfless, and unattached in order to love, yet protect myself from emotional mood swings and angry behavior. When I get my "monkey mind," that is, when my mind gets muddled, gets delusions, depression, and confusion, many questions arise, and I feel like my head is overloaded and going to explode.

In my Buddha mind, I see myself as a divine dragon, sent down to earth to be a teacher, an artist, and a poet who is unlimited and all loving. I'm a descendent of great warriors and healers. I work as ordinary men do in hopes of creating heaven on earth. I imagine a world of peace and understanding where all people can live as one in harmony. I believe the entire world, as a whole, is a great campus for all of us where everything is possible.

Throughout history, no martial artist has missed these steps in his or her training. Train the body to create energy. Train energy to create chi. Cultivate chi to create spirit. Train spirit to create humanity.

In nature, softness outlasts hardness like the bamboo which is soft and flexible but endures the great wind. The oak tree is strong and hard, it does not move when the great wind comes, so it snaps. To be free to do what you want to do is the greatest gift to mankind. Live life in ways that respect and enhance the lives of others, in order to break free of the ignorance and live free to pursue our dreams.

Tak Wah Eng was born in Hong Kong in the tiger year of 1950. He began his martial art training as a child on the rooftop of his home. When he was 16, he immigrated to New York, settling in what is known as Chinatown. He was fortunate to meet and become a student of Grandmaster Wai-Hong, who was the Father of Fu-Jow Pai Tiger Claw Kung Fu.

He found friendship in his teacher and a home in his martial art school. He loved learning everything about his Tiger Claw style, as well as learning from friends of his teacher. He has trained some who have gone on to achieve great success in their careers due to his lessons of harmony and balance. He continues to teach out of his small studio on the Bowery in Chinatown, where he has multiple generations come to continue learning Kung fu from the old way, He is proud to serve his community and all who wish to learn the beauty of his culture – Chinese Kung Fu.

Master Tak Wah Eng

True Leadership
Phil Torres

What is leadership? What are the ingredients that make for successful leaders? Are leaders born or is leadership purely a product of the environment? Is leadership ability automatically assumed when one attains a title, an office, or a specific job? How do those in leadership positions hone their leadership skills? What must we do? How must we act?

The Webster dictionary defines leadership as the office or position of a leader; capacity to lead; the act or an instance of leading. I define leadership as, having the discipline, courage, and foresight to act in the best interest of self and others, whether in a formal or informal setting. Acting to ensure that things that need to get done, get done on time and to standards, by yourself or with others, whether in an organization or an informal group.

It is directing, motivating, persuading, modeling, or coaching people to get tasks done. People, some in leadership positions and some not, rise to leadership challenges every day, especially when faced with emergencies or significant unforeseen challenges.

Leadership can be in the form of leading an army to conquer a country or it can be a casual driver on the way to work who sees a terrible vehicle accident and acts to save the lives of those involved. Leadership is action to affect others and organizations in their performance.

In this chapter I hope to communicate lessons learned through my experiences while serving in uniform for over 34 years, and since, while conducting team building and leadership workshops for private and public organizations in the U.S. and abroad, as well as learning from the experiences of others. I believe that an effective leader is not driven by ego or other similar internal or external stimuli. A true leader is driven by what is best for the organization and the people therein.

My yardstick for measuring the effectiveness of a leader has not changed in decades. I believe a leader is best measured by the success of his or her followers. For years, while I was still wearing a uniform, I learned to pay attention to how a person reacted when promoted or elevated to a higher office. The initial reaction was indicative to me of how effective a leader the person would later prove to be.

I usually asked a simple question, "How do you feel about this significant promotion?" If the answer was something to the effect of, "This gives me much more power and authority," I would watch the person closely, because I felt the person was ego-driven. If the answer leaned more toward a concern for the added responsibility, I would smile. My personal anecdotal observations proved me right more often than not.

I learned long ago from a General I worked for and admired, to never walk by a mistake. If something is happening in your environment that is obviously wrong and you have the capability of correcting it, correct it. Correcting doesn't necessarily mean physically interfering. It may sometimes be an observation that needs reporting or a phone call that needs to be made immediately. If you don't correct a wrong, it may appear to others that you approve of the action. To many, silence is consent. Be a problem solver, not part of the problem.

Learn to truly empower people. True empowerment is like walking into a room and turning on all of the lights to make the entire room bright, rather than just turning on one light (that of the leader) and therefore, have less illumination. True empowerment allows everyone in the organization to think and act in the best interest of the organization. It allows everyone to feel that he or she is a stakeholder in the organization. If you ever want to know if people in an organization feel empowered, don't ask the leader, ask the followers if they feel empowered.

I have seen organizations where the leader brags about empowering his or her people, and then you ask the people and get a completely different answer. Communicate to people what needs to be done, ensure they have the knowledge, resources, and equipment to get it done, and then let them do it. Be in the habit of telling people what needs to be done, not how it should be done. We all approach tasks slightly differently from each other. Allow people to use their ingenuity to perform tasks. That also means allowing people to fail. Many of us learned our greatest lessons from our failures. If an action does not create a safety hazard and doesn't hurt the organization, allow people to learn.

When I was a Battalion Commander, I had a sign on my desk, and one inside my hat that stated, "Today, be an obstacle remover." People work best when their leaders are blazing ahead, cutting the weeds out of their trails, and removing obstructions that interfere with their jobs.

That also means providing the training, guidance, and equipment they need. A leader's primary role is to be an obstacle remover. Remove obstacles out of people's way and allow them to sprint down the lane of success and be champions. A leader creates champions. The more champions in an organization, the better performing the organization is.

Regardless of what you say or how many times you say it, *people will pay attention to what you do before they'll listen to what you say*. Up to 93% of human communication is non-verbal. Your actions speak much louder than your words. Always set the example. Teach through example. Ensure that your actions and your words are consistent, because if they are not, it is not your words they will listen to.

Always lead by example. I also learned early on (in combat) that under extreme stress, it is imperative, as a leader, to stay focused and communicate clearly, in as calm a manner as possible. Emotions, like fear, become contagious. Control emotions and keep your head in the game.

A leader is constantly learning. You learn mostly by constantly stepping out of your comfort zone. Seek to constantly become familiar with the unfamiliar. Live outside your zone of comfort and you will keep learning forever.

Too many people get set in their ways and prefer to stay safely in their comfort zone. They quit taking chances, and therefore, quit learning anything outside of their own circle. You must get out of your comfort zone and be a lifetime student, learning everything you can from everyone you can.

As a leader, everything you do, or don't do, speaks volumes about yourself. Let us be mindful of the following quote:

> *Your beliefs become your thoughts,*
> *Your thoughts become your words,*
> *Your words become your actions,*
> *Your actions become your habits,*
> *Your habits become your values,*
> *Your values become your destiny.*
> *Mahatma Gandhi*

A life well lived involves risk. Learn to manage risks, not entirely avoid them, for only then will we truly learn.

When teaching, don't just tell, show. People learn best by doing. Research supports that people learn and retain most effectively when they participate *experientially* in the learning process. According to Edgar Dale's *Cone of Experience*, people remember:

> 10% of what they READ,
> 20% of what they HEAR,
> 30% of what they SEE,
> 50% of what they both SEE and HEAR,
> 70% of what they SAY and WRITE, and
> 90% of what they DO!
> Whenever possible, have people do!

The state of our mental and physical well-being is critical to how well we perform. None of us go to work, or participate in our daily activities, feeling at 100% of our mental and physical well-being all of the time. Sometimes we perform at less than 100% of our norm for a variety of reasons, both physical and mental. Be mindful of how those you lead and interact with on a regular basis are doing.

Understand that they may be distracted by some physical ailment or mental stress. Know your people well enough so that you can determine when someone may not be performing up to their norm, and allow for whatever may be distracting or hindering them to be addressed so that a person can feel supported and recover quickly.

How we feel, physically and emotionally, affects how we perform, and thereby, affects the organization. Find out how people are feeling, address concerns quickly, and you enhance their ability to perform.

An employee may have spent the previous night in the emergency room with a child and may be mentally exhausted. That employee may be safer at home rather than around machinery or on the road. As a leader, when you show that you are genuinely concerned for those you lead, they in turn give their best for you and for the organization.

When we attend a learning environment, such as a course or seminar for professional development, some of us allow different inner voices to affect how much we get out of a learning activity. Some may listen to a prisoner voice, "I really don't want to be here. I know this is good for my career, but I would rather be someplace else." No new learning can take place unless we are committed to learning the topics at hand.

Some may listen to a vacationer voice, "Finally! Away from the office and away from those people at the office. I'm just going to relax, have fun, see some sites, and maybe attend a few sessions." No new learning takes place if we don't make the effort. Some may listen to a sophisticated voice, "I don't see anyone here capable of teaching me anything. I'll take every opportunity to show everyone that I know as much, or more, than anyone here." No new learning can take place until the ego is kept in check.

Finally, some may listen to an explorer voice, "This is a new place, with people I don't know, and in an unfamiliar setting. I'm going to take every opportunity to learn as much as I can and take it back to the organization." The explorer voice allows us to be out of our comfort zones and make every effort to learn as much new material as possible.

Knowledge of how we develop our social construct and perceptions is important in understanding human behavior. Chris Argyris, an American business theorist, Professor Emeritus at Harvard Business School, and an organizational psychologist known for his seminal work of learning organizations, is the author of the following quote which describes how we perceive the world. The quote was later used by Peter Senge in *The Fifth Discipline: The Art and Practice of the Learning Organization.*

> *We live in a world of self-generating beliefs*
> *which remain largely untested. We adopt those*
> *beliefs because they are based on conclusions,*
> *which are inferred from what we observe, plus*
> *our past experience. Our ability to achieve the*
> *results we truly desire is eroded by our feelings that:*
>
> *1) Our beliefs are the truth.*
> *2) The truth is obvious.*
> *3) Our beliefs are based on real data.*
>   *The data we select are the real data.*

The following quote from *Scott Schuster, Founding Director, Executive Programs, Business Week,* best expresses how we individually process information, "The world is an internally created phenomenon. We take the inputs received through our senses and process that sensory data through our mentality and emotions to create what each of us experiences as the world.

Every person's world is necessarily different from everyone else's."

Be a leader who creates a craving for learning. As Peter Senge stated in *The Fifth Discipline*, "People in a learning organization reflect upon, continually clarify, and improve their internal pictures of the world, and see how those mental models shape their actions and decisions."

One of the most critical skills for an effective leader is listening, specifically, active listening. Active listening is not necessarily a natural skill; it is a learned skill that must be continuously worked on. In the book, *The 7 Habits of Highly Effective People,* Dr. Stephen Covey emphasizes listening as a critical skill when he writes, "Seek first to understand, then to be understood."

His son, Shawn Covey, captured listening in his book, *The 7 Habits of Highly Effective Teens*, when he wrote, "You have two ears and one mouth... Hello!" and, "Before I can walk in another's shoes, I must first remove my own."

The deepest need for the human heart is to be understood. Everyone wants to be respected and valued for who they are – a unique, one of a kind individual. As Shawn Covey taught, "People don't care how much you know, until they know how much you care."

Genuine listening requires that you listen to the whole message someone is communicating. Listen with your eyes, heart, and ears. Stand in their shoes. Practice mirroring (a mirror doesn't judge, it reflects). Communication consists of 53% body language, 40% tone/feeling, and 7% words.

Emphatic listening is important. Chances are, those who influence us most are powerful listeners. Whether instinctively or through practice, they developed the skill of empathy. A University of Maine researcher, Dr. Marisue Pickering, identifies four characteristics of empathetic listeners as:

1) Desire to be other-directed, rather than to project one's own feelings and ideas onto the other.

2) Desire to be non-defensive, rather than to protect the self. When the self is being protected, it is difficult to focus on another person.

3) Desire to imagine the roles, perspectives, or experiences of the other, rather than assuming they are the same as one's own.

4) Desire to listen as a receiver, not as a critic, and desire to understand the other person, rather than to achieve either agreement from, or change in, that person.

Dr. Pickering associated 10 skills with empathy:

1) **Attending, acknowledging:** Providing verbal or non-verbal awareness of the other, i.e., eye contact.

2) **Restating, paraphrasing:** Responding to a person's basic verbal message.

3) **Reflecting:** Reflecting feelings, experiences, or content heard or perceived through cues.

4) **Interpreting:** Offering a tentative interpretation about the other's feelings, desires, or meanings.

5) **Summarizing, synthesizing:** Bringing together, in some way, feelings and experiences; providing a focus.

6) **Probing:** Questioning in a supportive way that requests more information or that attempts to clear up confusions.

7) **Giving feedback:** Sharing perceptions of the other's ideas or feelings; disclosing relevant personal information.

8) **Supporting:** Showing warmth, caring in one's own individual way.

9) **Checking perceptions:** Finding out if interpretations and perceptions are valid and accurate.

10) **Being quiet:** Giving the other time to think, as well as to speak.

According to Shawn Covey, most of what we communicate (up to 93%) is non-verbal. People will "hear" your actions much louder than they will ever hear your words.

Please Listen
When I ask you to listen to me and you start giving me advice,
you have not done what I asked.
When I ask you to listen to me and you begin
to tell me why I shouldn't feel that way,
you are trampling on my feelings.
When I ask you to listen to me and you feel you have to
do something to solve my problem, you have failed me,
strange as that may seem. Listen!
All I ask is that you listen. Don't talk or do – just hear me.
Shawn Covey

People do not like working in the "dark." People want to be kept informed about how they are doing and be kept up to date as to the direction of an organization.

Providing proper feedback is an important component of effective communication. Before providing feedback, always ask yourself, "Will this feedback really help this person or am I doing it just to suit myself and fix them?"

1) **Give feedback in the first person** – "I'm concerned that you have exhibited a temper problem."

2) **Never attack the person, always address the behavior.**

Some people are not successful at executing their assigned roles in an organization. As leaders, it is incumbent upon us to assess and provide the necessary feedback to allow people to succeed.

According to Dr. John Maxwell, in his book, *Failing Forward*, there are the top 10 reasons why people fail:

1) Poor people skills
2) A negative attitude
3) A bad fit
4) Lack of focus
5) A weak commitment
6) An unwillingness to change
7) A shortcut mind-set
8) Relying on talent alone
9) A response to poor information
10) No goals

"The common denominator of success lies in forming
the habit of doing things that failures don't like to do."
Albert Gray

Good time management is an essential ingredient of effective leadership. Many leaders spend much of their working day putting out fires. They do so because they don't get ahead of the time management curve. All of us deal with important and urgent things most days.

It is critical for a leader to determine what is truly important in an organization and continually focus on doing what is important. An urgent item has a time stamp, like a report that must be submitted to higher headquarters or to a client by end of work today. An important item may determine the success or failure of an organization, but doesn't necessarily have a time stamp. Something without a time stamp is easy to put off until tomorrow, next week, or next year.

People like to work on things with a time stamp, even when those things may not be critical to the survival of an organization. There are things that are recognized as important and urgent to the organization and we must work on those first, but one of a leader's main functions is to determine what is important and ensure that everyone in the organization works on the important items first – every day.

We have to continually assess the criticality of every function we perform. Something that is important and urgent must be worked on first. Everything else that is important, but not necessarily urgent, must be worked on next.

Something that is urgent, but not important, must be dispatched with the minimum time necessary, in order to get back on what is important. Something that is not important or urgent is a pet project and needs to possibly be eliminated or have little time spent on it.

Many pet projects have little to no value to an organization and take time away from what is important. According to research by Dr. Stephen Covey, mediocre organizations spend about 15% of their time attending to what is important. Successful organizations spend between 65-80% of their time on what is important.

Those figures speak for themselves. An effective leader must first determine what is truly important to the success of an organization and then ensure people work on that the majority of the time.

A critical component of leadership is the Emotional Quotient (EQ) of the leader. It has been said that EQ is more important than IQ in a leader. Effective leaders connect with people through their emotions. "Great leaders move us. They ignite our passion and inspire the best of us. When we try to explain why they are so effective, we speak of strategy, vision, or powerful ideas. But the reality is much more primal. Great leadership works through the emotions." Daniel Goleman, *Primal Leadership – Realizing the Power of Emotional Intelligence.*

In his book, Goleman recognizes four closely intertwined domains of EQ within the "Personal Competence and Social Competence Spheres," which are:

1) **Self-Awareness:** *Emotional Self-Awareness*: Reading one's own emotions and recognizing their impact; using "gut sense" to guide decisions. *Accurate Self-Assessment*: Knowing one's strength and limits. *Self-confidence*: A sound sense of one's self-worth and capabilities.

2) **Self-Management:** *Emotional Self-Control*: Keeping disruptive emotions and impulses under control. *Transparency*: Displaying honesty and integrity; trustworthiness. *Adaptability*: Flexibility in adapting to changing situations or overcoming obstacles. *Achievement*: The drive to improve performance to meet inner standards of excellence. *Initiative*: Readiness to act and seize opportunities.

3) **Social Awareness:** *Empathy*: Sensing other's emotions, understanding their perspective, and taking active interest in their concerns. *Organizational Awareness*: Reading the currents, decision networks, and politics at the organizational level. *Service*: Recognizing and meeting follower, client, or customer needs.

4) **Relationship Management:** *Inspirational Leadership*: Guiding and motivating with a compelling vision. *Influence*: Wielding a range of tactics for persuasion. *Developing Others*: Bolstering other's abilities through feedback and guidance. *Change Catalyst*: Initiating, managing, and leading in a new direction. *Conflict Management*: Resolving disagreements. Building bonds. Cultivating and maintaining relationships.

Daniel Goleman goes on to discuss the results of a random sample of 3,871 executives. Goleman examined the relationship between leadership style, organizational climate, and financial performance. He identified six styles of leadership that leaders use to interact with their people.

An effective leader has a deep bag of tools to draw from. Effective leaders interact with their people based upon a lot of factors. A brand new employee may need a lot of guidance and direction, whereas a senior leader may need coaching or mentoring. Effective leaders use the right tool at the right time.

The Six Leadership Styles

Visionary
– *Builds Resonance* (emotionally in sync) by moving people toward shared dreams.
– *Impact on Climate*: Most strongly positive.
– *When Appropriate*: When changes required a new vision, or when a clear direction is needed.

Coaching
– *Builds Resonance* by connecting what a person wants with the organizational goals.
– *Impact on Climate*: Highly positive.
– *When Appropriate*: To help an employee improve performance by building long-term capabilities.

Affiliative
– *Builds Resonance* through the creation of harmony by connecting people to each other.
– *Impact on Climate*: Positive.
– *When Appropriate*: To heal rifts in a team, motivate during stressful times, or strengthen connections.

Democratic
– *Builds Resonance* by valuing people's input and gets commitment through participation.
– *Impact on Climate*: Positive.
– *When Appropriate*: To build buy-in or consensus, or to get valuable input from employees.

Pacesetting
– *Builds Resonance* by meeting challenging and exciting goals.
– *Impact on Climate*: Because too frequently poorly executed, often highly negative.
– *When Appropriate*: To get high quality results from a motivated and competent team.

Commanding
– *Builds Resonance* by soothing fears through giving clear direction in an emergency.
– *Impact on Climate*: Because so often misused, highly negative.
– *When Appropriate*: In a crisis, to kick-start a turnaround, or with problem employees.

I sincerely hope that these tidbits of information can assist you in performing as a leader. I will leave you with the summary of my criteria for success as a leader. These are the criteria that I have used throughout my military career, and which have served me well. As a retired Colonel in the United States Marine Corp, I have had ample opportunity to try each of these and have found them to be very useful in any leadership situation. I hope you will find them useful as well.

Here is a summary of my criteria for success as a leader:

1) **Genuinely Show Respect to Everyone** – Whether junior or senior, friend or stranger. Respect opens doors and is the grease in our social fabric to get things done.

2) **Nurture Relationships** – Good relationships are critical in getting things done and in working with other organizations.

3) **Clearly Communicate** – What needs to be done and by when.

4) **Ensure Everyone** – Has the right training, equipment, resources, and guidance to get the job done.

5) **Remove any Possible Obstacles** – Or obstructions that may interfere with someone's performance.

6) **Allow for Individual Creativity** – In performing a task as long as guidelines are followed.

7) **Be an Active Listener** – As discussed previously.

8) **Value Everyone in the Group or Organization** – Empower and make everyone in the organization a stakeholder in the outcomes and success of the group or organization.

9) **Recognize Individual Performance** – Do this at every opportunity. Research, going back to the Hawthorne Studies of the 1920's, shows that recognition, above all else, motivates people to perform.

10) **When Counseling or Reviewing Performance** – Always address performance, never attack the person. Hold people accountable for their actions and be consistent with consequences. Research shows that certainty and consistency of consequences has the biggest effect on a person's behavior.

11) **Provide a Clear Leader's Guidance** – and an intent purpose statement delineating where you are headed with the group or organization to include your end state goals. This is similar to providing a roadmap with a GPS destination. If people get lost along the way, they still know where they are supposed to wind up at.

12) **Repeat, Refuse, and Report** – Whenever I was in Command during my uniform days, I asked members of my Command to remember The 3 R's – Repeat, Refuse, and Report. If a member of my Command ever received an order or direction that was clearly illegal, immoral, or unethical, they were asked to have the order repeated to ensure they heard it correctly. If, after the order is

repeated, they still felt it wasn't appropriate, they were to immediately refuse to obey the order and report the incident to the proper authorities. As a leader, always behave professionally.

13) **Learning is a Lifelong Endeavor** – Always seek to learn so that you may continue to grow. Read as much as you can about leaders and leadership, about growth and self-improvement, and about developing and empowering others.

I learned much from the series of books written by Dr. Stephen Covey, by Dr. John Maxwell, and by many other authors. One of the best books I've read is, *Failing Forward* by Dr. John Maxwell. Every leader fails at something throughout his or her life, but the successful leaders do not allow failure to define them. They learn from the failures and move forward. Always move forward.

14) **Attitude** – Can be the biggest determinant in anything you do or fail to do. Attitude can be a force multiplier, and it can also be contagious. Affect everyone with a positive attitude. Greet, compliment, and smile!

15) **Always Remember** – That everything you do, or fail to do, speaks volumes about you, whether or not you are aware of how you are perceived by others.

Phil Torres rose from Private to Colonel in the U. S. Marine Corps and retired after an illustrious career lasting more than 34 years of active duty. Highlights among his responsibilities included Chief of Nuclear Security Policy and Chief of Command Security for the U. S. Strategic Command, Offutt Air Force Base, Nebraska; Commander of the Marine Corps Security Force, Naval Submarine Base, Kings Bay, Georgia – responsible for one of the nation's largest strategic nuclear

weapons site in the U.S.; Advisor to the Commandant of the Marine Corps on human climate issues, Headquarters Marine Corps, Washington DC; and Inspector (Inspector General) for Marine Corps bases Japan.

He served in Vietnam, to include the battle for Khe Sanh during the 1968 Tet Offensive, and was awarded the nation's third highest combat decoration, the Silver Star Medal, for actions as a Platoon Sergeant during Operation Meade River, the largest heliborne operation in Marine Corps history. He entered the Marines with a ninth grade education and retired pursuing a doctorate degree. Since retirement, he has been a Leadership and Management Consultant, a Security Management Consultant, a Team Building Facilitator, an Advisor to the Secretary of Defense on readiness issues, and an Advisor to the Secretary of Veterans Affairs on veterans' issues.

He is a lifelong martial artist with over 56 years in the martial arts. He currently holds the title of Kyoshi (Master) in Okinawan Shorin Ryu Kenshinkan Karate, and has practiced several styles of the martial arts to include Isshin Ryu Karate, Shotokan Karate, Motobu Ryu Karate, Bando Kickboxing, and Ju Jitsu. In 2014 Phil was inducted into the USA Martial Arts Hall of Fame. Phil is also a competitive shooter in the action shooting sports. He competes and officiates at world, national, regional, state, and local championships across the country throughout the year. Phil is also a motorcycle enthusiast and resides in San Antonio, Texas.

Master Phil Torres, Col. U.S. Marine Corp, retired

The Importance of Full Speed Reality Training
Bill Kipp

I have been fortunate to have studied a number of martial arts since the age of 15, two of which I have black belts or higher rank in. For the last 30 years, I have climbed into the most protective body armor available and allowed people with no formal training, cops, martial arts masters and grandmasters, and professional ring and cage fighters, to activate their adrenaline and unleash their beasts against me.

I have trained thousands of instructors, from virtually every martial art system, on how to teach this technology to their students and people in their communities. This experience has provided a rich laboratory of experience to see how untrained, and trained fighters alike, respond under the adrenaline rush. It has also shown the relative strengths and weaknesses of how traditional martial arts training translates into surviving real altercations.

From my experiences, I have found some important elements that need to be added to fully bridge how we train safely in the martial arts environment and the realities of surviving an actual altercation. This by no means should be taken as a slam on the martial arts. Safety is, and should be, a priority for any good martial arts instructor.

Obviously, we can't have our loyal students getting adrenalized and hitting their fellow students full force, or we're not going to have a school for very long. But I believe in the adage, 'We fight as we train," and there are some missing skill sets that any martial artist would benefit from having, which are not being taught in most traditional martial arts training curriculums.

The good news is, such training exists and is considered by many in the industry to be the missing link in traditional martial arts training. Reality-Based Self-Defense (RBSD) training has experienced a surge in popularity among the self-defense and martial arts industries. And there is little doubt that it is a great way to train in self-defense. It requires minimal training time and produces maximum retention. Yet much confusion still exists around it, which has, in some cases, caused more damage than good. Reality training is not necessarily about recreating a brutally real situation for the students to face and overcome. That would be akin to sending students out into the dark alleys and biker bars to learn to protect themselves. They might survive the experience, but more often than not, it is going to go wrong.

With just a few exceptions, the theme for reality training is to set up the student for success. *We do as we train.* If we train to fail, we are likely to fail under pressure. Conversely, if we train to win, a successful outcome is much more likely in a real-life altercation. Thus, the purpose of a scenario is to get the student to successfully learn and apply a particular set of skills or techniques under varying levels of pressure.

Scenarios should start with low levels of intensity and simple skills to set the student up for a success, with successive scenarios building on the previous success to imprint positive action modes in a safe and predictable manner. This reality springboard has proven to provide students of all abilities high levels of proficiency in a relatively short time.

Why Deal with Adrenaline?

The one thing that anyone can count on, no matter how much training they have, is in a real altercation, their adrenaline will be running sky high, because it's supposed to. The question is, will their training set them up for success in controlling that adrenaline or will it control them?

In my experience, most of the mistakes made in real fights are a result of the adrenal rush overcoming someone in the heat of the moment. For martial artists that haven't experienced the adrenal rush in training or in life, they simply just don't know how they will respond in a real adrenalized situation. With RBSD they will.

Can You Untrain the Adrenal Response?

Some systems try to untrain the adrenal response. I don't know if this is even possible, but why untrain an important survival response that has allowed us to survive as a species? Since you will, and should, be adrenalized in a real altercation, why not learn to control it and even use it as jet fuel to fight for the lives of yourself and your loved ones, if it ever becomes necessary? When trained correctly, adrenaline becomes the great equalizer, allowing a smaller and weaker defender to prevail against a larger, stronger attacker.

Train the Brain!

The truth is that the vast majority of incidents never warrant the use of physical force. Thus, a martial art, a gun, or any fighting science or implement, is never the go to default weapon. *Our brain is always our go to weapon of choice.* Yet when adrenaline kicks in, there are things that occur in the brain that can make it very difficult to assess the situation and execute a skillful response.

In short, when we are confronted by an aggressor, even on a verbal level, our adrenaline kicks in to gear. Breathing becomes rapid and the cerebral cortex (conscious high brain) goes offline and the primitive amygdala (emotional and survival lower brain) comes online and sounds a general alarm to the body for fight or flight.

Research has shown that this part of the brain is only capable of about a 10 to 12-year-old level of maturity. Plus, the amygdala is our emotional brain, which explains why people also have strong tendencies to act emotionally or to have a knee-jerk reaction in tough situations. If the defender is not able to bring the high brain back online, they will be operating at the level of a 10 to 12-year-old, highly emotional child. This happens to white belts and it happens to high-ranking black belts as well, because this brain switch is not dealt with in the traditional martial arts paradigm.

215

Martial arts training may be adrenalizing, and even scary at times, but that's not typically enough to cause the cerebral cortex to go off-line. Reality-Based Self-Defense uses scenarios to safely resource and adrenalize the student in order to bring their high-brain back online when triggered. This allows them to use their vast computer to analyze and problem solve the situation appropriately, not in a knee-jerk reaction. This is vital for someone in a serious life-or-death situation.

Is Adrenaline Good or Bad?

Adrenaline is one of the strongest chemicals or drugs on the planet, and it can be very good, or it can be very bad, in the heat of a threatening situation. If we are in control of it, it can infuse us with superhuman speed, strength, and mental clarity.

We've all heard the stories of women picking up cars off a pinned child and other stories of amazing feats due to adrenaline infused power and speed. This is called adrenal activation, where we consciously activate the low brain to control and focus adrenaline as our best friend in the world if we ever need it.

Bad – Amygdala Hijack

If we are not in control of the adrenal rush, we will quickly succumb to the negative effects of adrenaline: tunnel vision, distorted sense of time, lack of hearing, and loss of fine motor control. Our mental judgment will be at an emotional pre-teen level. This is called an amygdala hijack. All of a sudden, we are not only dealing with the threat, but a wide array of internal challenges as well.

Kiai or Kiap!

The core factor to whether one is adrenal activating or amygdala hijacking is *breathing*. The common response when triggered is to take a short intake of breath, and then to hyperventilate or possibly stop breathing altogether. This aggressively triggers the amygdala hijack response and the adrenaline takes over. The antidote is after that short intake of breath, to *breathe deeply and consciously*.

The very act of thinking about breathing brings the cerebral cortex back online where you can regain control. Or if you need your adrenaline to fight, the breathing manifests as a powerful yell to fully activate, control, and laser beam focus the adrenaline for verbal and or physical defense.

Although most martial artists do some sort of kiai in training, it is my experience that very few do it when adrenalized. They tend to hold their breath, lock all their power inside them, and succumb to the common knee jerk mistakes so many make. The kiai is the doorway to activating our warrior spirit. RBSD training provides this experience, which for many students can be transformational as they tap in to their newly discovered deep well of power.

Speed vs. Power?

It is my experience that, for safety reasons, most martial artists have developed excellent speed in their techniques, but true stopping power is often less developed. This would make sense from a safety standpoint, where they just can't be unloading on their fellow students, especially to vulnerable areas.

RBSD allows students to activate their adrenaline and hit with absolute full power to vulnerable targets on the attacker. This can be done with pads and with the proper instructor training with good results.

But you will get even better results with a properly armored instructor, trained to be both the aggressor and a coach. Let's say you wanted to train to throw a full force forward elbow. The steps would be:

Step 1 – You would practice several reps in slow motion to get the full range of motion, breathing, angle, etc.

217

Step 2 – Practice 3-5 absolutely full force reps with adrenal activation and forceful breathing.

Step 3 - The skilled pad holder, or padded attacker, helps activate the student's adrenaline with an intense semi-surprise attack. Perhaps you place a hood over their head or have the defender close their eyes, so the attacker initially has control in true predator/prey style. The defender yells to fully activate their adrenaline and applies whatever techniques are being drilled, in this case a forward elbow. The padded attacker keeps fighting until the student has really tapped into their adrenaline and unleashed their beastly elbows with focus, power, and speed.

Each successive scenario gets progressively more intense and the skill sets more complex, according to the student's abilities.

Applications for RBSD

There is a wide market for this type of training, from children's assertiveness training to corporate safety and conflict resolution, to law enforcement and military applications. For martial arts specifically, it has been used for anti-bully/anti-abduction training, anti-rape training, verbal de-escalation and boundary setting, travel safety, defense against armed and multiple attackers, defensive knife and gun training, and more. It has been inserted into traditional martial arts curriculums, has been used to fire up belt testing, and has been used for seminars to the public, and for private customized lessons.

Padded Assailant Training

Using mock assailants in the scenarios provides a level of reality for the student that is unmatched. It is important to note that the armored assailant is not just a padded dummy that gets kicked and punched. The padded assailant is highly trained to elicit the adrenal rush and provide an experience that pushes the students to the peaks of their abilities, but not push them too far in each step of the training.

The body armor has to be protective for both the wearer and student so that the students feel safe to flip the adrenal switch and go all out, as they must in a real attack.

After trying virtually every suit available, I use the *Predator Armour* which is the result of over 40 years of trial and error in pursuit of the very finest body armor for Adrenal Stress Response Training.

The result is an amazing collection of gear that provides adequate protection against *full force* strikes to vulnerable targets, specifically the head and the groin. These are targets that no attacker can make stronger and works for defenders regardless of size and strength.

There are a number of commercially available protective body armors on the market. Most of these padded suits were designed originally for law enforcement baton training to non-vital areas for liability reasons.

This common type of armor was never intended to take full force strikes to vulnerable targets. Sadly, stories abound of well-meaning instructors buying these suits and using them for full force scenario training and sustaining serious injuries.

Why Attack Vulnerable Targets?

For safety reasons, most martial art training uses strikes to the chest and other non-vital areas. An attacker can strengthen his stomach and chest muscles to absorb a lot of punishment. No one can make their head, (eyes, throat, nose) or their groin any stronger. These are the target areas we train RBSD students to go after full force. A fight should be avoided at all costs, but if this is not possible, fight with all you have got to any and every vulnerable target you can find.

Adrenaline Training:
The Crucial Missing Link in Traditional Martial Arts?

Our ability to deal with the adrenal fear rush in violent assaults is perhaps the most critical factor in effectively defending ourselves. Yet this is the one factor that is not adequately addressed in the traditional martial arts. Through modern technology, we can now experience the fear "rush" and learn to work effectively with it.

We can answer those "what if" questions without having to visit the local bar-room brawl house. We can even learn to use our fear as a powerful ally, transforming it in to the jet fuel that can help us fight for our lives, if ever needed. This is what adrenal stress scenario based training is all about!

Bill Kipp is a lifelong martial artist and former USMC Recon Team Leader, Bill has trained students and instructors worldwide in RBSD. His program FAST Defense was voted the Best in Self-Defense Industry and Bill is a Black Belt Hall of Fame Self-Defense Instructor of the Year. Bill travels the U.S. with his wife and 2 dogs in his RV, providing private customized training at martial arts schools nationwide.

For Predator Armour and Bill's Private RBSD Training, go to:
www.predatorarmour.com.

For RBSD Instructor Training, go to:
www.fastdefenseglobal.org.

For RBSD Firearms and Combatives Training, go to:
www.combatforceacademy.com

Master Bill Kipp

The Way of Healing is found in Death
David Nelson

*In a world where death is the hunter, my friend, there is no
time for regrets or doubts. There is only time for decisions.*
Carlos Castaneda

When Dr. Bohdi Sanders asked me to write a chapter about
healing and injury recovery for the older martial artist,
obviously I was honored. I thought, "Good idea." As I sat down
to write though, I realized that many tenured martial artists,
perhaps like yourself, already have a pretty good handle on
managing injury recovery and pain.

In fact, many martial art systems come with healing arts as part
of their curriculum, and the strategies I outlined in *Black Belt
Healing: A Martial Artist's Guide to Pain Management and
Injury Recovery*, work quite well regardless of age. So, I got to
thinking. "Beyond physical injury recovery, what's the real
problem or fear of injury as we age? What really enslaves us?"
Then it hit me like a hook punch to the jaw!

Death, of course! The Big D! The Enforcer! The Grim Reaper!
There is no escape, and in that no-escape, the keys of deep
wisdom and healing are found. Bear with me for a moment.
You're going to like where this is going.

When you get injured you rely on time to heal, and over time
your health is restored and your training resumes. But
eventually, there will be no more time to recover. Death is
hunting you, and you can hear his footsteps.

Death is usually accompanied with his dear friend, "Serious
Medical Condition." You aren't going to have time to heal from
his touch. It is going to happen. It will be time for the ultimate
"let-go" of all you know and care about.

There is absolutely nothing, and I repeat, *nothing* that will keep
you from being death's prey. It is a non-negotiable deal. No

matter how good you are at striking a deal, or prayer, or meditation, death will be on your doorstep one day. This hunter will not be denied his prey. Think about that for a moment and I hope this unsettles you a bit. If not, then you really need to get your head out of the sand.

As a martial artist, there is one thing you rely on – reality of direct experience. You can fantasize and conceptualize a battle or your martial art, but it does not become real until you embody it and apply it in direct contact.

A martial art without contact is just swimming on land, right? Same goes for dealing with death…and healing. Contemplating and deeply meditating on your mortality helps take you out of conception and into the reality that someday you are going to die.

There will be that moment when you exhale your last breath and that's it. Period. Direct experience of mortality is that awakening moment when you move out of simple conceptual awareness of impermanence to the direct experience of this moment-to-moment reality.

To truly see that you will die, and that the time and place are uncertain, will assist you in embracing life fully to its utmost. Even in this moment there is a possibility of death; and feeling this deep within the marrow of your bones has the potential to change you, transform you, and heal you.

If you keep this barebones fact of your mortality at the level of just "head-knowledge," it will forever remain just another piece of information floating between your ears.

This is what the Zen worlds call, "Putting another head on top of your own." When you take it deep into your bones, raw and open, the truth of the "knowing" is irrefutable. You will be changed forever, and you will never be deceived again by fear of injury or death itself.

A lesson from the Hakagure might help here:

The Way of the Samurai is found in death. Meditation on inevitable death should be performed daily. Every day, when one's body and mind are at peace, one should meditate upon being ripped apart by arrows, rifles, spears, and swords, being carried away by surging waves, being thrown into the midst of a great fire, being struck by lightning, being shaken to death by a great earthquake, falling from a thousand-foot cliff, dying of disease, or committing seppuku at the death of one's master. And every day, without fail, one should consider himself as dead. This is the substance of the Way of the Samurai.

As you can see it is very traditional for warriors, such as the Samurai, to contemplate death. In fact, that is one of the reasons why the Samurai studied Zen. They actively examined death and mortality, which helped abate the fear and uncertainty that comes with it. So, here are the big questions you should consider. What if you faced your mortality now? Can you "let-go" before you die? How would this affect your life now? How would this heal you? What wisdom can be awakened in this moment of no escape?

Our lives, nothing but morning haze
drifting above the ground.
Forgotten now
...with the rising sun.
Shinzen

Nobody really knows what happens after you die. All I know is that it is uncertain. Yes, there are countless religious belief systems that try to help you feel better about death, but that is while you are alive, now. And there are accounts of near-death experiences and numerous stories about what people saw and came back to report. But that is near-death. What happens after you've turned cold in the grave, or a pile of ash in an urn on a fireplace mantle? Nobody knows, so let's rely a little bit on a Zen story for a moment.

225

A man goes to visit a Zen priest to inquire about what happens after death, as he is gripped in fear. So, he asks the Zen Priest, "What happens after we die? I am so afraid." The Zen priest replied, "I don't know." The visitor is astonished, and in a pissed off manner says, "But you're a Zen priest. You're supposed to know of these things." Responding, the Zen Priest, retorts, "But I am not a dead Zen priest."

So, even if you don't know what happens to you after death, contemplating your mortality can still assist in your journey of healing. How? Well, meditation on death awareness is one of the oldest practices in many spiritual traditions, especially Zen, the "religion" of the Samurai. The historical Buddha is noted as saying,

> *Of all the footprints, that of the elephant is supreme.*
> *Similarly, of all mindful meditations, that on death is supreme.*
> *Buddha*

Contemplating your own death, while you are alive, can be very helpful in arousing and letting go of fears, which lie hidden deep within, especially the fear that someday you will be dying, and eventually dead. Can you imagine how your life would change?

> *There is no place on earth where death cannot find us…it is madness to think you can succeed. To begin depriving death of its greatest advantage over us, let us adopt a way clean contrary to that common one; let us deprive death of its strangeness, let us frequent it, let us get used to it; let us have nothing more often in mind than death…We do not know where death awaits us; so let us wait for it everywhere. To practice death is to practice freedom. A man who has learned how to die has unlearned how to be a slave.*
> *Montaigne*

Living free! Living in no fear. How cool would that be? But not the macho bravado of no fear t-shirt warriors, but the living free from all suffering! That is the true healing! In essence, you are

226

leaving the self of suffering behind with a strong vision of how impermanent this floating world is, and you're okay with it. This is where death meditations help.

Over thirty years ago, I read a quote that went something like this. A student came to a martial arts instructor and said, "I want to learn how to defend myself." The teacher, pausing, asked, "Which 'self' do you wish to defend?" I don't know about you, but this made me stop and think.

So, who are you? Who lives? Who dies? I am certain most of you are insightful enough to know you are not your name or label, no more than the map is the territory or the menu is the food, and yet we so desperately attempt to defend and improve this label or menu. Who are you beyond your name, your rank, your titles, or achievements? Maybe this will help.

Remember as a kid on the fourth of July, having sparklers to light and twirl in the dark? You could swirl and twirl these and make wonderful rings of fire in the air, right? So much fun! Even as a child, you know those rings of fire are an illusion of your senses and that if you tried to grasp or hold that ring of fire, there would be nothing there to grab. Just empty air. Yet there was "something" there.

Think of that ring of fire as the "self" you are defending. The senses of touch, smell, taste, hearing, seeing, and consciousness gathered together creates a sense of a "self." You are here and not here, simultaneously. When judgement sets in, liking this and that, it begins the twirling of light (self) leaving a trace of a "you." This twirling is what Buddhists call samsara, the wheel of suffering.

Now, imagine this. You want to improve your sparkling light show. You say you find circles boring, or not as good, and prefer figure 8's or ovals. Regardless of the changes, it is still a light show. Nothing is really there. The same goes for "self" improvement. It is just a change of a light show that is simply an illusion of the senses, which is why after accomplishing one

227

goal, another one pops up right behind it. This continues forever. Contemplation of death and your impermanence will allow you to really get a feel for this. It is very healing when you see this very self you are trying to defend, improve, or keep alive, is nothing but a light show twirling in the abyss. It only becomes delusional and full of suffering when taken for real.

Meditating upon your mortality and "no-self" will open your eyes to a stunning decrease in attachment to an interest in anything but this eternal now. Courage begins to blossom. When you are deeply aware of your own impermanence, every fleeting moment is recognized as precious. Your desire to be present in each moment amplifies, along with courage, faith, integrity, honor, and above all compassion.

> *Contemplating mortality*
> *The impermanence of this body*
> *I discovered my unborn face*
> *...Infinite, everlasting*
> *Shinzen*

There was this young man soon to be sent off to war. Obviously, he was scared. He was scared of dying. A friend of his recommended he go see the local Zen priest and discuss this with him, as Zen priests specialize in dealing with life and death. So off he went and found his way to the local Zen temple and availed himself of the priest.

He said, "Sir, I am afraid of death and dying. What can I do? Are there any special teachings you can give me to help? I am so scared and don't know what to do?"

The Zen priest, waiting patiently for the young man telling his story, paused, then said, "Pay attention!" The young man, astonished at just this advice, got mad, and said, "Is that all? Just pay attention?" The priest, looking the young man in the eyes, said, "No. There is more." The young man leaned towards the priest waiting for more words of wisdom heard, "Pay attention. Pay attention."

228

Presence is possible only when you pay attention to the totality of experience, both what appears to arise internally and what appears to arise externally. To realize no-self, you let go of beliefs – and that is, what you *think* you know.

Not-knowing becomes the path. This path is not easy. Your illusionary self is organized on the basis of being in control. Stepping into non-knowing means stepping out of this illusion of control. Even though illusionary, these habituated patterns do not go easily. Resistance often arises as fear. This is typically the fear of the unknown, like death.

A gap (mai-ai) opens in front of you, and you don't know what will happen when you step into it. Entering that gap is the essence of spiritual (and martial) practice. It is why meditation on death is so important. To step into that unknowing is to die to the life you *think* you know and control. To live awake means to face this dying in each moment.

During my years of formal Zen training, one of the genuine surprises was the extent to which the theme of impermanence and death permeated all that we did, from sitting on our zafus to washing the dishes. Direct awareness is practiced by letting all expectations drop away so that you rest in total awareness.

To let all expectation drop is to die in the moment. And that is healing! Therefore, meditation on death and impermanence plays a crucial role in preparing and sustaining a practice of paying attention.

Practice is not about achieving altered states of consciousness. I learned this early in my Zen training when I had begun having wild sensory experiences during meditation. Nonin, my teacher, informed me they were just altered states and also bound by the natural law of impermanence. One state is no better than any other. Just return to breath, be here. He was showing me how to use the raw material of my life *now* to deepen my relationship with life itself.

The essence of practice is presence. Presence is natural awareness. It is seeing the sparkling of no-self as just light. It is your human heritage to be at peace. Awareness of death and impermanence cuts through the veils of personal habituation and socially conditioned agendas. It puts you in touch with life itself.

I prefer the earthy mud of Zen
to the chorus of angels in the heavens.
I prefer the aches of my body
to the comforts of the privileged.
Let the rains come
and the knees throb,
this life is special
...why miss it?
Shinzen

One tradition of the Samurai I have adopted, and I highly recommend, is writing poetry. It is a phenomenal form of meditation upon death. Using my Dharma name of Shinzen, I write haiku, tanka, and other poems inspired by Japanese masters of Zen poetry, such as Ryokan, Basho, and Ikkyu.

From studying their work, I began to pen my own Jisei, or death poems. Typically, a Samurai, before his death, would write a haiku or short poem that transcended thought and created that "Ah, now I see" moment. It is designed to connect the reader with the "who-is-about-to-die" mind, poised at the end.

It is very healing to sit quietly, focusing on death, and then write a poem. Something about meditating in this manner brings about appreciation and compassion for this life as it is now. After all, you never know when you are going to pass. Contemplating mortality daily, and writing a poem reflecting that poised state of mind entering death, is a wonderful way to begin or end your day.

On the next page are some examples of Jisei from some noted Samurai.

Had I not known
That I was dead already
I would have mourned
My loss of life
Ota Dokan 1432-1486

Holding forth this sword
I cut vacuity in twain;
In the midst of the great fire,
A stream of refreshing breeze!
Shiaku Nyudo d.1333

Both the victor
And the vanquished are
But drops of dew,
But bolts of lightning –
Thus should we view the world.
Ouchi Yoshitaka 1507-1551

Not only did the Samurai write death poems, so did many Zen priests and poets. It was customary to brush a final poem as a legacy. Death poems can be written in advance of a priest's or poet's demise, but more often written from the deathbed.

Sick on my journey,
Only my dreams will wander
These desolate moors.
Matsuo Basho 1644-1694

In all the world
Who understands my Zen?
Even if Master Kido were to come,
He wouldn't be worth a penny.
Ikkyu Sojun 1394-1481

Grass, mist rising
Not a voice over the water
The day has ended.
Yosa Buson 1716-1783

231

As I mentioned earlier, writing a death poem usually was in the style of a haiku or tanka. Most of us are familiar with the haiku, the three lines of poetry written in syllables of 5-7-5 per line, respectively. Present in a good haiku is the removal of dualistic views, the division of beauty and ugliness, future and past, and life and death. Keeping it simple, I refer to Tanka as a Haiku with two extra lines of 7-7. So you have five lines broken into 5-7-5-7-7.

Jisei can be very dark or very uplifting, but typically has a nature element to represent this floating ephemeral world. Acceptance of life as it is, and death as it is, is a key element as well. The inevitability of death is noted and faced with the poised mind of equanimity.

This daily practice arouses deep courage to continue on in your life, and brings forth a new vision of life and death. It is truly an ultimate healer. I highly encourage you to purchase a journal for your Jisei and begin to write daily. Do not worry if it is perfect or not. Just write as it comes. The more you do, the more polished you will get.

I hope as you explore death as a means of deep healing and awakening, you enjoy your life as fully as possible. Remember, it is your deep thirst for survival in the future that makes you incapable of living now. Explore many forms of death meditations.

Even if I were to die now
It is okay -
I've had my coffee.
Shinzen

David Nelson, Sensei began his martial path in the great north woods of Wisconsin in 1969 studying Goshindo Karate with Paul Dean, Shihan. Over the years he has studied a variety of traditional, and not-so traditional martial, meditative, and

healing arts. Holding a doctorate in Natural Health, he is the author of Black Belt Healing: A Martial Artist's Guide to Injury Recovery and Pain Management published through Tuttle Publishing.

Using his Dharma name of Shinzen, he has also authored two books of poetry: Bushido: Verses of Consideration-Journey to the Interior of a Warrior's Spirit and Strong Coffee, Burnt Toast: Awkward Poetry of a Lost Monk. He received the precepts in Soto Zen under the tutelage of Nonin Chowaney, Heartland Temple in Omaha, Nebraska in 1994. He can be found on Facebook or feel free to contact him at davidnelsonphd@yahoo.com.

Sensei David Nelson

234

Dim Mak
Dr. Steve Cooper

As I was asked about writing this chapter, I immediately thought of the Shel Silverstein song "Lullabies, Legends and Lies." This pretty much sums up what is known in popular culture about Dim Mak. The term Dim Mak means death touch or touch of death. There is a record label and a clothing line named Dim Mak. There is a musical group named Five Finger Death Punch. I dare say that none of them ever played with Merle Haggard. If you can imagine it, it has probably been thought of on the topic of Dim Mak.

Who could forget the "Five Point Exploding Heart Technique" from *Kill Bill 2*? The topic is even addressed in *Kung Fu Panda*. Is this just an urban myth or is there really any substance to this theory. In China, they have heard the stories of Dim Mak, but they don't want to talk about it. I will try to delve into the legends and lies of Dim Mak without putting you to sleep with a lullaby.

Defined, death touch is any contact that causes death. That would include, but not be limited to a baseball bat, or a slug from a .45 caliber handgun. However, for this discussion, we will stick to the theory of pressure point Dim Mak. Pressure point activation is a viable means of self-defense, when taught and executed properly. The various methods of activation range from rubbing and touching, to striking.

One point may cause pain, two points may cause pain to meet in the middle, and three may cause loss of consciousness. In reality, one point may cause loss of consciousness under the right conditions. Pressure point applications disrupt the flow of energy or Qi in the body. With that in mind, let's take it a step further.

If there is enough energy disruption, in enough meridians, for a long enough period of time, there can be illness and/or death. Also there are points on the body, which are more dangerous than others. If an acupuncture book states, "Do not needle here or do not use on pregnant women," there must be a valid reason. These rules were around long before lawyers, so I would surmise that the warnings were not for malpractice reasons. It is indeed possible to injure or kill someone with Dim Mak, however, it is unlikely that it could be done at will.

The skill and time required to make it work are hardly worth the effort. It is much easier to just temporarily incapacitate an attacker than to "off them permanently." Not only do you still have to deal with the legal problems, but the karmic ones as well. There are cases of accidental Dim Mak every year or so. One that comes to mind is the occasional child that gets hit with a pitch or a line drive and dies.

There is a spot on the chest where a pressure point is located close to the heart, and if hit at the correct angle, the heart rhythm can be disrupted. Conversely there is a point on the back that fixes the problem. Unfortunately this has not become a part of mainstream first medicine…yet.

There are probably only a handful of martial artists with enough knowledge and skill to be able to perform a Dim Mak technique, and most of them are silent on the topic. I have smacked, whacked, and knocked out a lot of people in my time, but I would never teach a Dim Mak technique publicly, and most likely not even to my senior students. Even David Carradine was not taught the five-point exploding heart technique by his master Pei Mei!

Every martial artist worth his or her salt has a technique or two that he or she would classify as a kill shot. This is a technique that they consider deadly and to be used only in extreme circumstances.

Whether it involves pressure points or not, does not matter. What matters is that it is a "go to" technique in times of danger. There is a big chance that the technique in question was passed down from their instructor, but also a good chance that it has

236

never been field-tested. It is difficult to test techniques that may be deadly. Either you run out of test subjects or you run out of bail money!

Even the martial arts portion of The Bubishi mentions deadly techniques. Many think that The Bubishi is only a martial arts text, but in reality, it is an encyclopedic collection of rules for living; only a very small portion is about martial arts. We will never completely know what was passed down, or what was lost, as far as martial knowledge goes.

I taught a women's self-defense class at a major university for several years. I would always ask the young ladies if they knew any self-defense techniques. Usually one or more would raise their hand and tell me about the deadly upward palm strike to the nose. I knew immediately that someone close to them had been in the military. This bogus technique has been taught for years to our troops and they felt the obligation to pass it on to their loved ones.

The legend goes that if you do an upward palm strike to the attacker's nose, you can drive the bone into the brain and thus kill them. Total BS!

In all my years of medical training and anatomical studies, I will tell you right now that this is not possible in any way, shape, or form. The bone they are referring to is thinner than a potato chip on its edges, and the base of the skull, at that point, is much too thick. At best, a well-placed, upward palm strike will make the eyes water, the nose bleed, and the attacker will be greatly angered. If you are teaching this technique to your students, stop it!

A palm strike to the nose is a viable technique, but it should be at a downward angle to the point where the bones and cartilage of the nose join together. This may cause unconsciousness, but not death. It is safe to say that most martial arts instructors have never been in a real life self-defense situation, and that's alright as long as they are not going around acting like "Billy Badass," teaching things that just won't work. Do your homework before passing anything on to your students. Their life may depend on it.

One of the saddest things I have seen was a young wife being interviewed on the local news after her husband had been robbed and beaten to death. She said, "I don't understand. He had a second degree black belt." Unfortunately for him, it was in a sport-oriented style with little or no emphasis on self-defense. Sport Karate is fine, but don't try to pass it off as self-defense.

I have a very good friend who is a great tournament competitor. He called me one evening and stated that he was teaching a self-defense seminar for some ladies at his church and needed to know what to teach. At first, I was surprised, but then realized how smart he was to admit that it was not his forte. I was more than happy to help him out. It is important to know your strengths, but even more important to know your weaknesses.

Just like pressure points, before you poo poo the practice, let's look at the facts. These stories started for a reason. In his autobiography, *Karate-do My Way of Life,* Gichin Funakoshi recalls a story about the great karate master Sokon Matsumura. As the story goes, Matsumura was challenged to a fight to the death by another martial artist. The time came for the big event, and the offending martial artist was frozen in his tracks. Eventually, Matsumura defeated him with a yell.

To the average person, this seems like old wives tales. When I first read it, I thought the same thing. Years later, when I became familiar with transmission of Qi and sound through an art called Kiajutsu, I realized that this story possibly was true. We don't know what information has been lost or hidden throughout history. Every time I think I have seen it all, something else comes along to change my perception.

There are many things that affect the energy flow in our bodies. We also looked at the theories of Yin and Yang, and the cycle

238

of destruction. Theories that are applicable to a Dim Mak technique are yin and yang, the cycle of destruction, the cycle of creation, the diurnal cycle, mother child relationship, sound theory, and the disharmonic emotion theory.

Again, this is where most brains start to tune out, la, la, la, la, too much information. There are no simple answers to complex questions, so stay tuned. To simplify as much as possible though, the cycle of creation is the theory that one element helps create another. The diurnal cycle has to do with the time of day that each meridian is the most and least active. This is in two hour blocks.

Each element has a sound, or sounds, associated with it. These sounds can attack the normal energy flow. Grandmaster T.A. Frazer discovered the disharmonic emotion theory. Emotions have long played an important role in combat. Anger is the one most often recommended to avoid. Emotions affect our bodies in both positive and negative ways.

For example, anger affects the kidneys and the adrenal glands. Anger can be generated by the liver and also affect the eyes. Have you ever heard the expression, "I was so mad, I couldn't see straight," or how about the caution about "Coon Temper?" Supposedly, if a raccoon gets really mad, it defecates. I have not personally observed that one, but I have heard it all my life.

Anger also affects digestion. When someone is happy, they are referred to as light-hearted or if they are sad they are heavy-hearted. Different texts list about nine emotions, but for combat purposes, we only deal with three. The three are anger, psychotic happy, and grief. As Professor Frazer discovered, psychotic happy beats anger, grief beats psychotic happy, and anger beats grief. Emotions affect you, as well as your attacker. Maybe you have heard of the "evil eye" or "the eyes are the window to the soul?"

The eyes project Qi. This is why you should be looking at your target when you hit someone. I have always been taught to look between my hands when fighting. All of these old sayings came from somewhere for a particular reason. If you can create the desired emotion in your attacker, while controlling your own, you will have a definite advantage.

The reason I mention all of these things is because Dim Mak is the result of piling on. The more ways you affect the body's energy, the better your chances of doing permanent harm to your attacker. These theories have been tested in a careful manner.

Several medical studies at major universities have been done on this subject. One of those studies actually paved the way for a particular medical school to expand their curriculum to include an acupuncture program for their medical students. Obviously, the testing of actual death touch techniques is not legally or morally possible, but suffice to say, there are those of us with several "go-to" techniques that, given the necessary circumstances, we would not hesitate to use in a life-or-death situation.

I once knew a jujutsu instructor who said he didn't give much credence to pressure points, but when he was viciously attacked while teaching a seminar, he spun the attacker around and punched him in Gallbladder 20 point, thereby rendering him unconscious. That is pretty convincing!

From a physical standpoint, it is entirely possible to kill someone with pressure points. The possibility can be instantaneous or delayed. The pressure points can heal or hurt the human body. Some organ systems are more important than others. For example, a person can live without a gall bladder or spleen, but it is impossible to exist without a heart or a viable mechanical substitute.

The correct points, used in the correct manner, can completely shut down an organ or system. If that system happens to be gall bladder or spleen, the person may continue to live, but with some complications. If a more vital system were shut down, such as the heart or lungs, death would be fairly quick. If the liver or kidneys were shut down, death would eventually come, after the body's toxins poison itself.

There are points on the front of the body referred to as "alarm points." These points send an alert to the associated organ to let it know it is under attack. The system under attack is very susceptible at this point in time. So you can see, with the proper technique, it is possible to kill with Dim Mak, but personally, I think it is highly unlikely.

A friend of mine was working as a bouncer in an establishment, when a rather large individual grabbed him by the lapels and threatened to administer bodily harm to him. He told me later that he struck two points on the forearms to release the man's grip, and he was surprised that the attacker still held on. I asked him what he did next and he said he hit him again in the same points. At that time, the attacker released his grip and fell unconscious at his feet.

It seems that the first time he hit him, the attacker actually went into shock and lost control of his bowels, but his body was a little slow in completely dropping. The man was later revived with no ill after effects, except for the smell. I would imagine, at this point, his "scoring" possibilities with the ladies had diminished greatly.

This is probably a good time to re-emphasize the importance of safe practice when using pressure points and having someone present who knows what they are doing. It is irresponsible to injure your training partner either on purpose or on accident!

Let's take a look at the actual possibilities of using Dim Mak in a real life situation. I see it as either a premeditated strike or a fortunate accident. I really prefer the latter. If you are being attacked and are defending yourself, there are consequences for your actions. Sadly, the days of beating the crap out of an attacker are rapidly declining. There are way too many lawyers, video cameras, and "peaceniks" in the world. If you knock someone down, depending on the part of the country you live in, and they hit their head on the curb and die, you may be charged with a crime! Hopefully, you will be found to be justified in your actions, be given a cookie and a glass of milk, and sent home with no charges.

I was watching the news one evening, and there was a story about an "elderly man" being attacked. It seems that this "elderly man" was about the same age as me. That made me angry at first, until I realized that this would be something I could use to my advantage in a self-defense situation.

I frequently get the response, "You don't look like a Karate instructor." I always thank them because I know that will be my biggest surprise when attacked. I see the headlines now, "Thug gets his just deserts from an elderly gentleman!"

The chances of accidentally "death touching" someone is much more likely than the chances of doing it on purpose. Just remember, with all the modern forensics today, it is almost impossible to get away with anything. All force must be justified and reasonable according to the local laws of your area, or the area where the incident occurred.

My personal belief, not to be confused with the beliefs of the publisher of this book, or to be disseminated as advice, legal or otherwise, is if someone wants to harm me or my family, all bets are off. I will do whatever it takes to completely end the threat! If the attacker dies from the encounter, well ain't that a shame! I guess it was his time to quit sucking up good air. This does not mean that I would kill them on purpose, but accidents happen. Better that they happen to him than to me or mine!

Now, let's look at pre-planned Dim Mak. It is possible to plan an attack using Dim Mak to kill another person. Only a very skilled martial artist could pull it off, but why would a very skilled martial artist want to? To take another life, in a premeditated way, whether it is done with Dim Mak, poison, or a gun, is not right.

242

Movies and TV shows attempt to glorify violence and the skills thereof, but they don't seem to address the after effects of such action. If caught and proven guilty, you are most likely going to be spending the rest of your life in prison for murder. Like I said earlier, there are very few techniques that modern forensics can't detect.

After years and years of training, the goal of martial arts is not just to improve physical technique, but also to improve the character of the martial artist. Training is a crucible that helps us hone our character and morals, and to become wiser, calmer, and better people. That is our daily struggle and is much more difficult than perfecting techniques.

Those who seek out martial arts training only as a means to hurt another person, usually don't last very long. They grow weary of the discipline involved or a smart instructor sends them on their way.

One of the things I enjoy about not running a large commercial dojo is that I can be very picky about who I teach. I don't depend on new students to pay the rent. I don't teach kids, and I don't teach people who "want to take Karate." I only teach the ones that are in it for the long haul.

Whether you teach a large commercial school or not, part of your job as an instructor is to instill your students with, not only physical skills, but morals as well. I had a friend of mine who was bemoaning the fact that he didn't want to listen to everyone's problems; he just wanted to teach Karate. I told him that being a listening ear comes with the territory. I have found that students will tell their instructor things that they wouldn't tell their parents or a priest.

Now, let's look at the possibility that you committed the perfect crime and got away scot-free. There is always an after effect. Even in wartimes, soldiers are haunted by their actions. Later, many suffer from post-traumatic stress disorder. One of my favorite uncles served with General Patton during WWII. He gave me a souvenir he had brought back. When I asked him about the particulars, he would only say that the guy he got it from no longer needed it. I knew this was his way of telling me he didn't want to talk about it.

Another friend served in Viet Nam. When a plane flew over his house a little too low, late at night, his wife would find him under the bed. I am sure this was a reflexive response from trying to survive a life-threatening situation.

Although I know of several Dim Mak techniques, and I know of several people that probably deserve it. I also believe that I have a karmic and moral responsibility to my fellow man. I also do not want to carry a load of guilt and remorse around for the rest of my life because some asshole deserved it.

So you see, the practice of Dim Mak is much more than a collection of killing techniques. If you study the human body and pressure points long enough and deep enough, you will find not only how resilient the human body is, but also how fragile. Dim Mak is not a merit badge to be earned or a particular belt to be awarded, but a life-long study in the arts of healing, as well as hurting.

Those who claim to know the secrets of Dim Mak, and are supposedly teaching them to anyone with money, are not only irresponsible, but most likely fraudulent. To state that a technique might kill someone is different than saying a technique will definitely kill someone. The latter assumes that it has been tested beyond a doubt. In my humble opinion, Dim Mak is a real thing, however, so is "Dim Wit." There are many out there who want to claim proficiency in the arts of self-defense for strictly financial gain without any regard for the final product.

My old Wado instructor, Tatsuo Suzuki, referred to this type of a person as a "mushi bushi," or mouth warrior. Keyboard warriors can be added to the mix, so don't be fooled. Research what you want to learn and who is teaching it in your area. If this is a chosen field of study for you, do so with sincerity, respect, and responsibility. Study with the idea that healing someone is much better than hurting.

There are people who need to be hurt to protect our loved ones or ourselves, but hurt them without malice, and only to the degree that it takes to stop the attack and render them no longer a threat. Train with a sincerity that will enrich you and your students, so you don't just perpetuate the "lullabies, legends, and lies."

Grandmaster Steve Cooper began his martial arts training in 1973. He spent 25 years training in Wado Ryu Karate and 20 years in Ryukyu Kempo. During that time, he also trained in many styles of Jujutsu and eventually founded Zanshin Ryu Jujutsu. His most influential instructors are Sensei Tatsuo Suzuki, Professor George Dillman, Professor Wally Jay, Grandmaster Shane Lear, and the late Grandmaster Ed Lake. GM Cooper now teaches two classes a week at his home dojo and travels around the country teaching seminars.

GM Cooper is also a Doctor of Chiropractic and a professional acupuncturist. His knowledge of acupuncture has led him to be an expert on the art of using the points of the body for both self-defense and healing. He also donates his time as a professional Santa Claus during the Christmas season.

Grandmaster Steve Cooper

Hard Core Martial Arts versus Competition
Peter Freedman

I grew up in Boston's Mass South End. Not to be confused with Southie. I started my training very young by way of my father. He taught me how to box, and later, how to bare knuckle box. It is very different. I got involved in martial arts as I got older and fell in love with Ketsugo Jujutsu, and later, Arnis. I now teach both martial arts as a combat method to help those people who feel they need to learn something in today's crazy world.

First off, before anybody starts a martial art, my advice to them would be to first ask yourself, "Why do I want to study this art?" What is driving you to take part in this type of physical activity?

I have noticed there are different people who study martial arts for different reasons. Some do it for a social event. They just want to find a place to go so they can socialize and hang out. Now, this is okay for them to do, but on the other hand, it may interfere with other people who study there for a different reason.

Some people become very needy and lose track of time; and by doing that, they lack the respect of another person's time. If you are merely socializing, please be aware that other people's time is valuable too, and you need to respect it. Socializing is okay, but do it after class is over with. Do it off the mat area, so you won't interfere with those who wish to get in extra practice after class.

Then there are people who just want to get into good shape. They care about their health and they want to improve their flexibility and coordination. They want to do something artistic with their body and mind. They want to learn how to deal with stress through movement and meditation, with proper breathing techniques. And what better to do that with, than a martial art! It can definitely do that for them. What a great stress reliever it is!

You can blow off steam by hitting a bag or having someone hold some hand pads and move them around. You can chase them or learn to avoid them, while practicing your striking techniques. Your mind is now off of all your problems of that day, trying not to get hit or trying to hit a moving pad. You can sweat off all your troubles, while getting into good top physical shape and improving your fitness daily.

Learning a new form, or kata, a pre-arranged series of body movements, where you are using footwork, along with blocks and strikes, on the different directions of a compass, can also relieve stress.

Believe it or not, you can't imagine how rewarding it is to learn a new series of movements and to practice these forms or katas to the point of self-perfection. Some of these forms or kata are just made up for exercise, while older ones have hidden gems of deep-rooted martial science secrets hidden in their movements, that only a knowledgeable master teacher can reveal over time.

One thing that all these forms and kata do for you, which I feel most don't give enough thought to, is they keep your joints healthy and flexible. They help keep your internal organs working properly. They keep your mind in a state of focus, because you must learn to remember all the different movements and in which direction on the compass you are going.

We tend to lose our ability to remember things as we age. Your forms and kata help you to retain that important part of the brain that maintains your ability to think clearly and to stay active and in good shape.

Some people want to study a martial art just for bragging rights. They want to be able to brag how they study a martial art and what a bad-ass they are, or think they are. Hopefully, they will find a good instructor that will snap them out of that way of thinking. I feel they are so insecure, because they care too much about what others may think of them. So they try to be tough guys, or gals, bragging about how tough they are or who they can beat up. They may even walk around with a bad attitude, or what is known as a chip on their shoulder.

We have all seen the movie *The Karate Kid*, where there is the good sensei and a bad sensei. Most of the time, a student will resemble his or her teacher. So it is important, if you teach a martial art, to watch how you act and conduct yourself daily, and not to limit your good behavior only to your dojo school of thought.

We, as teachers, if we talk the talk, must also walk the walk; meaning we must live up to what we teach others. You are responsible for shaping new minds and spreading an ancient, deep piece of culture from different lands. Honor it by teaching it the right way, by changing people's attitudes to have faith and to trust themselves.

Help your students kick their bad habits by replacing them with positive ones. That is your job as a keeper of old knowledge. Your job is to help them develop wisdom so they can slowly rid themselves of their insecurities and become good, positive citizens.

Some people like that hormone known as adrenaline. They love that rush they get when it starts flowing through their body. It is the fight-or-flight affect. These are the kinds of people who want to constantly test themselves, and what better way to accomplish that than through a sports type of martial art. You will definitely get your rush either way.

These people usually love sports and live their life around their sports. They enjoy getting together with friends and hanging out discussing the outcomes of each event. They love to work out, and they love a good fight.

They like that feeling of punching someone in the face or knocking someone out with a well-placed kick. Some prefer the grappling game, while others like the striking game.

However, a shadow seems to follow these combat sports. That shadow is in the form of ego and really bad behavior. Now, I am not saying that all who partake in a sports type of martial art are troublemakers, but a lot are.

I love to watch a good fight on television as much as the next guy does, but I love it even more when both fighters conduct themselves like gentlemen or ladies. This tells me that the fighter is well-disciplined and I respect that. I can't bring myself to respect a jerk. That is what needs to be changed in all sports today. It seems like most athletes have lost something and all they care about is money and fame. It is sad but true.

I have seen a great deal in my lifetime. It seems that things have gone haywire all over the world. People are killing people over money and religion. These are crazy times we now live in! Which brings me to the other type of person who studies martial arts – those who want to defend themselves and their families.

This is what we do in my dojo, our specialty. I am not going to say one martial art is better than another, because it is not. It all depends on your reasons for studying. People come to us because they have had something really bad happen to them or they are afraid something in the future is going to happen to them.

Whatever the reason, we do our best to help each person figure out what they are looking for, and we try to steer them in the right direction. I have actually told people to go somewhere else because what they wanted was not what we do in my dojo. I helped them research what they wanted, and they went elsewhere. We teach a combat martial arts. Here, you may wonder what the difference is between a regular martial art and a combat martial art.

Well, we are not a self-defense school. We are a school of combat. With that being said, I need to be careful to whom I pass this knowledge. What we teach here works. It has been tried and tested by those who go into harm's way to protect our great country. You will learn anatomy here. You can't hurt nor damage what you don't understand. For example, by learning Arnis, which is a Filipino martial art system, you learn how to use a stick. So what are you hitting with that stick?

I teach people, in our Arnis class, the skeletal system, because that is what you are hitting with your sticks. I show them where, on the skeleton, it is easiest to break bones, and which angle to hit that bone to make it break.

By learning this, and allowing each Arnis student to see the actual skeletal system, and having them swing at it at the different angles, they have a better image, or target, in their mind's eye about what they are striking. They also learn why they get so tired during training and why they lack both strength and proper energy. So we teach them about proper nutrition. If you eat right, you will have the right kind of energy in a fight, not to mention, you increase your life span.

Each student must also learn the history of where their martial art comes from, how it was developed, and why. They are taught how to use their minds to develop a quick thought response to match each of their aggressors' attacks. They have to learn how to see everything around them as a potential weapon, and that their true weapon is their mind, everything else is just an extension of their mind (weapon).

We also have discussions about the laws. No, I am not a lawyer, but we do have a lawyer come in from time to time and teach the rights of defense, and what not to do. We have paramedics come in and teach our students how to do "ditch medicine," in case they have dress a gunshot or a knife wound. They learn how to make up a medical kit and what each thing in their medical kit is used for. We tend to train for life and how to survive all the different things that can occur in today's world. We do our best to keep the training very practical.

The difference between a self-defense course and a combat course is we teach people to attack when threatened or if they feel their life is in danger. A self-defense class teaches you to wait until your attacker actually attacks you before you take action. There is also a difference between these two and a sports type of martial art. Sports martial arts have rules where you win without actually injuring the other guy.

Combat martial arts have one rule, to win – to survive at all cost. Do your best to either cripple your attacker or kill him, but know the law! Also, people who study combat martial arts seem to be the kindest and most down to earth individuals. They are very humble and caring, and a confrontation is the last thing they want to have, but they are ready if that situation arises.

Grandmaster Peter Freedman is a native of Boston and has committed his time to the lifelong study of martial arts. His father was a professional boxer and a bare knuckle fist fighting competitor. Thus, from an early age, he was heavily influenced by his father's concepts of boxing in the ring, as well as by his own experience outside of the ring on the streets.

During the course of his life, he constantly searched for more information on various systems of martial arts to find better ways to improve his methods of self-defense skills. Included in his studies were boxing, wrestling, Judo, Aikido, Goju Ryu Karate, Shotokan Karate, Tae Kwon Do, Savate, Muay Thai, Fu Jow Pai Kung Fu, Tai Chi Chuan, Ba Gua, Xing Yi, Pencak Silat, Arnis, Kali, Escrima, Dumog, as well as his main discipline of Ketsugo Jujutsu.

Until recently, he continued to expand his knowledge of the martial arts through Guro Grande George Brewster, who taught a Filipino martial art, Arnis. Mr. Brewster, a veteran of D-Day and the Battle of the Bulge, passed on at 81 years of age 2006, but his legend continues to live on. Currently, the combative system of Brewster Arnis, which was perfected by GM George Brewster, has been entrusted to Sensei Freedman. Guro Grande George H. Brewster, the founder of the Brewster Arnis method, appointed Peter Freedman as the new Grandmaster of Brewster Arnis in 2000. To this day, GM Peter Freedman teaches each and every Arnis and Jujutsu class in Weare, NH. His school is a private martial arts school that promotes the higher learning of the inner teachings that was passed down to him. He maintains a small private group, to prepare new holders of old knowledge, to someday become teachers themselves. Please feel free to check out his website at www.BrewsterArnis.com. And feel free to write him with any questions you may have.

Grandmaster Peter Freedman

The Seven Virtues of Bushido

254

Internal Healing
Harry Mok

Throughout my martial arts career I've been asked many times, "What is the best fighting art to take?" My reply is, "A punch is a punch and a kick is a kick. It's all about the individual who applies it. All martial arts have something special to offer."

As I turn 60, this year of the Dog, 2018, I reflect on the 52 years that I've been involved in martial arts. I look back to my childhood, when I was about eight, and there's not a great amount of memories that I chose to remember.

Although, what I do clearly remember is the miserable days when I had become sick with colds and flu. The reason why those awful memories stuck in my mind is because my mom would boil these awful herbs from San Francisco's Chinatown for hours, and then have me drink the herbal tea to help fight off my cold.

I remember, I always had to have a chaser to wash down the terribly bitter taste of the dry, dark, potent teas. As I recall, after drinking this terribly bitter concoction, I was never sick for very long. As I grew up, I would have a better understanding of why I was never sick for long.

As I continued throughout the years with my training, various injuries would occur, whether I twisted my ankle, sprang my wrist, bruised my shins, or burst open my knuckles, injuries of all sorts. My dad would bring out the old bottle of Dit Dow Jow, (A Chinese herbal liniment handed down from hundreds of years), and rub it deep into my injuries.

Other times, my mom would take a Chinese coin with vegetable oil and began scraping my skin with the coin until it turned blood red. All I could do was go along with it no matter how much it hurt. White Flower Oil would be used to rub on my temples and upper lip and I was barely able to keep my eyes open from intense effects which were similar to Vick's Vapor

255

Rub. There were remedies of all sorts. As I matured in life, and in martial arts, I realized the necessity of self-healing, and that is what I will share with you here.

Decades ago, Great Grandmaster Al Novak, once told me, "A well-rounded martial artist is one who can cause serious damage to his opponent and then heal them from their injuries at the same time." For those of you who knew GGM Novak, you know that he was at every major tournament in California. Mr. Novak's comment left an impression on me that would influence my way of thinking for the rest of my life.

It began to make sense, those bitter tasting herbs had a purpose. I began researching my ancestry, and herbal formulas that would help redefine my decades of martial arts training, while finding ways to heal myself and detoxify my body. What I found amazed me, and I dove deeper into the ways of the healing arts.

Spiritual Attitude

Mind, body, spirit, and soul – we have all heard of the term, "You are what you eat." This term also extends to who you are as an individual. You are who you surround yourself with. You are who you are influenced by. If you think positive and project positive energy, then, in most cases, you will have positive things in your life.

Although, in some cases, when one person puts out as much positive energy as possible, negative energy still seems to come knocking at the door. One must recognize this negative energy and make changes to transform the negative energy in order to receive good energy.

This attitude can be used in all aspects of life, both internally or externally. Internally, for self-healing, and externally, when dealing with anything, or anyone, outside of your self being. If you choose to hang out with thugs, you eventually become a thug. If you hang with drug addicts, you're influenced in certain ways that may become harmful to you because of that relationship. If you're driving a car, and your buddies just happen to go in a store and rob it, and you drive off, what happens if you get pulled over by the police? I'm sure you'd all agree that the driver is going to join his buddies in jail for being an accomplice.

So in life, if you do positive things and stay positive, then you are positive. God forbid a doctor informs you that you have cancer. If you're convinced that you were just given a death sentence, most folks would go into a depression, and not long after, the body will slowly start to shut down.

Death begins to eat at your mental attitude. I've seen this happen many, many times; although, I've also seen the positive aspect of some very strong willed individuals that literally healed themselves because they refused to be beaten by such a disease.

This is where your body, mind, spirit, and soul comes into effect from having a positive attitude, working together as one entity with a completely positive effect. Find a solution and don't become the problem. I will discuss this throughout this chapter.

Understanding Your Body

We all have taken our bodies for granted at one point in time in our lives, some of us even on a daily basis. A very good friend of mine, Dr. Colin Dong, (God rest his soul), created a cure for arthritis through diet. He said to me, one day as I followed his regiment on one of his bestselling cookbooks, "Why are you following recipes in my cook book?"

I must have been in my late twenties early thirties at the time. He laughed at me and continued, "You're young, eat what you want and enjoy your life, but this I will say to you, when you begin to reach your mid 40's, you better seriously consider changing your diet."

Wow, this has stuck in my mind to this day. In the 1950's, one out of seven people in the U.S. was dealing with cancer. Today, one out of two people will be dealing with cancer during their lifetime. What does this tell us? Are we listening to our body? Do you know your body? How well do you think you know your body?

What are the signs that your body is trying to communicate to you? We are all guilty of taking our health for granted, up until something bad goes wrong and the coin is flipped. At that time, there is a 50/50 chance as to whether or not everything is going to work out or not.

So, why allow the coin to be flipped. This is where we can all stand up and be proactive. Listen to your body, in fact, learn what makes your body feel good. Remember, we are what we eat and most everything we eat is contaminated. Go back to the basics and minimize your food intake.

I always tell people, if you eat to where you are overly stuffed, you will gain weight, if you eat to where you are satisfied, you will maintain what you have, and if you eat to where you are still hungry, yet satisfied, you will eventually begin to lose weight. Understand and know your body. Don't wait for the worst to happen, be several steps ahead of life. Get a check up on a regular basis.

Pinpointing the Issues

Our body speaks to us in multiple ways. If you train hard and find that you pull a muscle to where the pain is nearly unbearable, what caused the problem? Did you not warm up properly? Did you not stretch well enough? Or were you not completely focused on what you were about to attempt and was not aligned properly?

Recently, a very dear friend passed away from a heart attack. We all know heart attacks are caused by many issues, high cholesterol that causes blockage in the arteries and which can cause a weak heart. This can possibly reflect years of a bad diet. Well, my friend passed away from a heart attack, not because his arteries were clogged, but because his kidneys had failed. So, the question is, why did his kidneys fail? He was a diabetic and failed to take the needed medication. This all goes back to diet and what we consume. Stay on top of your body, know it so well that you can pinpoint the issues and immediately address the issues before it gets the best of you.

Two years ago, I was given a wakeup call and was told I was borderline diabetic and had high blood pressure. My initial response was, "Are you serious!" As fit as I thought I was, how can this be? I took action and cured myself of high blood pressure, and my border line diabetes is now normal. All done without any medications. I'm sure, had I continued on the path I was on, I'd be taking multiple medications as I speak.

But I immediately began to research my diet and realized I was taking in too many carbs. So, I changed my diet and began cutting out white rice and replaced it with brown. I cut out my bread, pasta, and noodles, and added more protein and complex carbs such as green vegetables, in my diet.

I cut out all sugar filled drinks and cut down on my cafe mochas. I started doing meal preps and ate more proportioned meals throughout the day. One of my favorites is a turkey breast patty over a bed of steamed spinach with garlic and topped with salsa. Within a matter of only 2-3 months, I was normal again and feeling great, not to mention, I dropped an additional 12 pounds without even trying!

I like to jumpstart my body in the morning by drinking one to two glasses of warm water. During my meals, instead of drinking a cold liquid, I drink hot tea. If you ever have traveled to Asia, you'll notice, at every meal, hot tea is served. Think of our body's system as that of a sink. What happens when you pour grease down the sink followed by cold water? We know the outcome because I'm sure some of you had to deal with clogged sinks. Although, if you pour grease down the sink

259

followed by hot water, the grease will emulsify and find its way down the drainage pipe.

I did some research in China, looking back at some of my ancestry, and found a province where the average lifespan was 100 years, with little to no health issues. In researching their diets, I found that it consisted mainly of fresh fish, vegetables, and rice. How could you go wrong with this lifestyle!

Find the solution that works for you *before* you become dependent on medications. If you're already on meds, then be very aware of your diet and work towards a healthier lifestyle. Eat clean! Get on a training regiment, join a local gym or martial arts school. If there's a will, there is a way. Don't wait for the worst to come; take the proper steps to a healthy lifestyle today. God forbid losing a foot or leg or staying on dialysis for the rest of your life.

Some of the Solutions to Self-Healing

The Cure for Arthritis

Arthritis affects tens of millions of individuals on a daily basis. Is there a cure or do we get on meds that only temporarily help alleviate the pain. Arthritis is a toxic residual that lingers within our body due to all the contaminants that we introduce throughout our lifespan. Tired of the meds that only put a band aid on what the real issues are?

Well, here's a solution to cure the pain and rid yourself of this nasty toxin. It entails a change of diet and may be considered drastic to some, but what's so wrong about good healthy eating? As a martial artist, we never want to limit our performance due to the suffering of arthritis.

What does eating clean mean? It means, when you shop for your groceries, you need to put back anything that has preservatives, artificial flavoring, or colorings. Anything that you can't understand when you read the ingredients means you

260

shouldn't be putting it in your mouth. Next, cut out all fruits except for avocado. Yes, it's considered a fruit. Eat all veggies except for tomatoes, and depending on how severe your arthritis is, you should also cut out asparagus. Cut out all your red meats and stick to poultry and seafood. Organic chicken is the best. And cut out farm raised fish.

Here is a meal prep you can do for the day. In the evening, take a whole chicken and boil it until it's fully cooked, save the broth. Steam your rice and veggies of your choice, the greener the better, and make sure they are organic. If you are diabetic, use brown rice. In the morning prior to your daily routine, boil two cups of the chicken broth.

Warm up your chicken breast and veggies. Chop up some chives, garlic with pepper to your liking, or any other types of herbs that you like. Place the hot soup broth in a blender with a cup or two of rice, your chicken (sliced in chunks), veggies, and chopped herbs. Cover and pulse 2-3 times quickly. Do not purée; the objective is not to drink the concoction, but rather to slightly mix as this will be your meal to eat throughout the day.

Place in a decent size thermos and have with you for lunch and snack. For your evening meal, prepare your dinner accordingly as you normally would and make sure you're sticking to the rule and eating clean. Thousands of individual around the world have cured themselves of arthritis based on this diet. Search out a bestselling book entitled, *New Hope for the Arthritic*, by Doctor Colin Dong.

Complete Body Detoxification

There are many formulations of detox programs. One that I have been using for the past 15 years is the Master Cleanser, it's also called the Lemon Juice Diet. It's a very deep detox that lasts for 10 days. I do this detox three times a year for 10 days, and I have even done it for up to 23 days. I call it the inflammation killer. I have seen others I've shared this detox with, lose anywhere from 8-40 pounds in 10 days and some have been cured from some very specific pains, arthritis, chronic cough, migraine headaches, and more. Buy yourself a Nutra Ninja and start juicing greens with various fruits. If you're already one who has joined the diabetic regiment, then stick to the greens for the most part and eliminate some of the fruits and carbs, pasta, bread, white rice, etc.

I have been training in iron fist since the early 80's and I've been told that my hands would be filled with arthritis from all the years of pounding. Well, at 60 years old, I continue to pound on metal, rocks and wood. This is all due to my detoxification regiment to rid myself of these toxins *and* using Dit Dow Jow. I continue to punch and kick as though I was in my 20's.

You must fast for ten days for it to work deeply and effectively. If you're only trying to eliminate a chronic cough, then you can do the fast for half the time, depending on how severe your cough is. You may experience a headache within the second or third day. Don't be alarmed, as this will go away. Also, you can mix a half-gallon at a time by using half the formula. You can also refer to the booklet, *Master Cleanser: The Lemon Juice Diet*, for more details.

The Master Cleanser Formula

1) Fresh squeezed lemon juice: (Organic is the best for you, but not necessary) 2 cups fresh squeezed lemon juice per gallon of spring or filtered water.

2) Organic grade "B" maple syrup (you can get this at any natural food store). Mix in 24 tablespoons of maple syrup per gallon of water.

3) Cayenne pepper (You can get at most any store.) 1 teaspoon of cayenne pepper per gallon of water. Drink this throughout the entire day as your breakfast, lunch, dinner, and in-between snacks. If you feel weak, drink. If you feel light headed, drink. If you feel hungry, drink.

262

Morning or Night Intestine and Colon Wash

1) Sea Salt (you can get at most grocery stores or health store) Use 2 teaspoons of sea salt per quart of fresh water. Dissolve the salt and drink. This should equal approximately two tall glasses. Make sure you are near a restroom for the next hour or two. Your body will start to flush. If this is too much to handle for 10 days, then alternate with the following dieters tea.

2) Laci's Dieter Tea (you can get at Rite Aid): This is tea you can drink every night in preparation for the morning flush or alternate every other day with the sea salt flush. This will force a bowel movement and may cause a little cramping. Because you are not eating, your body will not have a bowel movement. This is why you must force a bowel movement to cleanse the toxins from the intestines and colon.

3) You can drink as much water as you like throughout the day, as well as pure green tea hot or cold. Once you have reached the end of the 10 days and feel great, if you want to continue, you can do this for up to 40 days, my wife and I have done 23 days ourselves and could have easily done 30 days.

4). Please remember, the longer you fast, the longer you need to take while transitioning back to solid foods!

Slowly Transition back to Solid Food

On the 11th day you can start to drink organic orange juice. You can also continue to drink the lemon juice mix or even mix the two together. On the 12th and 13th days, continue the orange juice and begin a juicing program with vegetables and fruit or you can do a vegetable soup broth.

Then you can start with oatmeal in the morning; it is good with almond milk. Stay away from dairy, I would suggest dairy be left out of your diet completely.

On the 14th day, you can go back to eating your regular meals. Keep the portions small. Your stomach shrinks after no food for 10 days. You can have 4-5 small (protein & carb combo's) meals a day if you were overweight and want to keep the weight off. Cut out the fatty, greasy foods, and cut back the heavy carbs.

I would avoid red meat for a while, especially if you're trying to get your stomach and intestines back into shape. These foods are very difficult to digest and take a long time. Red meat should eventually be minimized in your diet later in life. Eat clean and healthy!

I am also including a formula for Dit Dow Jow to be used for *EXTERNAL PURPOSES ONLY*. It is used for healing bruises, sprains, joints, iron hand, and iron fist training. Use as recommended by rubbing on effected area. *DO NOT* use on open wounds and *DO NOT INGEST*.

It is written in Chinese, so the Chinese herbalist can accurately fill the order. Once the herbs have been acquired, you will need a large *GLASS* container, (not plastic), that can hold upwards to 3-5 Gallons. Purchase two gallons of cooking rice liquor and three bottles of 98% rubbing alcohol. Pour the rice liquor and rubbing alcohol into glass container. Stir, mix, and allow to soak in a cool place for a minimum of one year.

跌 打 药

Dit Dow Jow

264

Dit Dow Jow Recipe

跌打方

零仙	一錢	川芎	三錢
生地	五錢	紅葱	三錢
續斷	二錢	歸尾	三錢
田七	三錢	詭同	二錢
椿皮	三錢	龜板	二錢
獨活	二錢	牛七	三錢
鬱金	三錢	鳥药	三錢
莪术	二錢	杜仲	三錢
赤芍	二錢	血竭	三錢
三苓	四錢	桂技	三錢
羗活	二錢	枝子	二錢
防風	二錢	乳香	三錢
秦芄	二錢	木瓜	三錢
末菊	三錢	巴戟	二錢
桔梗	二錢	京芥	二錢

How effective is your body releasing waste. Have you had your colonoscopy done lately? Last year I had a colonoscopy done and the doctor said to me, "I don't need to see you for another ten years." This was strange because at my age, you are supposed to have a colonoscopy every five years.

What does this tell me? I've been using psyllium fiber (Metamucil), for the past 30 years, not because I have issues with bowel movements, but because psyllium coagulates the waste in the colon and gets everything out, leaving no toxic residue lingering on the side walls of the intestines. Therefore, my next visit for my colonoscopy will be when I turn 70. I utilize one to two servings a day, one in the morning and one at night. It comes in capsules as well if you prefer that instead of drinking it.

Making Changes and Preventative Measures

Sometimes making changes in your life is as difficult as a person trying to quit smoking after 59 years or a crack addict trying to kick the habit. In either case, it's a life changing challenge and a commitment to a healthier lifestyle. I've always imagined what a martial artist should look like. When I saw my first Bruce Lee movie, I was immediately convinced that the ultimate image of a martial artist was that of Bruce Lee.

So for 42 years of my life, I dedicated my training to build my physique to match and surpass Bruce Lee's physique. (Not to say that all martial artists need to look like Bruce, this was only my own personal thoughts.) I've heard many negative comments throughout the years about martial artists who were overweight. It is not the weight that dictates the individual's capabilities as a martial artist, though it does set the stage for potential health issues that can shorten one's lifespan.

How many people do we know that have left us way too soon? I have lost count. Change can happen at any given moment and time. It's the will that motivates and stimulates the mind to act upon just about anything we set our mind to. This is the gift we have all been blessed with.

Do __YOU__ need to make Necessary Changes?

My colleague, Dr. Ba, has been developing herbal formulas for decades to help the body fight off cancer, with promising results. One year I was able to assist my friend's wife, who was diagnosed with ovarian cancer.

The herbal formula assisted her in the chemo treatment and she did not get sick, lose her hair, lose her appetite, and her white blood count did not drop while on chemo. In addition, miraculously, her cancer was gone. She was advised to have her ovaries removed, and because she was later in her years, she agreed. For nearly two years, she has been cancer free until recently when the cancer returned.

266

What does this tell us? When a person has been diagnosed with cancer and is treated and survives the chemo regiment, these folks need to understand that you cannot go back to the same lifestyle that you have been living your entire life. This is why I teach about making lifelong changes in your life.

It has been proven that cancer cells cannot survive in an alkaline, balanced body, but will flourish in an acidic body. Do your research on how to balance your body and make it more alkaline. I use an ionizer at home to alkaline my drinking water to 9.8 alkalinity. Take preventative measures, seek out a nutritionist, and make the changes that will allow you to be proactive in living a long, healthy lifestyle. Make that change!

As martial artists, we are here to set examples for all who will listen, to be respectful, humble, courteous, teach all aspects of the art, learn to heal what is broken, be preventative, live the way of the Budo, and to focus on self-improvement. In closing, your health is your health, it's all about the individual that applies themselves to live a long, healthy life. All cultures have something special to offer for a healthy lifestyle.

Harry began his entrepreneurial career in the entertainment industry early on due to his well-known expertise in the martial arts field. He has been inducted into 16 Black Belt & World Masters Hall of Fames, has received the "Presidential Gold Champion Award," and the "Presidential Lifetime Achievement Award." Harry began his early training at the age of 8, performing Lion Dancing (Martin Jue) and studying Shotokan (Norman Fong), Choy Lay Fut (Doc Fai Wong), Sil Lum (Wing Lam), Kajukenbo/Jukendo (Earl Boles Sr.) and holds the rank of 9th degree in the Kajukenbo Gaylord Method under SGM Pete Morales.

Compelled to express his martial arts talents and bring martial arts awareness to the screen, Harry began working as an actor/stuntman, performing and/or starring in such films as

267

Rambo II, Uncommon Valor, TC 2000, Talons of the Eagle, Femme Fontaine, For Life or Death, College Kickboxers, The Vineyard, Tiger Claws II, Ninja Busters, Forbidden Power, and others.

In 1987, Harry created and produced his first full length feature film, The Vineyard, starring and directed by veteran actor James Hong and released by New World Pictures. Thereafter, Harry was subsequently requested to utilize his considerable talents by producing for Atari Games/Time Warner Interactive, creating action fighting games.

Harry would go on to direct music videos and commercials for the burgeoning music industry, producing, directing, and writing the majority of his work, acquiring an unparalleled reputation for his creativity and technical experience. In 1998, Harry received directing/producing awards for the first ever Jimi Hendrix music video for Universal MCA Records and Experience Hendrix. Recently, Harry completed an animated series and comic book novel for Lions Gate Entertainment starring Shaquille O'Neal, based from his creative concept entitled, Hoopfighter, where he successfully integrated full contact martial arts with basketball.

Today, Harry is on the producing team of Blue Dream Studios animated feature film entitled, Animal Crackers, starring John Krasinski, Emily Blunt, Sir Ian Mckellen, Sylvester Stallone, Danny Devito, Gilbert Gottfried, Patrick Warburton, Harvey Fierstein, Raven Symone, Wallace Shawn, Tara Strong, and more. Harry's latest adventure with Blue Dream Studio's is Pet Robots, currently in Pre-production.

Harry recently completed development of a feature film that he has written and will be produced and directed by Harry, entitled, Lion Dance. Harry calls it, the Kung Fu version of the Karate Kid. At the age of 60, Harry has not showed any signs of slowing down and continues to train 5-6 days a week and gives seminars when his busy schedule allows.

Grandmaster Harry Mok

The Good, the Bad, and the Ugly
Dana Lynn Hee

The warrior spirit within is a great equalizer when it comes to facing good times, bad times, and times when it's just plain ugly. As an enthusiastic, long-term student of the martial arts, particularly Shotokan Karate, Moo Duk Kwon Taekwondo, and Olympic World Taekwondo, I have learned the most important lesson in life – your attitude matters.

Abandoned and abused since I was three years old, raised and terrorized in an orphanage for nine years, surviving alcoholic, suicidal, maniacal relatives for three more years, all was not easy. At the age of fifteen, I decided the streets were a safer bet for me.

Police decided otherwise and I ended up in a government shelter until I was adopted as a sixteen-year-old by a high school friend's parents. From a very early age, I discovered it was better to live in my dreams, than my realities. My favorite dream was one I made one desperate night, upon a single star. Little did I know, that this same dream would save my life one day.

My mother did finally get back in touch with us at the orphanage. She would occasionally write or call, with promises that she would come visit, or come and take me out of there to live with her. And I remember the rare times when I would receive a letter during mail call, and I would gallop all around the dormitory, waving that letter high in the air. And then there was the time that I actually got to talk with her on the telephone, and she said she'd be coming to get me the next day to go spend the summer with her. I was so excited, I couldn't sleep all night long.

The next morning I convinced my housemother to let me wait for her on the front steps. Shortly after breakfast, I sat down on the cold stone steps, waiting, watching, and hoping. As each car entered the long circular driveway, my heart would beat a little faster, and I would shield my eyes from the glare of the sun and try and make out who it was. And, as each car left with their excited, laughing children, my heart would sink a little lower. Finally, the bell rang for lunch, and I pulled myself to my feet, and went off to the cafeteria. "Perhaps later," I said to myself. After lunch, my housemother, told me that, "No one will be coming to pick you up," and that I would remain at the home once again during the long summer vacation.

It was late that afternoon that I sat in the deep grass and clover on the playground, beneath a huge, sweet-smelling Magnolia tree. I watched the few kids that were left, playing a game of jump rope. And, as I sat in thought that morning, the familiar pain of abandonment wrapped its tight hold around my heart and a feeling of hopelessness spread through my soul. The bell sounded for us to gather in our groups and head inside the building, so I quickly wiped my face and walked across the lawn towards the huge stone steps.

I walked up the steps with the other children, then paused for a moment before entering the doorway. I turned around to take one last breath of the fresh, sweet air before heading inside to the dark, musty smelling dormitories. It was then that I noticed, there on the horizon in the twilight, just above the tree-line, a single star glittering brightly. Quickly, I closed my eyes, crossed my fingers, and whispered to myself, "Starlight, star-bright, first star I see tonight. I wish I may, I wish I might, have the wish I wish tonight. And I made that wish, just before the hall monitor smacked me on the backside with a ruler and ushered me inside.

Later, in the quiet of the night, I held close to that star in my mind, as the tears fell like rain down my cheeks. Muffling my sobs in my pillow, I paused for a moment as a thought suddenly appeared in my mind. It was three little words that I had heard in a Sunday school church sermon, "Be not afraid!" Taking a deep breath, I thought about those three words, and the light they held within began to lend me their courage.

Quieting down, I dried my tears with the edge of the sheet, and finally fell asleep, dreaming of my wish on that star. It was a wish that I repeated, year after year. And it was a wish that always gave me a glimmer of hope, even in my darkest hour, for as a child, I believed in the power of wishes, stars, and the three little words, "Be not afraid." And my wish was for love, a place to call home, and a happier tomorrow.

This choice I made, to hide within my dreams, was probably a desperate way to salvage my ravaged mind, and it was one of my better choices. I consider it a grace of God. It was not until later, through martial arts, that I learned that we all have choices, regardless of our circumstances.

Growing up in rural Louisiana with strict Southern Baptist teachings and the principle rule being, never let others know the bad things, I generally believed I had no choice. Whatever happened was up to God alone. Fortunately, in my twenties, I discovered a better way of looking at things.

I do the best I can with what I have and the rest is up to God. But that is another story. Growing up was definitely hard, and even today, I'm having to keep reminding myself to put my "big panties" on. I just hope I continue growing up until the day I pass on from this life.

Well, that's just my mind wandering. Let's go back to my age of sixteen. Being adopted for a few years was very fortunate for me. Although my sense of self was not even knee high to a grasshopper, my foster family showed me what a loving, caring family can truly be about. Little by little they helped mend my wounded self-confidence. They gave me hope. So much so, that I began shedding my cocoon-like shell and testing my butterfly wings for the first time in my life.

By my junior year of high school, I was participating in choir, social activities, visiting our high school football games, and I even became one of the wall flowers in the shadows at our school dance events. Best of all, I began practicing in the track and field event of high jump and excelled at it. That is where my dream of Olympic gold truly began. Deep down in my soul, I somehow felt that if I could become an Olympic gold medalist then I would truly be someone, then I would be loved and cared for.

I used to eat my cheerios in the morning, reading the Bruce Jenner Olympic information on the back of the cereal box, over and over again. My dream of Olympic gold was not very rational, I agree. But hey, that is what imagination is for. And just look at what my dream did for me.

Following my Olympic dream for the high jump, I trained harder and harder. By the time I graduated high school, I was clearing 5'9" and I had a top Stanford University coach interested in training me. He also believed in my dream.

But first I had to get my GPA up and complete additional educational courses. I moved out of my foster home (it is truly hard to feel like you are not a burden, when the people in your young life have always convinced you that you are), and I moved in with a brand-new fiancé, my first love.

I began taking an overload of classes at the local junior college. I worked part time at night and I trained in the afternoons with my track coach. Yet my newly found positive attitude began crumbling under all of the pressure I had put upon myself.

It was just like that old saying, that the higher up the ladder you climb, the harder you fall. I had fallen so many times in my young life that I found it easier to give up rather than feel that anticipated familiar pain.

As the pressure mounted, I began to fail. First, I dropped out of college. Second, I split with my fiancé, whom I discovered had been cheating on me; then I walked out on my high jump coach at a disastrous showing at a Bruce Jenner classic event. Then, I drowned my sorrows in alcohol and planned to kill myself by driving off of a cliff. It was a low time.

It was warm that evening. It was just about midnight. Seething with self-disgust and emotional turmoil, I sat on the edge of my bed and rocked back and forth in silent agony. As the minutes ticked by, my distress increased, almost to the point of hysteria. I just couldn't take it anymore! With a heart-wrenching sob, I suddenly sprang to my feet, grabbed my car keys and ran down the stairs to get my car. Pealing out of the driveway, I raced off towards the nearby mountain highway.

With tears streaming down my face and my throat tight with constriction, I forced the accelerator down further and the car slid screeching around the mountain turn in the inky blackness of the night. With my face rigid with anger and self-loathing, I braced my hands on the wheel as I fish-tailed out of the curve and head down the last straight-a-way and towards the death-defying, hair-pin turn 500 yards ahead of me. I cleared the last stand of tall pine trees and raced into the night sky.

It was then that I was suddenly hit with the most beautiful, panoramic view of twinkling stars on the beckoning horizon. Still on auto-pilot, I punched the accelerator all the way to the floor. Suddenly, my mind flashed back to childhood and to the many nights I had gazed in hope at the stars in the night sky. One image from the past stormed into my mind with the impact of thunder. It was the evening when I saw that single star. The evening when I made a wish, I was only six years old, but that simple wish gave me the hope and courage to walk into the following years with a tiny spark of hope.

"What happened to me!" I shouted in rage. "I don't believe! I don't believe! I...." My thoughts and speech were suddenly blocked by a single booming phrase that thundered through my mind, "BE NOT AFRAID!" My mind cleared. One thousand one, one thousand two...I switched my foot over to slam on the brake. As the tires screeched eerily on the dark pavement, my car slid at frightening speed, straight toward the flashing yellow guard rail. It was a flimsy barrier overlooking a vertical drop off of thousands of feet of solid rock. "Too late," I hissed to myself.

That night changed my life forever. For the first time, I realized that I had spent my young life running away from any chance, challenge, or dream. I realized what a coward I was being by trying to cut my life short.

That night, standing trembling outside my smoking car and the flashing yellow lights of the guard rail, I swore to myself, NEVER AGAIN! It was as if I had drawn a line in the sand, made a stand, and decided to fight for what I wanted in life. It's therefore, interesting that the next decision I made was a God given interest in martial arts.

Of course, I had always enjoyed the Bruce Lee Kung Fu films with martial artists jumping up into tall trees and spinning through the air. Yet what really caught my attention about a month later was when I was walking through the deserted junior college campus after practicing shooting with bow and arrows in the outfield.

I passed a large group of students in stunning white uniforms, all moving and shouting in precision. They were led by a diminutive Filipino man who exuded a huge aura of powerful energy. I became mesmerized, watching day after day until he asked me to join his class, which of course I did. It was truly another great decision of my life!

Little by little, I gained power, speed, precision, strength, and most of all self-confidence. How this came about is another story. Yet from this very solid application of basic martial arts, I discovered a whole beautiful and powerful side to myself. And when, at advanced brown belt, I met my husband to be in an inter-school fighting match, I had no hesitation to switch to his style of Moo Duk Kwon Taekwondo.

There, I eventually became a black belt and I fought in my first few Taekwondo tournaments. And it was there that I discovered I now had a second chance to make my dream of Olympic gold come true. Only this time it would be in the full-contact fighting sport of Taekwondo in the 1988 Olympic Games in Seoul,

Korea as a demonstration sport. It was as if God Himself slapped me on the head and said, "Here it is again you little fool. Now don't back out!"

Again, the details of the journey to Olympic gold are too long to go into at this time. Just know that *none* of it was easy! It was just my knowledge from martial arts to keep moving forward and to keep picking myself up when I was down, along with my stubborn, Chinese, "Year of the Ox" persistence in making my Olympic dream come true, that kept me from quitting when the going got tough. That, and God's voice whispering in my ear, "This time, you cannot give in to your fears!"

Since winning Olympic gold, my life has been both a thrilling and terrifying, wild, roller coaster ride of public relation events, and spending 20 years as a top Hollywood stuntwoman, traveling the world and doing car hits, stair falls, fights, crashes, and burns for the leading ladies on blockbuster films like Batman, Charlies Angels, and The Terminator. I have met people, presidents, and dignitaries from all over the world, while, of course, dealing with normal life issues that tend to pop up when we least expect them.

WOW! My adventures have been incredible! They also had their challenges – over 20 concussions (if I remember correctly), plus many other injuries, and mental and physical failings, and as the years progressed, health issues.

Yet, through it all, I always retained my martial art ethics of humbleness, respect, courtesy, doing any job 100%, and always picking myself up when I got knocked down. All in all, I would do it all over again if I could. (Personally, however, I would just try to make a name for myself doing precision driving (one is generally safer inside a car, rather than being hit by one).

In my case, back then, my macho sense of pride encouraged me to defy death with car hits, stair falls, fights, crashes, and burns. My interior goal was to face my worst fears. No wonder I sustained so many concussions.

As time wore on, and my neurologist was screaming, "NO MORE CONCUSSIONS," I began realizing I needed to do something else. But what?

Mostly, I wanted to do something to give back. I had received very little help my entire life. And working as a stuntwoman is a very selfish endeavor. Yet, I truly felt blessed to have been able to accomplish all of these wonderful things – most especially turning my life around by learning to face my fears instead of running from them.

So, I decided to start sharing my experiences with others. Eventually, I became a top motivational speaker, sharing inspirational stories with audiences of up to 45 thousand attendees. And believe me, that journey was also tough, yet so much fun! Again, I used my martial art principles of focus and determined persistence. Even so, after a while, life again started taking another down turn.

The economy fell, my ability to focus and market became increasingly inefficient and I began making irrational and risky decisions with my money, my time, and my relationships. Before I knew it, I was broke, drinking far too much alcohol, became involved in violent relationships, and basically destroyed anything and everything in my path. It wasn't until I began losing friend after friend, and doing some really crazy things, that I realized I needed help.

Somehow, in that crazy process of derailing, my martial art warrior instinct became lost in that demonic bottle of alcohol, and the ever fading natural barrier in our frontal lobe that keeps us from standing in front of oncoming trains. And I'm sure that a crazy mental inheritance from both parents did not help!

My mom was extremely bright, yet had some serious personality issues. My father was a genius level Lockheed engineer with anger and paranoia problems. Both of my brothers were genius level. As for me? I was not even expected to graduate high school. My brain seemed wired for failure.

(One of these days I will write about the crazy things I did as a result of this re-wiring, or PTSD, or whatever they want to call it).

Needless to say, I finally lost all hope. I was at the bottom of my well, with no light above. Even my belief in God had paled to an almost invisible, ghost-like memory. Fortunately, because of my sound martial art training, I refused to give up. Instead, I researched and called, and called, and asked, until I finally found some resources that could help.

That process towards recovery took over two years, and I am just now still struggling to fight my way out of the death grip that the evil darkness wants to hold over us. Yet, even though things are still rough, I feel good now.

I know that the battle is already won in my favor! I finally rediscovered my faith – my faith in God, my faith in myself, my faith in my future (regardless of what it becomes), my faith in goodness, and my faith in taking just one more step forward.

We all have a human side of us that is good, that is bad, and yes, that is sometimes just plain ugly. Yet, we all have the *choice* to make as to how we live our life regardless of our circumstances.

When I was lost and desperate as a child and teen, I relied on wonderful dreams to block out the terrible realities. When I wanted out of this life, my star dream gave me a brighter hope for the future. When I doubted my ability to win Olympic gold, my martial art motto of, "Never give up," kicked in (that and God's voice whispering in my ear, "DON'T EVEN THINK ABOUT IT!")

When I felt I was on top of the world with Olympic Gold and Hollywood, I reeled in my ego, retained my humbleness and giving nature, and performed my jobs with 100% effort, and helped those wanting to succeed by giving them a hand up. I never let a fall keep me down. Even when I lost my faith, my

279

beliefs, and felt that all was lost – God lifted me up and reminded me of my inner strength as a true warrior.

And, as a true warrior, even darkness cannot hide that inner light. You just keep your focus on what you *can* do, not on what you cannot.

You just keep taking one more step forward. There are many awards, activities, and sports out there that can make you feel like a hero. Yet there is only one that can make you a warrior – martial arts.

I will leave you with a poem that I wrote when someone asked me why I would do a stunt like being hit by a car.

Is the Thrill of Victory Worth the Agony of Defeat?
Dana Hee

Is the thrill of victory worth the possible agony of defeat?
To me it is, because...

Too many times I said no to conflict...
and I felt like a coward.
Too many times I said no to challenge...
and I felt like a looser.
Too many times I said no to risk...
and I felt like I had lost out on something important.
Too many times I said no to my dreams...
and I began to lose faith in them.
Too many times I said no to an opportunity in life...
and I had regrets.
Too many times I said no to life...
and I almost ended mine.

What I discovered is that, it's the chance, challenge, and dreams in my life, which gave me that sense of meaning and purpose that keeps the light of hope shining at the end of the tunnel.

And, whether I succeed or fail with my goals, I have found that the sense of pride and satisfaction I gain from having the courage to step forward in pursuit of happiness, well, that gives me a lifetime of pride and satisfaction.

In truth, it was my martial art training that taught me to keep stepping forward, to say yes. Too many times, I said no. So now, I say YES! It is the way of the warrior.

Dana Hee beat the odds by making her dream come true of winning an Olympic Gold Medal at the age of 27. Dana then went on to become a stuntwoman in Hollywood, working on such blockbuster films as, the Batman movies, Lethal Weapon, Terminator III, etc., doubling for Nicole Kidman, Uma Thurman, Rene Russo, etc. She became one of the top stuntwomen in the business and won the prestigious Taurus Award for her work for Cameron Diaz on Charlies' Angels.

Forced to take a look at her choices after being seriously injured three times in a row while filming on Alias, for Jennifer Garner, Dana made the decision to pursue a new course of action. Today, although discovering that change is definitely hard, and creating a new career even harder, she nevertheless uses her Olympic and Hollywood "recipe for success" to help her make her new dream come true.

Currently, she is working on going from good to great as a motivational speaker, doing TED Talks, and more; and despite the difficulties, she maintains the positive attitude of one who knows that success IS possible, that dreams DO come true.

Master Dana Hee

Out of Control Egos in the Martial Arts
Alan Goldberg

The martial arts world has changed in many ways since I entered its halls of honor, respect, and integrity. Don't get me wrong, in some ways, it has changed for the better, but in my opinion, that only covers a small percentage of what is going on in this fractured industry. As the publisher of *Action Martial Arts Magazine* for the last 25 years, I have seen a lot of situations, progression, and digression, which many others may not have had the opportunity to see.

First, the growth of eclectic arts has exploded. In my 58 years in the arts, I have seen this happen exponentially. When I started, there were only a dozen arts that were known to the Western world, now there are thousands.

Yes, I understand the progression of many that want to set their place in the martial arts world. But there should be standards for this advancement. It should require a high rank, many, many years in the arts, active years, and experience in multiple factors that play a part in the martial arts.

I have a problem when I see a 25-year-old martial artist wearing a 10th Dan and calling himself a Soke or Grandmaster. It gets under my skin when a non-established organization gives out rank, and I do mean "gives" rank. It just adds to the problems we are having in the martial arts world today. When I started in martial arts, there was Karate, Judo, and Kung Fu, with some subdivisions. These were our main separations in arts at the time.

Now, in today's martial arts world, we have the MMA world, sport martial arts, reality martial arts, traditional martial arts, non-traditional martial arts, day care martial arts, and the business school of martial arts, and many more divisions within the many ranks and styles. My theory is, the more players in the arts, the more people we have jockeying for the higher positions in the food chain.

One of the crazy attachments to these titles are the non-traditional aspects of uniforms, colors, flags, stripes, etc. That's not so bad; it's kind of flashy and interesting, but along with this comes the belts and ranks.

When I started in martial arts, there were only three belts – white, black, and red. The red belt represented a Grandmaster, which at that time, there was only one, Gogan Yamaguchi "The Cat." Now there are so many colors and decorations on the belts that I would need another two pages just to list them all. This is getting a bit ridiculous!

With the belt situation, I suspect it's all about jealousy – who has the biggest belt, the coolest belt, or the most stripes. There was one group out of Ohio that decided to have custom belts made. They sent in the article about their convention and included a photo.

When I saw the photo of about 20 so-called Grandmasters, all wearing these six inch wide, multi-color belts that looked more like they were wearing some kind of sumo wrap, I wanted to laugh aloud. With that thought, it then became apparent that almost every one of them was so overweight that it did actually look more like a sumo wrestler convention than a martial arts photo.

My editor saw the photo and started to crack up! He made a great analogy, stating that, "The martial arts was turning into a big penis contest." Looking back, he was right on the money.

An event comes to mind which illustrates how this over-compensation has gone wild in the martial arts. About 10 years back, I was at the Arnold Classic with my buddy, Chuck Zito, the late Joe Lewis, Nasty Anderson, and Tokey Hill. We were all walking through the event, when two gentlemen came up to me and said, "Sifu Goldberg, you need to do a cover on this Grandmaster. It would be our honor to introduce you to Dr. X, the only 14th degree black belt in the world."

Well, like magic, three of my friends that were walking with me heard this claim and just disappeared. They just turned and walked away abruptly, leaving Tokey Hill and me standing there, with dead stares on our faces.

But, if you know me, you know I'm a little bit of a wise ass in situations like this. In reaction to the gentleman's statement and claim of having a 14th degree black belt, I reached out and shook his hand and said, "An honor to meet you sir, but one question before I even contemplate doing a cover on you. Who was the 15th Dan that tested you and gave you this rank?" There was no answer. Two seconds later, Tokey and I just walked away to catch up with our friends, all the time shaking our heads in disbelief.

My pet peeve concerning this is the use of titles such as Dr. or Ph.D. by martial artists who did not *earn* these titles or degrees in a college. Let me be clear, this is a *JOKE* and against all the laws of higher education within the United States.

There are some organizations that give these false titles away, sell them, or simply award them. Besides being a complete sham, it is illegal under the law. If you claim to have a doctorate in martial arts, you are not legitimate, period.

Wearing my publisher's hat, I met a martial artist from Baltimore that insisted he had eight, yes eight, Ph.D.'s under his name! Besides the fact that he was only 50 years old, his martial arts experience was so negligent in so many factors, that he should not have even had a high rank in any art.

So I mentioned to him (me being a wise ass), that he looked great for a 120 year old man, as he would have to be 120 years old to have earned eight Ph.D.'s. But yes, he was part of the good old boys club, you know, those guys who slap each other on the back and give each other rank and titles, and sometimes, even doctorate degrees. SAD!

My dislike for the unauthorized use of these titles comes from an incident during my publishing days. I received an article from a group out of Baltimore and Ohio (yes the same group with the Sumo convention), about an event they had just hosted. In the article, there was a list of all the martial artists that had received an award.

I was blown away by the fact that so many in this group had the title Dr. or Ph.D. attached to their names. It was like looking at the list of names with their titles was more like looking at a list of on-call doctors at the local Hospital. As the publisher, I would have been liable for printing that list, due to it being an illegal act. Most people don't know that it is illegal to call yourself a doctor if you aren't legitimately a doctor.

My second issue was with giving this group a platform, which would have verified their titles, because it would have been in print. My editor changed all the titles to Grandmasters, out of respect for the group, and because of some of the positive results the group had produced during their existence.

We went ahead and published the article in good faith. To my surprise, I was attacked by the board of directors of this group. I shrugged it off and moved on with the statement that we published in our bylaws, which states that, "We have the right to change or adjust any article sent to our office."

I have seen many of these less than legitimate things in the martial arts, but the straw that broke the camel's back was when I found out that a martial artist that runs a so-called "hall of fame," was giving out Ph.D.'s as if they were real doctorates. I think he called them Doctorates in Asian Studies, basically meaning a Ph.D. in Martial Arts. This guy actually gave one of my students a doctorate degree and I was furious!

I hired a lawyer and got the penial codes for using, giving, or selling these degrees. This false, and illegal, use of these titles comes with up to one year in jail, and/or a $1,000 fine, in many states, per each incident.

Ten years ago, when every Tom, Dick, and Harry sent me paperwork for my Hall of Honors with these false titles on the paperwork, I had to convey that they could not use them due to the fact that they were against the law. I lost many new inductees those first few years because of this, but what the hell, these people were delusional in their idea of what standards of the martial arts are anyway.

After these incidents, and uncovering these frauds in the magazine, I was verbally attacked by a few of those wannabes on social media. They didn't even have the backbone to do it under their real names; they used fake profiles like a coward. But I was able to track them down and confront them face-to-face. Because of this situation, none of them use the titles anymore, and even a few of them have come back to me and thanked me for stopping that insanity.

I just recently received an email from a gentleman using the title of Grandmaster, Soke, Dr. X, Ph.D. I contacted him about using these titles on his paperwork and never heard back from him. Oh well, another one bites the dust. I ask you, what happened to simply using the titles of Sensei or Sifu?

I will end this chapter by stating that there is no such thing as a Doctorate of Martial Arts. I even put my money where my mouth is concerning this. Sifu Jeff Wagner and I placed a bounty of $10,000, over 10 years ago, for anyone who could prove to us that they have a legitimate doctorate degree in martial arts, approved by the USA Higher Board of Education.

It cannot be some fake degree from some mail order, martial arts scam organization, but from an accredited college where they had to write and publish a thesis. Please come forward and collect your money if you have one! Needless to say, no one, to this date, has been able to show us such a degree. So I ask once again is there a Doctor of Philosophy in Martial Arts in the house? No? I didn't think so.

Over fifty years ago Alan Goldberg would set forth a path in martial arts that some of us could only dream of. Master Goldberg's early training was in the art of Shotokan Karate. Having the honor of studying with such famous masters as Manard Miner and George Cofield. He would later on learn the traditional and non-traditional arts of Five Animal Kung Fu. In the 1970's, Alan started training with Sifu Lau as the disciple of famed Shaw Brothers stable Master Jiu Wan. Sifu Lau and Master Goldberg would form a student and Master bond that has lasted over thirty years

When Sifu Lau left New York City in the early 80's, Sifu Lau suggested he train with the late Sifu Moy Yat of the Yip Man family and he started his Wing Chun training. This would give Master Goldberg the opportunity to study Wing Chun under two different sifus. Master Goldberg is now known as a pioneer of Wing Chun in the United States.

His students include actor Joe Piscopo, Heavy-weight World Champion Dimitrius "Oak Tree" Edwards, world renowned orthopedic surgeon Dr. Richard Pearl, and others. Master Goldberg is the holder of Black Belt Magazine's "Kung Fu Instructor of the Year 2004" and holds over 70 other hall of fame awards. He holds positions on many boards in major martial arts federations. He is a founding member of Martial Arts Grandmaster International Council (MAGIC), a founding member of World Black Belt along with, Chuck Norris and Bob Wall, and a board member of the International Sports Hall of Fame with Dr. Bob Goldman and Arnold Schwarzenegger

He is the publisher of Action Martial Arts Magazine, the largest free magazine in the U.S. today, he created one of the nation's hottest martial arts fads such as The Action Martial Arts Magazine Collector Cards. Master Goldberg created Law Enforcement Survival System (LESS), which was the only self-defense course taught to the NYC Emergency Service Unit of the Police Department. He has made appearances in several martial arts movies, is one of the promoters and Vice President of 21st Century Warriors, which showcased some of the

288

legendary martial artists of our time. This event saw the return of Don "The Dragon" Wilson, Royler Gracie, Orlando "The Warrior" Rivera, Dan "The Beast" Severn, and others battling it out on Pay-Per View.

His proudest moments are yet to come this January at Atlantic City's Tropicana Casino and Resort, when he will again produce his MEGA Martial Arts weekend. The Action Martial Arts Magazine Hall of Fame Banquet, the world's largest martial arts trade show and expo, Jan 25-26,27 2019. Check out this year's event www.actionmagstore.com or contact Master Goldberg at ActionMa4@gmail.com.

Master Alan Goldberg

The Road to the Top:
The Building of a Female Martial Arts Champion
Malia "Dacascos" Bernal

The Gift

In the 1960's and 1970's, when I started martial arts, women were not supposed to engage in an "unlady" like sport such as martial arts. Women were supposed to marry, have children, and manage and run her home. I fit that description to a "T." I was good at my job, so why was I in search of a martial arts school?

It was my mother's idea. Mom was glued to her TV set every Friday night, watching Friday Night Boxing. She was a big fight fan. She felt that since I was a young lady, raising a small son, and my husband worked the night shift, I should know how to protect myself, family, and home. Can you believe that?

I thought that was my husband's duty. In time, I understood my mom's reasoning. She could see what I was blind to. My husband was not cut out of "fight material." He was a business man, older than me, whose only interest in life was work and money. On my birthday, my mother convinced my husband that they should purchase a gift certificate so that I could learn self-defense. That was the beginning of an adventure I will never forget or regret.

The Search

I made it a priority to do my research before I committed to any school, which was a smart move on my part. I had no clue there were so many different styles. I remember seeing a large sign in my neighborhood with the words KARATE SELF-DEFENSE.

I decided to pay them a visit. As I walked out of that first school, I knew it was not the school for me. However, I was better prepared with questions on my next stop.

What started out as a neighborhood search, ended up sending me miles from home. My excitement was slowly dwindling away. Fortunately, I learned some things on my first day, it was that: 1) I did not want to be slammed to the floor 2) I for sure did not want someone's butt stuck in my face 3) That my body has always been loose and limber, so the thought of having to become ridged with my body movement would not work.

I had had enough! I turned my car around in the direction of home. "There's always tomorrow," I told myself. My tomorrows basically presented the same scenario – nothing. I was headed back home and decided to find something to eat.

As I was driving along, I spotted what looked like a Chinese restaurant. It had a big, beautiful, red pagoda in front. It appealed to me, so I parked in front of the building and began to look around.

I saw a man hanging from the roof, fixing something. I pushed open the door, entered, and immediately knew this was no restaurant. I stood quiet and just looked around.

A young woman approached me and asked, "May I help you." "Yes," I said, "What is this place? It's certainly no Chinese restaurant." She laughed and said, "No, but it's in the Chinese family. It's a form of martial arts called Chinese Kung Fu."

She took me on a tour of the school, and I really liked it. She was about to teach a beginning class and invited me to watch. I was impressed. She gave them a good workout and what she was teaching was different from what I had seen in the other schools.

I watched her teaching Kung Fu and it was beautiful, powerful, soft, and flowing all at the same time. Without a doubt, I knew this was for me. Before leaving, I thanked her and asked a few more questions. She handed me a schedule, and I knew I would be back. So began my training in the art of Kung Fu.

The Beginning

I was excited and nervous at the same time, as I stepped onto the floor for my first class. I was officially a student in the school of Chinese Kempo-Gung Fu! Never had I done anything even close to this. Snow skiing, water skiing, and wind surfing had always been my sport. I was excited to meet the instructor.

The students could tell it was my first day and were very kind. They did a quick rundown on what I should do. I lined up and stood still. I could tell they were excited for the instructor to arrive. I had the feeling that I was in the wrong class, as they looked advanced. Good Lord, leave it to me to show up on the wrong day!

About that time, the door opened and in walked the teacher. It was the man I saw hanging from the roof on that first day! He was the instructor, Sifu Al Dacascos. I could see that he was young, powerful, and on the lean side. It crossed my mind that no one would be stupid enough to mess with this man, he knows what he's doing. He was definitely a man of confidence.

Since I was not asked to leave, I assumed it was alright to stay. There were about 30 students in class, 10 were women. The only words spoken to me were "follow along." I realized it didn't matter if you were female or male, or even if it was your first class, all were taught the same. I have never been so thankful that I was strong, tough, and fit. I didn't know what I was doing, but that's okay, I was able to keep up.

After 2½ hours, class ended. I loved it, the teaching was awesome. As I was preparing to leave, Sifu (I learn that's what I had to call Al; it means teacher) approached me and welcomed me into his school.

He made a joke about that first day that I saw him hanging from the roof and thought that was funny. I felt foolish. He also complemented me on how well I did in class. I was flattered. He said I was very strong and asked what other sports I do.

I trained 3-4 times a week. Each session was becoming harder. We didn't use mats; Sifu said reality is taking the fall to the floor. We trained with shoes, as he would say, "If you get into a fight, you're not going to stop and take your shoes off." Of course, he was correct. There were about 20 women total in the school.

The students were a mixture of Filipino, Chinese, African American, and Caucasians, all very mean and tough. Soon the training became too hard for the other women and one by one, they all dropped out. I was the last man standing you might say.

It didn't take long for me to figure out the guys wanted it to stay that way; they wanted to see only men in the class. They pushed me harder and harder, trying to get me to leave. But, their bullying didn't affect me, it only inspired me to kick harder, punch harder, and push harder.

I was learning beginning techniques – movement, flow of the body, dropping to the floor, kicks, and punches. The conditioning exercises were amazing. I entered the school with strong arms and legs, but with all the bag work, I became even stronger. Control was not taught in Sifu's classes. He would teach how to respond, to avoid being hit, hurt, or injured.

As a beginner, my reaction time was not so fast. I took a lot of falls and felt the end of a punch or kick many times. My family, friends, and husband started complaining because I looked like a truck hit me. My husband was concerned that people were going to think I was being abused, so I started covering up.

People and children would stare at me because of all of the bruises, and it made me feel uncomfortable and my mother, wouldn't stop nagging about it. Finally, I told them both to stop, "You guys bought this for me; you wanted me to learn. That is what I'm doing." I reminded them they didn't give me this much trouble when I started water skiing and wind surfing, and I couldn't even swim!

First Tournament

I had been a student for six weeks, when Sifu approached me and asked if I would be interested in going to a tournament. I looked at him with a blank stare, not knowing what he was talking about. I asked him what a tournament was. The tournament he wanted me to enter was only five days away and I told him that I would think about it.

The night before the tournament, he asked me to stay after class; he proceeded to explain about tournaments. He taped off a ring, brought in some of the students to officiate, and my sparring partner was his wife. This is the first time I had seen this. It's not what we practiced.

I had been using no control and moving around in wide open spaces. He would always say, "Use what I've taught you; go with your body flow, move, hit, and strike." Now Sifu was telling me that in tournaments, you must use control and stay inside the ring.

It was too much for me; I felt uncomfortable. I didn't want to go because I felt I was not ready. However, Sifu had other plans. He said, "You're going." So I did. Curiosity got the best of me. I thought I could go and just observe, and then back out.

On the day of the event we all carpooled together. That was my first mistake; always take your car so you can leave! The parking lot was full, and I saw people all arriving in uniform. I had on street cloths looking like I'm going on a date. I felt foolish.

However, little did I know, that would become my trade mark – arrive looking like a lady and when I got there, change and look like a warrior. It felt right. When we entered the building I saw a lot of women. I noticed their uniforms were white and I wore a black uniform. I began to get excited thinking I could do this. I changed into my uniform and Sifu told me to go find a quiet place and warm up. The atmosphere was tense and filled with anticipation of what was about to happen. The man on the microphone was announcing, "All women over here."

I saw that they were separating the women into light, middle, and heavy weight groups. I decided to stay to the side since I didn't know what to do or where to go. Soon I looked up and Sifu was by my side. He was relaxed and asked, "What's going on?" He told me not to leave the area. They began lining up the ladies in one of the divisions and I noticed they were lined up by size.

The official would say, "Okay, you two look the same, you stand here, you two over there." That was the procedure on down the line. I asked Sifu "Why are the ladies being lined up by size and not by belt." His reply was, "Do not worry, it will be okay."

I was angry because Sifu knew this, but left out this most important point the night before. It was now my turn and I was lined up with a blue belt. I turn to Sifu and told him, "I'm leaving. I'm not going to do this. She's a blue belt; she has obviously been training longer than six weeks."

Sifu told me to be quiet and watch. I thought he understood that I was not fighting. I heard some of the other ladies talking, and it seemed that they were not aware of this either. I focused on watching the fighting that was going on in another ring, it was a joke!

The line dwindled down to my weight class and soon it was my turn. I thought Sifu was going to say that I was not fighting, but I was so wrong. I was not prepared for what he did when the officials called my name; he pushed me into the ring! I stood there looking like a deer frozen in position. Everyone was waiting for me to walk forward and bow. Somehow my legs moved and I was where I should be.

I went through the motion of bowing and getting into fight position. Suddenly, it was like an explosion. She charged me and I went flying backwards on my butt. That woke me up! I thought Sifu said this is a controlled event. I jumped up and went back to the line and continued. This time I was prepared and had the right mindset, and felt like I was back in the classroom.

If I was going to lose, it wasn't going to be because I was scared or didn't try. I went in swinging hard and fast, and was disqualified. It went so fast that I wasn't sure what just happened. Sifu told me that I hit her in the mouth.

My next tournament I was paired up with a brown belt. I was kicked so hard in my rib cage that I ended up in the hospital that evening because I couldn't breathe. This was to be a repeat performance in all of the following tournaments Sifu put me in. Because of my fear, or passion, I would just strike out and get disqualified, or lost because I didn't know what I was doing. I was so disappointed in myself and was ready to give up.

One evening after class, Sifu took me aside, and we talked. "You're not going into any more tournaments," he said. He told me that he believed I could be a good fighter and his plan was to restructure my training. He pointed out that I have to learn how to play the game.

His plan started with us just going to tournaments and watching. I was beginning to understand what he meant and learned how to play the game. We watched all the matches, with Sifu pointing things out to me. I knew that sooner or later, I would have to fight that person. By watching, I was able to learn so much about their fighting styles.

I began to understand the importance of timing. It taught me when to come in, counter, and score. Sifu pointed out to, "watch their body language." I didn't know what he meant. He explained, "Some set you up with fakes; watch for that. Others telegraph their movement before they release." Sifu pointed out the importance of speed saying, "Get in. Get out." He told me to move around the ring, like in class. Remember a moving target is hard to hit.

His plan was for me to develop a few good techniques, along with a couple of techniques I used only for emergencies. I no longer feared the color of the belt. Sifu was so correct; I had to step out of the ring and watch from the outside.

I was going back to the training room with a whole new attitude. Sifu was going to teach me everything – fighting, forms, and weapons. He made a joke and told me he was going to recreate "Mary Lou" and then unleash her into the world of tournaments.

The Making of a Champion

Even though I started out a loser, deep inside, I knew I could do this. Being a beginner didn't stop me from dreaming. I had high expectations of myself. I wanted to be the first woman with a huge reputation in this sport called Karate. However, I had this thought in my head that was hard to shake. This sport of Karate was a man's world; women were only being tolerated. This was going to be one hard fight to win.

I remember seeing several magazines in school, which I didn't pay much attention to until I started really training. I could see myself on the cover and inside the magazine. In short I wanted it all; I want to be #1. Crazy as it might seem, I knew it would happen. I was so convinced that I told the students that one day, I was going to be the first female champion on the cover of Black Belt Magazine, which was known to only have male athletes at the time.

Winning trophies was nice, but I wanted more. My training for tournaments was now starting. Sifu had me sparring four nights a week with the guys; it was hard, but very good. Sifu started teaching me my forms that I would be doing in competition. The flow and graceful body movement was beautiful. Overall, I felt pretty good about things.

Some time had gone by and I had been training very hard. I had been practicing all that Sifu pointed out to me and I learned to take a punch and give it back. My kicks were right on target, and fast. It was all good! One day I asked Sifu if I could speak to him. I told him how excited I was with my progress and that I was looking forward to my next tournament. But there was something I wanted to talk to him about.

I told Sifu Al, "You recreated my fighting style. Now I want to change my look." I rushed into explaining my dream. He didn't say a word. I explained all women look the same in the black uniform. I'm going to change mine. Of course, that didn't go over well. He said the uniform was tradition, and I had to wear it, but his reaction didn't stop me. Once I started talking I was like a water faucet, the words just came flowing out.

I told him that I thought he had the best students and that he was the best martial artist; and that, along with me building my reputation, he should build his. Go into tournaments with me! Make your school famous and your style wanted by all. I had seen enough to know he was unique. For one brief moment, I had a feeling of fear, as Sifu had a look on his face I will never forget.

What I just did showed no respect for my teacher, even though it was a huge compliment coming from his student. After a moment of silence, he spoke. He had this crazy smile he flashed at me and said, "Not a bad idea." I was speechless.

Not meaning to, I was later to learn that, with that one suggestion, I had actually opened a new door, and that, in time, we would change our lives and we would become partners. We became Al and Malia, the Sonny and Cher of the martial arts world – the most powerful husband and wife team in the sport of martial arts. But that's a whole other story.

After my talk with Sifu, my hard training continued. I know Sifu said that I had to wear a traditional uniform, but I was busy making uniforms and trying different hairdos, just in case. I was trying to focus, but it was really hard. I still had a husband and child who needed me. At times, I thought that I had bitten off more than I could handle. After I had it all together, I asked Sifu to have a look and please approve what I was about to show him. To say he was jumping with joy would be a lie.

He just stared. "What is all this," he shouted, "You can't wear that!" He just got up and walked out. I had been working hard to build his school's reputation, and mine, so I went marching after him. You said you wanted to reinvent me, well I have. I'm wearing this, even if it's against your wishes as my Sifu. I walked out and did not return for two weeks.

The break from aggressive training felt good to my body and I got some well-deserved rest, but I was beginning to miss my classmates and training, so I got myself back to school. Nothing was said about my behavior or my absence. Life simply picked up as before. One evening, Sifu called me into his office. I was thinking that he was going to ask me to leave, but I was wrong.

He blurted out, "If you're changing your look, then we have to change your name. You are now Malia." This is how my name is pronounced in Hawaii. In Hawaiian, Mary is Malia. I thought what a beautiful name and I liked it. I was about to leave, when he asked me to stay a moment, and told me that on my very first night in class, he was impressed.

He always wanted a strong woman to train and compete, and he felt he had just met her. He then added, "It's not just the uniform, the look, or style, that is the easy part, now go out there and leave your mark. Show them who you are. By the way, you should have asked me to help with your uniforms. I'm a tailor as well." These are words I will never forget.

Soon all my hard training was going to be put into motion. My first tournament was coming up as Malia. I had my classmates and my Sifu all behind me. I wished I could remember the name of the tournament I entered as Malia, but I can't. All I can remember is that I won. I was trembling with excitement. This was not an easy win. That day I fought seven times. I was punched, kicked, and bounced around, but I held my ground. My roundhouse kick was fast and right on target. My punch was making solid contact. I won first place in fighting!

It was announced that I had won first in forms, but the judges realized I had made a mistake because my final bow was to the audience, not the judges, so second it was. There were over 20 women in the forms division, all from different styles. I believe I was the only Kung Fu competitor. My form was not perfect, but it was liked.

Sifu wanted me to leave my mark, and I believe I did. My name, my style, and my look, was soon being noticed by all. I started entering every tournament out there, big or small, inside or out, it didn't matter. I just wanted to compete. In time, I was to learn that my hardest competition was myself.

I was winning almost every tournament that I entered, only very rarely did I lose. The more wins, the more experience and the more exposure, was my way of thinking. I was beginning to have a taste of what I wanted and it felt good. My dream was becoming a reality. For a long time, I stayed only in Northern California, as everyone was coming here to compete.

I started hearing about a major tournament held in Long Beach, California every year. That was when I started competing outside of Northern California. It was a good decision; I started winning in that area as well. Over a period of time, my reputation continued to grow. I was asked to do magazine interviews, television shows, performances, and even movies. I started having fans who would cheer for me at the tournaments. What a feeling!

Sometimes there were so many fans that I would hide under tables where no one could find me. I was trying to concentrate on my events, as it was hard doing three events in one tournament. In time, it didn't feel like a competition anymore because I was always competing against the same ladies. One day, I asked if I could compete against men in kata and I got my wish.

I will never forget the look on the faces of the men when I walked into their ring. They would say, "Malia this is men's division." I replied, "I know." Sifu Al and I started entering tournaments together. And, in time, my life would change. I would move from California to Denver, CO. My winning streak continued, I won all major events in that area as well. I would travel to Hawaii and soon, to several other states; and I never left empty handed.

My chapter in America would also come to an end. I moved to Europe and started a whole new adventure. The world of martial arts has been so much more than receiving my black belt. From day one, when I started my training, it has taught me the meaning of life and how to live it.

When I look back today at my martial arts journey, I am amazed at how far I have come from where I started. I set my goals with determination, followed through, stuck to my guns, and achieved more than I ever dreamed of. Dreams do come true! My thanks go out to God, because without Him, I would not have been able to survive my life adventures.

Malia Bernal went on to open and run her own Kung Fu school in Hamburg, Germany during the mid 1970's. On June 15, 1997, Malia Bernal became the first female to be recognized for her own style called Xian Dai Gung fu, by the founder of the Kajukenbo Self-Defense Institute Inc., Sijo Emperado. She was promoted to Master, 7th degree black belt. She is also a 9th degree black belt in Wun Hop Kuen Do Kung Fu. After becoming a champion herself, Malia began training other champions. Some of the world renowned champions, in both martial arts and in the film industry, are Karen Shepard, Christian Wulf, Emanuel Bettencourt, and her own son, Mark Dacascos. Malia is still involved in both the martial arts and

fitness world. She is available for motivational speaking, training, and seminars. You can contact Malia at: maliamaliatnt@aol.com.

Grandmaster Malia Bernal

Empty Hands

Revealing that which is Hidden
William Powell

It is very important, as a martial artist, to reveal that which is hidden. Your training should be dedicated to and focused on smashing through any façade, illusion, deception, plateau, or puzzle that attempts to keep you from getting to the heart of the matter by uncovering the truth.

To compound the warrior's already difficult traverse in pursuit of the Way, there are challenges to be met, puzzles to be solved, choices to be made, and trust to be earned between you and anyone that claims to have something to "teach" you. Is what you are being taught real? Does it work? Can you understand and execute that which you are learning in front of, and outside of, the teacher's view? Is there a better way?

Is there another way that is easier to grasp? Why spend 7-10 years of continuous training in an art like Kenpo Karate when you can get a black belt in another art in 1½ years? If you achieve black belt by completing a set of standards by that school or this teacher, aren't you a real black belt? Who's to say that you are not? No one can tell you that you are not a black belt if you believe you are and can back it up if necessary.

The great UFC Champion Royce Gracie once said, "A black belt covers about two inches of your ass. It's up to you to cover the rest." The only teacher that can alter your truth is reality. And the world's reality will be the teacher that matters most.

One of my favorite teachers, GM Tom Updegrove of martial posture studio in Philadelphia, handed me a handwritten note on a post it note when I moved from Philly to Chicago in the mid 80's, which read:

"The more you practice, the less accepting you are of "accepted practices." The more you see and hear, the less likely you are to believe what "experts" write and say." I will never forget that.

Reveal that which is hidden before the world reveals it for you. We live a life made up of an indeterminable amount of time. We all know that we are going to die. But when and how? Some say that your time is already written and is simply a matter of fate. Others would say that there is no grand scheme and the time and place of our death has not been set, that it's a random thing.

Whichever philosophy you believe, one thing is for sure, death will put a crimp on your lifestyle. Since we do not know the exact moment of our death, that means that we have an indeterminable amount of time to live.

As warriors, we try to gobble up life and live in a way that exemplifies that high ideal. Training in the arts gives us a chance to do so with minimal concern, by understanding fear, pain, and their relation to death. Those that are afraid of getting hit because it hurts, are going to be in for a rude awakening when the Grim Reaper comes calling. How do you want to die?

At the moment of death, do you want to be in a panicked, frenzied, fearful state, or do you want to meet death with a calm understanding that it is a part of life and without fear? Warriors will choose the latter. Life and death philosophy has been debated for ages, with no clear answers provided by much greater minds than mine. So I will tell you what I do know.

When you go to a martial arts school for self-defense, you will have an indeterminable amount of time to train for an attack that has not yet occurred. There is no way to see the future, so there is no way to be sure that your training will be sufficient for the moment that it is needed.

Therefore, you must make every moment count in your training. Try to imitate, then emulate, your teacher's movements, thinking while you are learning, since there will be no time for thought when the real life situation happens. This way you can observe, learn, study, practice, and train your techniques until they become truly yours. Wash. Rinse. Repeat.

Realize and understand that the very martial arts technique that you learned today, no matter how new they are to you, may be the very one that you need to work that night, when attacked by a mugger. You have to understand that you can't know everything that there is to know about any and all possible attacks when you first start training. Maybe you will know enough, maybe not. But what choice do you have, as the dirt bag drug addict is about to plunge a filthy, kitchen steak knife repeatedly into your chest, stomach, and face?

As you drift away from life, through blood pouring out of your body onto the street, you think, *and they were gonna teach us knife defense next week! Too bad that I missed the first edged weapons class because I was on a date*. The karma train is rolling on. I hope you get my point.

Train until you die! The way of the warrior is death. Life ends in death. That is the fact of the matter. The Vikings exalt, "Rush to meet death before someone else takes your place."

You have an indeterminable amount of time on this earth. Use every moment well, as if what you do at this exact moment is your last act on earth, and do it right.

There is a very important word in Bushido, the way of the warrior, and that word is respect. As human beings, we are born with dignity, as a pristine representation of God's love on earth. But while growing, we get bumped, banged, and bruised by life, and then we learn and earn respect. To me, one meaning of respect is:

*R*emember that
*E*veryone knows
*S*omething and
*P*erhaps can
*E*ven teach you
*C*ertain
*T*hings

307

It is absolutely amazing what people know. No matter what you are an expert in, there are infinite topics in which you are totally ignorant in. I mean that with all due respect. Know-it-alls are not only idiots, but can be quite annoying. No one knows everything about everything.

You may know the genus and species of a South American Bizarre Looper Moth, but couldn't tell the difference between the angle of a right hook to the chops, and the right angle to hook a tuna in the deep sea. So know what you know, learn what you can, and then share all that you know with anyone who cares to know what you have learned.

In learning the martial arts, you can read books, magazines, watch DVDs or demonstrations, and listen to audio tapes and hear what the experts say. But you must *experience* it firsthand in order to *understand* it.

Once you have invested the time and effort required to master an art which you have trained in, then start on another, from the beginning, as a beginner. With this philosophy enhancing your personal educational model, you can learn more about the martial arts and more about the Way. Enjoy the process, since the only end to learning is death. Some say that the journey even continues after that.

Respect is a concept that should be instilled in our children early in life. Teaching the difference between respect and weakness is very important as well. An essential element in teaching the idea of respect is that the child first learns the importance of self-respect. If you do not respect yourself, you will not respect others; you will fear them. Martial arts education and training starts with respect, and self-respect is at the core.

Bullying is recognized as a major social problem that inhibits student growth, restricts creativity, and normal human social development through physical, mental, and emotional fear. Stymieing imagination and creativity is the last thing we want for our children. The entire pre-college educational system is set up in a structured, uniformed platform for bully-enhanced failure.

The whole K-12 educational system is based on older, bigger, and stronger students being educated in the same building as younger, less mentally, physically, and emotionally developed ones.

This leads to the idea that bullying is just part of growing up in the school system. It is not! Bullying is wrong and is the direct result of parental failure to instill basic core values of respect and self-respect in their children. Looking for a reason that we have bullies? Look at his or her parents or parent.

With my two children being trained fighters since birth, if I ever found out that they tried to intimidate or bully another child, there would be hell to pay. They know that because that is how they were raised.

The toll taken by bullying has never been greater. In previous times, when school let out and you got home, you were safe and the torment ended. You had a sanctuary to recover from the damage, unrelated to academic stress. Now, with social media tied directly to your home, school computer, iPad, and cell phone, the bullying is 24/7.

This has led to record numbers of youth suicides and school shootings tied directly to cyber-bullying. While it is impossible to shield our children from the ever more efficient technology of instant communication to a massive audience, we can influence, and therefore, affect its impact.

Teach your children simple core values, the difference between right and wrong, and how to develop the intestinal fortitude, (guts in plain English), to stand up to bullying, either for themselves or in defense of others. It is not easy, but it can be done and it must be done!

A secret is just information withheld for a purpose, between a select group, individuals, or both. One such secret of the martial arts masters is revealed here, and is known as "The Gyroscope of Self-Defense."

When you first learn real self-defense, you are like a baby in the woods. Hopefully, you can stay hidden in the leaves or behind big trees long enough to grow, become self-aware, knowledgeable, strong, and be able to defend yourself out in the open.

At any time you must be able to take actions in defense of self, since an attack can come at any time and in any manner; therefore, the techniques and forms of the martial arts are naturally endless. With this base, here is the theory and training model known at Powell's Way of Kenpo Martial Arts School as the "Gyroscope of Self-Defense."

When you first enter a real martial arts school, you have brought with you various degrees of skill, courage, and fear. In the most common scenario, you are standing alone in the center of the room and someone is throwing, let's say a brick, at you.

At first you watch helplessly as the brick hurtles toward your head and, if you respond at all, it's most likely to close your eyes, turn your face away, and raise your hands in a feeble attempt not to get your skull smashed in. With classes come the addition of new skills and focused repetitions.

You learn to see the brick before it is thrown, watch the timing of its release, and the speed and accuracy of the thrower. As the brick is released, you use your new skills to keep your eyes open, execute more purposeful hand, foot, and head movements, and succeed in keeping the brick from rearranging your face. The damage level is reduced to maybe a scratch of your wrist skin. You are pleased with your progress, and rightly so. Your training continues and builds defensive and offensive capabilities emanating from the very center of the gyroscope, which is you.

Soon you not only easily evade any brick thrown at you, but you find that you are no longer even in the room when a brick thrower is present. So you have learned to defend against an attack coming directly from the front. 12:00 if you were to paint a large numeral clock on the ground in front of you.

Substituting a punch as the attack, instead of a thrown brick, you now learn to develop a similar defense against this type of attack, (or any frontal attack for that matter), when it is launched from 11:00, 1:00, or any "time" on the clock, creating a circle of self-defense.

As your skills improve, you can substitute different defensive techniques for any attack coming from any particular "clock point." So you can now defend against any single person attack from any clock point on the dial.

You are at the center and the hands of the clock (or direction of attack and responding defensive techniques) emanate outward to a corresponding time on the "floor clock."

Now that you have gained proficiency defending from any time on the floor clock, imagine taking the clock and standing it up on end, like balancing a quarter on its side. You now have a "standing clock" as an exact duplicate of the one still on the floor before you.

The standing clock is your vertical reference for the attack or defense launch points, just as the floor clock is your horizontal map for proper foot movement and attack or defense directional motion. In many cases, the floor clock will relate to lower body foot movements with the standing clock utilizing upper body, arm, hand, and head maneuvers.

You might step to 2:00 with your right foot, pivot to 8:30 with your left, and then block or attack with the left hand to 3:00 and right elbow strike to 8:15. For now, use the clocks in their most basic application of directional reference points of attacks and defenses, rather than a guide for individual body movements.

311

Looking at the standing clock in front of you, you are still at the epicenter with the 12:00 time point, directly overhead, the 6:00 point directly below you, and the 3:00 and 9:00 to your right and left respectively. You now learn to defend against an overhead strike (more than likely a punch coming down from the ceiling) or a groin kick coming from below at the 6:00 time point. You can now replicate the technical proficiency of defensive and offensive movements learned from the floor clock, now applied to the angles of attack along the time points of the standing clock.

After you master the flow of both clocks, the clocks begin to spin both on their own axis and on a spinning axis similar to flicking a quarter on a tabletop with your finger and watching the spinning circle it creates. In other words, the floor clock spins and the 12:00 point may move to the 4:00 position and continue in a clockwise motion. The same for the standing clock which may be spinning like the Wheel of Fortune.

With both clocks spinning on the base axis, (with you at the center), the standing clock may tilt 45 degrees and continue to spin, while the floor clock begins to rise in imitation of the standing clock to perhaps a 30 or 40 degree angle. In any event, the sphere that the spinning clocks create never stops moving until the attack is thwarted and the quarter slows down to then reveal the content of its clock angles.

As you train and become more comfortable with the nuances of attacks and defensive techniques, coming from and going to different angles and points of flow from any and all points on the never ending spinning sphere, you will fear no attack while recognizing the unpredictability and effortless destructive power of the Kenpo warrior.

What you have now designed is a near impenetrable "Gyroscope of Self-Defense," allowing you, at its center, to attack and defend on any axis at any time, from any point on the spinning globe shape which you have created in your ever expanding martial arts portfolio.

Even after you learn this, fighting still hurts. The more times you fight, the more likely you are to get hurt. The only reason people fight is that they think they have something to gain. This could be perceived as the need to gain respect, honor, revenge, money, or more nobly, to defend a principle, yourself, or others.

Some would argue that there is never a reason to resort to violence to settle a dispute. This is mostly said by those who are not able to defend themselves. Humans are born to fight. We are born into this world fighting for air, food, love, security, knowledge, achievement, and health. Then we prepare for a fearless death.

Americans are taught from the very beginning to, "Fight for what's right!" We hear, "You have to fight off that cold," "They fought back from 30 points down," "Fight the good fight," and so on.

The problem with this overemphasis on fighting as a good thing, is that it often ends up being a bad thing. You give a whooping to some jerk who clearly deserves one, with the crowd cheering you on, and then the bad guy falls, cracks his head wide open, and he dies or is paralyzed.

The cheering stops and you are the one now in bad trouble. Hopefully, it was in self-defense and not just two guys in an agreed upon fight. In some states, you do not have a "Duty to Retreat," but, as a trained fighter and martial artist, you had better have a good reason why you didn't. If not, you are in big trouble.

We often hear the saying, "I would rather be tried by 12, than carried by 6!" And it's true. But be aware that, as they close your cell door, that will not comfort you very much. Besides the legal fees, time spent in jail, lack of female physical contact, you gained nothing. I will take that back. You did gain an abundant supply of hardened criminals, murderers, sodomites, and rapists that would just love to join in your affinity for fighting.

So it is paramount to your health and safety that you refrain from fighting if at all possible. If you have to fight, make it a one-time thing and win decisively. Which leads us to the next secret – *leave a lasting emotional imprint in the enemy*!

Before addressing the next topic, let's clarify the importance of this one by reiterating that, if you are forced to fight, make sure the attacker is thwarted, his anger and hostility is nullified, and his will to fight is crushed. In other words, *fight one fight per fight.*

The importance of leaving an emotional imprint in the enemy is essential in dealing with an aggressor, both now and in the future. An emotional imprint is the neurological component of a memory. It is similar to a feeling of euphoria and well-being when you think of a pleasant experience, or the dread, impending doom, and physiological reactions, when the thought is attached to a memory which is negative.

It can manifest in any number of forms, physically, mentally and emotionally. In my case, when a strong negative experience pops into my mind, subconsciously, some nerve synapses fire in my brain that cause my hand to involuntarily and automatically form a strong, perfectly formed, tiger claw, fist, or chop. The mental words that accompany this are, "Ok then. Let's fight!"

Don't ask me why, as I don't know. But I can surmise that the involuntary reactions on all my systems was the result of an emotional imprint from one or more negative experiences ingrained in me. Those mental, physical, and emotional actions, and reactions, are usually the extent of it. Once I realize that negative thoughts are taking a shot at seizing control, I counter with the powerful Hindu mantra, "NETI. NETI. NETI."

This simple, yet potent, set of words translates to, "*I am not that thought. I am not this thought thinking about that thought. I am not thought.*" Usually that is enough to change my mental direction and return my body systems back to normal. If left unchecked, emotional imprints will dictate your mindset, mood, demeanor, attitude, and view of life. Don't let this happen. As the great Bruce Lee once said, "Negative thoughts are the weeds that strangle confidence."

When involved in a fight, you must leave an emotional imprint in the enemy! If you are in a confrontation, and let's say that you knock the other guy out with a single, perfectly timed, right hand to the face. Since you are a trained fighter, that is not beyond the realm of possibility. If you win a fight, in this manner, it makes sense to feel that you prevailed in *your* mind.

It seems pretty clear. When two humans voluntarily engage in combat, one wins, one loses, or it's a draw. So if you knock your attacker out cold, you win right? Maybe.

If the punch was sufficient to leave an emotional imprint of defeat in your attacker's mind, then yes, the fight is over and you have won. The emotional imprint on the loser will be sufficient enough that he will always remember the loss, have mental and physiological reactions to that defeat, and its *association with you*. There is a good chance that this is the end of it.

But if the knockout was the result of a lucky punch or a sucker punch, in the mind of your foe, it will not leave the proper emotional imprint, and the fight will not be over. Every time you come into contact with that person, the animosity will remain, the conflict is unresolved, and the chance of a flare-up is probable.

To leave the correct emotional imprint, the victory must be so decisive, so clear cut, and so devastating in his mind, body, and spirit, that you have left no doubt about the outcome of this, or any future physical attack. Only in this manner can you achieve victory and hopefully, a lasting peace.

Conflict resolutions of this type also have an effect on any future would be adversaries who are there at the time. Swift, effective, and absolute defeat of another "equally matched" human, also leaves a less painful, but no less significant emotional imprint on all those present.

> *All great leaders know that a feared enemy must be crushed completely. Sometimes they have learned this the hard way. If one ember is left alight, no matter how dimly it smolders, a fire will eventually break out. More is lost through stopping half way than through total annihilation. The enemy will recover and will seek revenge. Crush him, not only in body, but in spirit.*
> *Robert Greene*

Another important concept that will increase the likelihood of winning a personal confrontation with a competent attacker is the strategic and tactical plan of coming from darkness.

The term "dark," means secret; not clear to the understanding; the quality or state of having a veiled or uncertain meaning; not explored because of remoteness; relating to grim or depressing circumstances; a time or place of little or no light; the quality or state of having a veiled or uncertain meaning; not explored because of remoteness."

The last definition is one definition that describes the Kenpo principle of darkness, as it applies to self-defense. There are other aspects involved as well. In the simplest sense, darkness is somewhere where you cannot see well. An attacker is most successful when you are caught by surprise, as he *comes from darkness*.

While this may mean it happens at night, where vision is compromised by lack of light and when violent crimes occur, it is not necessarily so. An attack in broad daylight can come from darkness by an assailant hiding in a doorway, alley, or from any angle not covered by your range of sight.

Of course other senses play an important role in your situational awareness and ability to quickly perceive and react to an attack from darkness. Other factors relating to an attack from darkness are the speed of the approach from darkness, and the ability to recognize the threat and defend yourself accordingly. This is difficult and requires extensive training in the martial arts.

We have all been startled at the movies, when an imminent victim is searching through the darkened house alone with no weapon. The music is haunting and ominous. Then AHHHH! We all jump and are shocked by an event we were already prepared for. It ends up being the cat jumping off the refrigerator.

We know it is going to happen, are trained enough in life, and with a semblance of common sense, realize that this is a movie that we paid to see and that there is no real danger, yet most people will jump anyway.

A lesson can be learned from the above movie reaction scenario. While we are mentally and physically recovering from our natural fight, flight, or freeze reaction to the startle, the real attack usually follows shortly after. If you are startled by something or someone, stay alert until you know that you are safe.

So darkness, in this context, is environmental and situational. The attacker may not even have touched you yet, but the surprise has already put you on the defensive. And while it may sound weird, being on the defensive is not the best self-defense. Being on the defensive limits your situational awareness and the correct perception of reality, similar to "tunnel vision."

Training in this aspect of darkness means learning about your surroundings by actually looking, listening, smelling, and feeling what is really going on. This is harder than it seems. There is such an overwhelming rate of stimuli in any given moment, knowing which are relevant to you and your safety are paramount. You can find many sources of training and instruction on this topic, and it is suggested that you do so.

Another aspect of darkness is the instant information it provides and what it tells you about the attacker who comes from behind and makes physical contact. For example, if someone grabs you from behind with a right armed chokehold, it is most likely that he doesn't have a weapon in *that* hand. It should also scream to you, "Where is the other hand and what's in it?"

If the attack was a choke to make you unconscious, he would be using *both* hands. Why only the right hand attack? Is this really a strong arm robbery? There is a reason for the one arm choke attack. But what is it? Does the attacker not know a proper rear, naked, choke technique? Or is there a knife or gun in the free hand? It is important to get this information quickly and accurately to know what right action to take.

Your reaction will be different if the other hand holds a gun that is being poked into your lower back, than if the free hand is just late in joining the other for a strangle choke. In this scenario, the latter is what you find. The bigger attacker has come from darkness launching a two-handed, rear choke, but has not locked it tight due to the tardy trailing hand. Showtime!

After ascertaining that there is no weapon employed (yet), it's just a fight. Hopefully, you are a trained fighter and know what to do based on that training. If not, you are in trouble and about to be another crime victim statistic.

Understanding darkness also provides assistance through simultaneous, and quickly useable, information to your battle systems. How big is he? How strong is he? How determined is his attack? What is his fighting skill level? Is he surefooted and tactically aggressive with skillful techniques or a lout trying out for mugger school? All these questions need quick answers to give you a chance at surviving an attack from darkness. If the attacker is leaning down to choke me, I know he is bigger.

318

If only one arm is strong enough to hold me in place, he is stronger (at that give moment). If the neck grip is not that strong and the initial impact of our contact is weak, he may be unsure, nervous, not a fighter, or just a bad mugger. In that case, the information gleaned by my familiarity and training in the realms of darkness will also tell me the direction and weapon choice of my counterattack.

Being grabbed from behind and that sensory information should tell me not to defend with a right front thrust kick into empty air. You need a full repertoire of self-defense techniques that work, and that you understand and have practiced intensely.

When you have reached this level of self-defense training, you will be learning to reveal that which is hidden, in this case, within the realm of darkness. You will then know how to respond appropriately when entering into and when leaving the darkness.

Kyoshi William Powell is a 7th degree black belt under Grandmaster Shorty Mills. He is the founder and head instructor of Powell's Way of Kenpo Martial Arts School, founded in 1985. He has been training in the martial arts for over 42 years. He also holds a 4th degree black belt in Okinawan Karate-do, a 1st degree black belt in Japanese Aikido, and a 1st degree black belt in American Judo.

He was a Gold Medalist in the 2001 Pan American Games in International Jiu Jitsu and won the Bronze in 2000. Kyoshi Powell is also the author of Growing Tigers in a Terrarium: The Importance of Martial Arts in an Unraveling Society, which is on permanent display at The USA Martial Arts Museum in Belen, New Mexico. He was inducted into the Action Martial Arts Magazine Hall of Honor, Hall of Fame for his lifetime achievement in the martial arts in 2017.

319

Kyoshi William Powell

Training and Mindset for Realistic Martial Arts
Bill Logan

There are arts that work well in today's society, and there are those that *can* work in a pinch, if used with the proper mindset. All arts can offer something of value, be it conditioning, technical skill, mental toughness, or a great stress outlet.

Martial arts are originally war arts and self-defense is a byproduct, but in the realm of combat effectiveness, some things have been lost, or omitted, to make it comfortable and safer for competition and sport, as well as to keep students coming back.

If you look at the progression of training methods for combat to what is being taught today, most are a shadow of or a fantasy of sorts. To make this clear, let's look at combative training: first, is actual fighting or killing, second, is combative training with very hard contact and injuries common, third, is training with controlled contact and fewer injuries likely, fourth is training with super light to no contact, and fifth, is envisioning training with no contact or physical conditioning at all.

Done properly, each stage has value, but taken out of context can lead to some problems. Teaching martial arts combat effectiveness using only one stage, especially stages 4 and 5, "the comfort stages," is fantasy and leads to the charlatans and mystical silliness we see propagated today. It is very plausible that many will have a false sense of security, until faced with actually having to defend themselves.

Most styles are in the stage 3 training range, good for basic self-defense and also provide good physical conditioning. Most of these will have superb conditioning and good technique, and others will have excellent technique and adequate conditioning. Stages two through five, when properly utilized in training, and with proper mindset, can prepare you for stage one self-defense situations.

Realistic martial arts should use simple movements and reflexive responses, as well as physical conditioning. Movements may become natural after extensive training and muscle memory drills, but again, we cannot get complacent and just go through the motions, no matter how mundane and seemingly boring they may be.

We must train with intent. Your mindset when training is a key factor in how well you do in self-defense and is also training your reflexes in instantaneous, proper responses. That is why systems like Krav Maga, Kenpo, and Kajukenbo spend so much time developing it, and so does several other systems such as Hapkido.

"You do not rise to the level of your expectations, but fall to the level of your training," is a popular axiom, but I would like to add that you must have a proper mindset while doing techniques in training, both as the one doing them and in having techniques done on you.

You can see this when you watch students working in class. You may have one doing all the moves correctly, but with no intent or snap, just being too soft to make it work. And then you see another student doing the techniques with power and precision, his uke slapping out with authority over and over, but not getting injured because he mentally chooses not to. Mindset!

True realistic martial arts must have sparring. It teaches timing and distance control, as well as trains the reflexes and teaches you to move outside the comfort of a scripted technique. Techniques fall apart when they are only practiced against a cooperative partner, and then you have to make it work against a not only resisting, but combative opponent.

Martial arts systems that promote proper mindset and actual contact in class prepare the student to work through the shock of being hit. It also teaches the student to not quit at the first sign of pain or blood. The brutal reality of a true life-or-death self-defense situation is not the place to find out if your double flip, jump spin kick works or not.

Real street effective systems need to teach strikes, and where to strike to incapacitate, not to score points or to look like Karate breakdancing moves. Strikes should target the weaknesses in the human anatomy. For maximum effect, a primary chart of eyes, throat, temple, knees, and groin is a good methodology. There is a huge difference between fighting and competing!

I was a bouncer for many years, and I would see guys that I knew were black belts in certain styles get into an altercation with a non-martial artist who liked to fight, and lose. And I don't mean just lose, but lose badly and end up in the ER.

I started to ask, "Why?" These black belts had years of training and some had decent rank, but were getting trashed in these fights. I asked to come by a couple of their schools to visit and watch. And after watching and listening, I noticed they were doing exactly what they did in class in the fight, a lot of unnecessary movements, throwing strikes with no real intent, etc.

They probably beat their opponent on points, but got their rear ends kicked because the other guy only had one thing on his mind – to stomp them into the ground as hard and fast as possible. That is a realistic mindset- victory over overly softened, controlled programming. Now obviously these situations did not require killing blows being struck, but effective fight-ending strikes, properly delivered, would have drastically changed the outcomes.

In this discussion of martial arts that work, the question of hard versus soft comes up regularly, and will continue to be debated, probably for eternity. Most hard styles are striking based and many soft styles have a strong grappling component. But don't mistake the soft systems as being weak; they are immensely powerful, but take a long time to master, sometimes a lifetime.

Some hard styles are Kyokushin, Yoshukai, Uechi-Ryu, Shorin-Ryu, Shotokan, and some of the soft styles are Wing Chun, Tai Chi Chuan, Aikido, Ju-Jitsu, and various Kung Fu styles. Then there are the blended systems of GoJu-Ryu, Kajukenbo, Kenpo, and its various systems, and Wun Hop Kuen Do, as well as the hybrids of Krav Maga, Pancration, and Sambo.

All of these have something to offer, but to be utilized effectively, you must have the proper mindset of *persevere at all cost*, not just not losing. The Filipino arts like Kali, Escrima, Panantukan, and sub-systems, are great arts for building skill sets outside of traditional Asian based systems and their use of weapons makes them excellent for self-defense.

Also, the Indonesian Silat systems will open your eyes to movement and angles of attack, as well as weapon use you might never see otherwise. These systems will help you develop a sense of timing that no other arts can and have a very well-developed self-defense mindset.

Truly effective, realistic, self-defense systems must be taught with adequate contact and conditioning, but also must be able to work in all four ranges of unarmed contact, as in kicking, punching, trapping, and grappling. To be effective, the system should not specialize in only working one range, as in Tae Kwon Do, boxing, and Brazilian Jiu Jitsu for competitions, even though they teach a winning mindset and have prevailed in some instances.

You must develop the skill sets to never have to fight the other guy's fight and adapt to an ever changing situation. The striking systems require somewhat less refinement of motion and reflexive instinct than most grappling arts, making them a bit faster to use for self-defense in most cases. But the strikes and their targets must be thoroughly practiced until they become second nature to be effective and relied upon. Many grappling arts are not suited to multiple attackers or weapon based attacks, but are well developed for one-on-one conflicts and control based professions.

To be prepared for real self-defense in today's world, systems need to be able to work against multiple attackers, knives, and firearms, using realistic defenses, not the silly stuff on the internet, which will most likely get you killed or maimed.

In the real world, the attacker, or attackers, get to pick the time and place, which is a huge advantage. We must respond with training and the proper mindset. So, in essence, they decide how it starts, but we decide how it ends. How hard you train today, decides your tomorrow.

Bill Logan has been training for 37 years in martial arts and is a 7th Dan in Kenpo, a 7th Dan in Kajukenbo, a black belt in Combative Jiu Jitsu, expert level 2 instructor in Krav Maga, an instructor in Escrima/Kali, and a Certified Law Enforcement Defensive Tactics instructor. He is also a CQC firearms instructor, worked as a bouncer for eight years, and was a kickboxer for four years.

He sits on the board of directors for the United States Martial Arts Hall of Fame, was the state director for the International Kenpo Council of Grandmasters, and is on the Board of Directors for GM Vera's International Realistic Mixed Martial Arts Association. Bill has been teaching professionally for 23 years and is the owner of Logan's Martial Arts Academy in Tallahassee, FL.

Master Bill Logan

The Martial Arts Hater Mentality
Frank W. Dux

In terms of combat, politics, and social structure, there always exist hard and soft power. This duality of our existence is never more transparently clear than when it comes to the human intellect.

On one side is the civilized, cultivated mind that is refined, possesses analytic and flexible intellect, and is capable of growth and change. On the other side of intellect is the thug mind that is so steadfast that it keeps one from ever being enlightened.

This is because the steadfast draws on all things that support and agree with it, to the degree that, though there exist overwhelming evidence and morality to be found on the other side, based on the thought process involved, it neglects and despises this revelation. The truth will never be *their* truth.

To protect itself, a thug mindset invents invalid arguments and distinctions to suspend logic and truth – sets aside and rejects most everything contrary to that mindset. As Sir Francis Bacon observed in the 16th century, "Consumed by prejudging the matter to a great and pernicious extent in order that its former conclusions may remain inviolate."

The thug mindset, the mindset of the hater, is a 1997, American lexicon, invented by Will Smith's *Gettin' Jiggy Wit It*, where he rapped that he had, "No love for the haters," because they were, without reservation, motivated by envy.

The R&B group, 3LW, equally provided context for understanding haters, by telling us, "Playas gon' play [and] haters gon' hate." in their song *Playas Gon' Play*.

Michael Strangelove describes haters as, "People, or groups of people, who express hatred in public forums," in his 2010 book, *Watching YouTube: Extraordinary Videos by Ordinary People.*

The *Urban Dictionary* describes haters as, "A person that simply cannot be happy for another person's success. So rather than be happy, they make a point of exposing a flaw in that person." It goes on to explain, "Hating, the result of being a hater, is not exactly jealousy. The hater doesn't really want to be the person he or she hates, rather the hater wants to knock someone else down a notch."

The fascinating thing, however, is that the psychological process that propels the hating, consumes the hater. There are a few cognitive biases that may be helpful in explaining the hater, but one constant always remains the same, and that is, haters are not dispassionate and objective people when it comes to the target of their hate.

In essence, haters are emotionally, and sometimes even financially, so invested in their hatred that they are motivated to cling to and assert their identity through their hate.

For example, white supremacy folks cannot tolerate those viewed "lesser than themselves," enjoying a success, because these haters are invested in the idea of them being part of a dominate, superior race.

This same attitude is prevalent in the traditional Japanese martial arts world, where those who study Koryu (pre-Meiji era), see themselves as being superior to those who have no lineage or cannot prove it.

One cognitive bias is what is known as *motivated reasoning.* This is where an emotion-biased, decision-making phenomenon occurs, where decision-makers are inclined to *arrive at a particular conclusion about their target of hate*, by engaging in biased processes with regard to accessing, constructing, and evaluating new and old information.

In essence, the hater readily embraces, or searches for, negative information about the hated person, even if that information is of trifling consequence and a matter that is so small that no reasonable person would wish to even consider it.

Therefore, it goes without saying that haters are susceptible to *confirmation bias* – the tendency to search for, interpret, focus on, and remember information in a way that confirms their own preconceptions.

Not surprisingly, the tendency to have their perceptions affected by their recurring (negative) thoughts about their target of hate, is exhibited by haters. This is what is called, in medical circles, as *attention bias.*

Similarly, *expectations* about the hated target affect the hater's perception of information about their target. This is a tendency that haters engage in. This is referred to in psychology as *selective perception.* It is to be anticipated that haters tend to place undue weight to certain aspects of events, namely those aspects that cast a negative light on the target of their hatred.

Haters also strenuously resist positive information about the target of their hatred, no matter how overwhelming that information is. Because of the hater's investment and the aforementioned psychological conditions, they are unable to revise their beliefs sufficiently when presented with new evidence.

That is why it is an observable reality that, any positive information about the target of haters will always fail to alter the hater's opinion. This largely has to do with the *Semmelweis Reflex*, which is the tendency to reject new evidence that contradicts a paradigm.

In fact, efforts to change the hater's opinion with disconfirming evidence, more than likely, will simply strengthen their beliefs, which is called in psychology, the *backfire effect.*

All these mental processes that haters possess have nothing to do with how educated or intelligent the hater is, or is not. As the eminent psychologist, Ziva Kunda, noted:

> *People do not realize that the process is biased by their goals, that they are accessing only a subset of their relevant knowledge, that they would probably access different beliefs and rules in the presence of different directional goals and that they might even be capable of justifying opposite conclusions on different occasions.*

Indeed, if anyone can confirm this to be true, it is me. Since, I have more than my fair share of haters in this world, just like anyone else who has really accomplished something that motivated others to stand up and take notice of them.

If you are hated for the sake of envy, then let me congratulate you, as being hated means you have arrived, my friend – *you have left an indelible imprint in this world.*

There is only one surefire way to deal with a hater, and that is to choose to rejoice in the knowledge of your success, not to turn that hate inward, because to do so is to fail to realize your greatness. There is nothing incorrect or wrong with being confident, successful, and proud of what you have accomplished. Only a fool thinks he should be above all forms of criticism, envy, and hate.

Grandmaster Frank Dux inspired millions to study martial arts and is considered the father of MMA. Victor Moore, gave Frank the title of, "The Ultimate Fight Champion," because he was the only person Moore could not defeat.

Grandmaster Dux has been an adjunct faculty member of The Criminal Justice Center and the trainer to undercover officers of the NEOA. He is the unprecedented, 2-time keynote speaker for Federal Law Enforcement Officers Association, and is a named source contributor in creating the US Navy SEAL Combat Fighting Course manual.

In addition, Dux is also world renown as an intelligence strategist/analyst and international business consultant who has interacted for 40 years with world leaders and captains of industry, with Dux being mentored by Howard Hughes "alter ego," former FBI/CIA legend, Robert Aimes Maheu. Frank Dux is intimately knowledgeable of the power elite, their secrets, methods, and what otherwise would go unsaid. His autobiography, The Secret Man, details his life in clandestine service to the country.

Frank Dux has his own national column for Artvoice.com. He created his own proprietary technology that enhances all martial art systems, called Dux Ryu. It's component, DUX FASST (Focus-Action-Skill-Strategy-Tactics), led to the founding of the first American System of Ninjitsu, if not, first Western Gendai (Modern) Ninjutsu system, that is being commercially taught outside of Japan, founded in 1975.

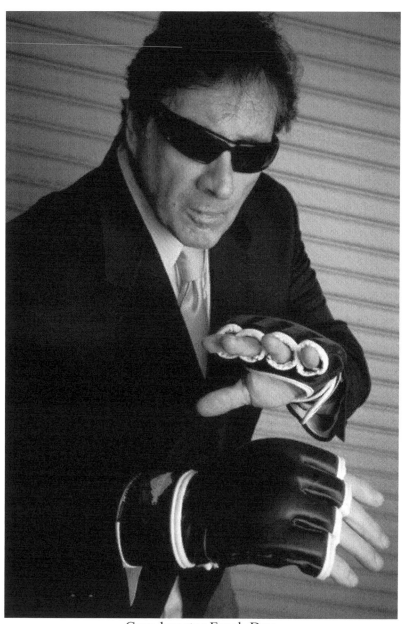

Grandmaster Frank Dux

Don't Teach Undesirable People
Bohdi Sanders

I have always taught that a responsible martial arts instructor should not teach people who show bad character. Even when I first started teaching martial arts, I refused to teach anyone who was a bully, a thug, or who exhibited bad character traits. Many of the original martial arts masters had the same attitude. The original masters would not teach someone until they first knew their character.

Moreover, even when they were willing to teach students, they still would not teach them some of their more advanced or secret techniques, until they had tested the character of the student for years. Some of their students were never trusted enough to receive the training that was reserved for only the most trusted students.

This was very common practice among the original pioneers of what we call martial arts today. They certainly would not want to teach a student, who they did not fully trust, all of their techniques. If that student turned on them, and the instructor had taught him everything he knew, he could possibly defeat, or worse, kill his master.

We all know through experience that the majority of people are not trustworthy. I feel sure that most of you have had an incident where someone you thought was your trusted friend screwed you over in one way or another. We have all had that friend that we trusted, who later, turned around and betrayed our trust.

If we can't trust people who appear to be good people, how much less can we trust people who blatantly expose their poor character? Character matters! Trust matters! You need to know the character of your students *before* you teach them some of the deeper secrets of the martial arts.

The ninja master, Masaaki Hatsumi also teaches this concept,

333

and doesn't mince words about the topic, saying, "Don't teach undesirable people." There is a reason that the old masters would not teach people who displayed poor character. They knew that if someone displayed poor character, he probably could not be trusted.

If you cannot trust your student with the knowledge you are giving him, especially in the martial arts, there is a high likelihood that he would use his skills for the wrong reasons, possibly to bully or harass someone, or worse. A guy with poor character, or poor judgment, may easily use his skills in ways that they shouldn't be used. It is not wise to arm a bully with better techniques to harm others.

Not only did the masters not teach people with poor character, they warned to keep your distance from those people, period. Takuan Soho taught, "Keep your distance from unvirtuous people." It would be hard to keep your distance from these people if you are teaching them martial arts!

There are many reasons that you don't want to teach undesirable people. You don't want to enable a thug to be more dangerous to innocent people. You don't want to arm a bully with better techniques. You don't want to give the secrets of the martial arts to someone who will abuse them or use them to hurt other people.

You have a responsibility concerning who you teach your skills to and how you teach those students to use those skills. It is irresponsible to teach a young child lethal techniques. He is not mature enough to understand what those techniques could do, thus, he may lose his temper in a playground fight and really hurt another kid. I don't know of any credible martial arts instructor who would give a young child this kind of knowledge.

But, many of those same instructors will teach whatever adult walks in off the street, as long as he has enough money to pay for the training. Their focus is only the money, not on being responsible for who they teach. This is wrong thinking when it comes to teaching the martial arts.

Money should not be the deciding factor when taking on a new student. As Master Hatsumi stated, "You must observe one's true character." Don't just teach anyone and everyone your art. It is this practice which has "dumbed down" the martial arts today. The love of money truly is the root of all evil.

Being a black belt used to mean something. Today, in many dojos, it simply means that person paid for enough classes and belt tests to reach his black belt. This is such a shame; it should outrage every true martial artist. The martial arts have been sold to the highest bidder, along with many martial arts instructor's honor.

Yes, you can make more money if you simply teach everyone who comes to your dojo. But is that the right thing to do? If known gang members came to your dojo and asked to learn, would you teach them how to fight and destroy the human body?

Marcus Aurelius taught, "To expect bad people not to injure others is crazy. It is to ask the impossible." If you are teaching people of low character in the martial arts, you are merely enabling them to hurt someone else. That is the bottom line, whether you want to admit it or not.

Does this mean that you should do an extensive background check before you sign up any student? Of course not! It simply means that you should observe the students character before you teach him more than the basics. You will have plenty of time to observe someone's character during the first few weeks or months of training. Then trust your instinct.

When I was teaching Shotokan Karate in Missouri, I taught mostly school age kids. I was also a teacher back then and had access to inside information on each of my students. I knew some students that I would not teach. They came to me and asked for classes, and I flatly refused to teach them, and told them exactly why. I let them know that if I saw changes in their character, I would reconsider.

Usually, there was no thought of changing. Instead of a student saying that he would change and prove me wrong, the usual response was, "F-YOU!" This response basically proved my initial feelings about the student.

I held my students to a much higher standard than any other school I had been associated with, with the exception of Shihan Bob Allen's Shotokan dojo. I required them to be courteous and polite, not just to me, but to their parents, teachers, and other students. Then I followed up and got reports from both their parents and teachers about their behavior. Across the board, parents and teachers stated that the student's behavior and manners had greatly improved because of my classes.

Could I have made more money by accepting every student who wanted to learn martial arts? Sure! But money is not supposed to be the main focus when teaching martial arts. That is a fairly new development in the martial arts world. It wasn't always that way. Martial arts didn't start out as a profession.

My students were held to a very high standard, and most rose to meet that standard. Their behavior was better; they were better mannered, and their grades increased, which was also a requirement to be in my classes. Overall, they became better people, which is the true goal of Karate to start with, according to Master Funakoshi.

Henry Ward Beecher is famous for the quote, "Hold yourself responsible for a higher standard than anyone else expects of you. Never excuse yourself." How much better off would the martial arts world be if all martial arts instructors held themselves to a higher standard, if they were selective with whom they taught, if they made their students earn their ranks instead of getting rank as some sort of participation trophy for being in the school for a certain amount of time? Too many martial arts instructors focus on making money instead of doing what's right, and that is exactly what has created the mess that we see in the martial arts world today.

We need martial arts instructors who will refuse to lower their standards to accommodate those who refuse to raise theirs. We need instructors who refuse to teach people of low character, even if that does cost them a few dollars. Many martial artists complain about the state of the martial arts world today, but few personally take steps to change it. As Confucius taught, "We must first set our hearts right."

When you sign up a young student, from that day, monitor his or her character. See if their character improves as they go along. Hopefully, you are teaching character traits as a part of your classes, if not, you are a big part of the problem. It is our jobs, as martial arts instructors, not to just teach self-defense, kata, and cool techniques, but to also mold our students into good human beings, to teach them character traits, honor, respect, courage, good manners, and courtesy. Masami Tsuruoka *stated:*

> *I have seen the best karate.*
> *All that really matters is what*
> *kind of human being you are.*
> *Masami Tsuruoka*

If you are not helping your students to become better human beings, then you are not only wasting a golden opportunity, but you are not fulfilling your responsibilities as a martial arts instructor. That may be a strong statement, but it is true nonetheless.

You have the responsibility to both *not* teach people of low character and to help foster good character traits to the students that you do teach. Too many people think that martial arts are only about fighting or self-defense. That is also a modern invention. True Budo is spiritual, mental, and physical. It is about balance. Character plays a huge role in true Budo, but that has been neglected in today's world. It is time to change that! Take your responsibilities serious.

Take the time to teach your students how to behave; teach them to become men and women of honor, character, and integrity. They are your legacy; their behavior reflects on you. If your students do not have honor, integrity, character, and respect, your peers will think that you don't either. Your students' behavior reflects on you. This is another reason that you should be selective when it comes to your students.

My friend, Steve Gamlin states, "I refuse to lower my standards to accommodate those who refuse to raise theirs." This quote should be in every dojo, and it should be taken to heart by every martial arts instructor. Refuse to lower your standards to accommodate those who refuse to raise theirs.

If a student will not conduct himself as he should, send him packing. If a student is constantly getting in fights, cursing his teachers, disrespectful to his parents, etc., refuse to teach him. It is time for those in the martial arts world to raise their standards. Start putting character and what's right, before the almighty dollar!

True martial arts are not for everyone; they never have been and never will be. Martial artists should hold themselves to a higher standard. They should constantly seek to improve themselves – spirit, mind, and body. They should work to perfect their character. They should be the most respectful, courteous, kind, and honorable people that you meet.

It is time to get back to that standard. It is time to raise our standards as martial artists. Be selective concerning who you teach, and truly *teach* those who you do take on as students. Let's bring honor, character, and integrity back to the martial arts. Let's get back to teaching true Budo in our dojos; it is your responsibility and duty as a true martial artist.

Dr. Bohdi Sanders is a multi-award winning and bestselling author of 15 books and 100's of articles, and is an 8-time Martial Arts Hall of Fame inductee. He started training in martial arts in 1984 under Bob and Nikki Allen and now holds the rank of 5th Dan in Shotokan Karate from Shihan William Jackson. Dr. Sanders was awarded the official title of Shihan by Soke Richard Hallman, along with Soke Stephen Barber, Soke-Dai Scot E. Philips, and Renshi Young Author Smith, III.

He has also been awarded the honorary title of Hanshi, (teacher of teachers) for his teachings and writings on the martial arts, by Sifu Al Dacascos, Col. Phil Torres, Grandmaster Eddie Mapula, Shihan Bill Holman, Soke Richard Hallman, Grandmaster Richard Hackworth, Grandmaster Joy Turberville, Grandmaster Terrence Shea, Shihan Dana Abbott, Grandmaster Dan Tosh, Grandmaster Harry Mok, Grandmaster Harry Greene, Grandmaster Dave Johnson, and Grandmaster Eric Lee.

Dr. Sanders has won multiple national book awards for his books. He has written three #1 Bestsellers, and six of his other books have climbed into the Top 10 on Amazon's Best Sellers List. His books have won 1st Place awards from the Indie Excellence Book Awards and the USA Book News Book Awards. In 2011, he was named Inspiration of the Year by the United States Martial Artist Association Hall of Fame. In 2018, Dr. Sanders became one of the first five Westerners elected to the World Martial Arts Congress in Beijing, China. He is also a member of the Golden Dragon Ohana, and the Independent Warriors Association.

He also holds national certifications as a Specialist in Martial Arts Conditioning and as a Certified Fitness Trainer. In addition, he is a Usui-Tibetan Reiki Master and a Master of Acupressure. He has a doctorate in Natural Health and Naturopathy, along with a BA in Sociology and a MA in Education. Dr. Sanders is also a columnist for Taekwondo Times Magazine and has written articles for several magazines and websites. In 2017, Dr. Sanders was inducted into the Elite

339

Black Belt Hall of Fame and also awarded a Lifetime Achievement Award for his contributions to the martial arts. Dr. Sanders is available for inspirational and motivational public talks and may be reached through his website, www.TheWisdomWarrior.com or through his social media pages.

Shihan Bohdi Sanders

What it takes to be a Master
Rondy McKee

When I was a 3rd degree black belt living in Korea as a member of the Korean Tigers Professional Demonstration Team, I asked what it takes to be a master. I had heard that 4th degree was the "turning point" and you became a "Master." I had hoped to test to my 4th degree before moving back to the states, so I asked my teammates, "What does it take to become a master?"

I should have known better than to ask a couple dozen guys, all equivalent to being my little brothers. They said, "You know when you book your ticket to fly to America?" "Yes," I listened patiently for this magical moment of master making. "The plane lands and the door opens," "Yes, yes, go on." "You raise your right hand, and say, "Hi everyone, I'm Master Rondy." And, from that time on, you will be called Master Rondy." Well, it did happen that way, but of course there was a whole lot more that went into it.

Let me back up quite a few years. Why did I start marital arts? I often tell students, why you start and why you stay are probably two completely different reasons. I started martial arts out of fear.

I was working during the day in agencies, and working extra hours in my first business before I was 20 years old. My specialty was marketing and advertising. I was actually an artist, but I didn't want to starve to death, so I learned how to adapt my eye for art into a lucrative business through marketing, advertising, and public relations.

I had been artsy my whole life, and strict military parents instilled a sense of discipline and responsibility in me. This unusual combination of traits made my work very marketable. My marketing campaigns were effective, and I quickly made a name for myself in the field. But my gender, my smaller size, and my late hours, also made me an easy target. I started to think about getting a gun for protection.

Living in Detroit, you would think it would be easy to get a gun. But I wasn't really sure how to go about it. I was already taking scuba diving classes from the Detroit Police, so I asked my instructor how I could get my hands on a gun. He quickly advised against it. He said I was too small and too timid. He said the next time I had trouble, the bad guy would just take away my gun and have it to use against me.

I understood where he was coming from and asked about pepper spray. He said, "Have you ever been sprayed with pepper spray in the face? Because you will if you decide to get some." It became apparent that he was not going to help me. I needed to find something the bad guy could not take away from me. The thoughts of learning self-defense entered my mind.

My first impression of entering a martial arts school to ask for information was not a positive one. There was a dozen or so balding men, every single one was overweight, no women anywhere, and the smell was a problem as well. The outfits that I had imagined being silky and colorful were stiff, off-white canvas, and everyone had on flood pants.

Then the guy in charge barked, it sounded just like a bark, and the men started doing a drill that looked very much like leap frog. And they were all barking too! The guy in charge noticed me just inside the door. He started in my direction, and I bolted as fast as I could. What was I thinking? This was not for me.

So it took another "incident" to realize I really needed to do something. This time I was injured. My hand, my drawing hand was in a cast. It was going to be a while before I was able to work. I could not barricade myself in my trailer forever with my kitchen chairs wedged under the front and back doorknobs.

I had been working at an agency on the other side of town. Every day, I passed by a school in a strip mall that had a sign in the window which read, "3 Lessons and a Uniform for $19.99." I summoned the courage to go in. This place was much different. I soon learned that this was Taekwondo, which I had never heard of. "It's Korean Karate," they told me. In this school, the students were young adults, and it felt more my style. There was a teenage girl in class with a green belt. I was mesmerized by the fluidity of her movements. Surely green belt must be the highest rank!

I plopped down the $20 and took my first lesson with the instructor in the corner of the mat. I had never done any physical exercise or sport in my life. I was the artsy kid. I was labeled early on, as the last kid to be picked for the team, the slowest runner on the track, and the only kid who did not know the rules of basic sports.

The instructor, either a marketing genius, or I'd like to think, he saw something in me, said, "You could be good at this." Notice he did not say you *will* be good at this, but just the glimmer of a chance that *I could be* good at anything physical was all it took. Where do I sign up for the longest program you have!

I received my student manual and read the entire book cover to cover that night. I saw how much time it took between belt colors and calculated my testing dates. I did not even know there were so many color belts. And to my surprise, green belt was not the highest.

I trained hard, practiced at home and progressed quickly. I put painter's tape on my carpet to make lines to practice stances. I made north, south, east, and west signs for the walls so I could practice forms. I created a make shift stretching machine by stepping on glossy magazines and sliding on the carpet, a rope with a loop hung over the dowel in my closet to help stretch for side kick. Back at work, I stuffed my scarf down my coat sleeves, as it hung on the coat rack. This partner with "arms" helped me practice my self-defense moves.

The day had come; I was ready for my first tournament. I had joined to learn some self-defense, but my instructor really thought I should compete for the school. I had never enjoyed watching sports of any kind, but this was different. It was exciting, and I realized that I was learning; I actually understood the rules and knew what was going on.

I also noticed something else. I noticed some things were not right, something was off. I knew the rules; I had read them over and over many times. Yet, the rules seemed to be altered, and decisions were overturned when some other master came over to talk to the judges.

I asked my instructor what was going on. He explained the hierarchy and rank. And some things are just because one outranked the other. It was not right; it was not fair. And on that day I decided I needed to earn rank.

My training had taught me how to compete, but it also taught me to be more aware of my surroundings and my situations. My newly found confidence enabled me to stand up for myself when I was not comfortable, and I was not comfortable with the amount of attention I was receiving from my instructor. It was time to move on.

I was not willing to give up my training, so I looked in the phone book for the head master's school, the one from the tournament. His students were very skilled, and he seemed to be very respected by all the other instructors. He was located on the other side of town. It only took a day to secure employment close to his school.

I was just a yellow belt, so the transition was smooth. This school was much different, much stricter, and had tougher students. I loved it. It took a while to get used to a Korean instructor and the accent, but I really enjoyed learning the culture.

It was at this school where I started learning Hapkido and demo stunts. At blue belt, I asked my instructor when we would learn to teach. "Saturday," he said. That was not what I meant, but you did not say no to my instructor.

Saturday, I showed up bright and early, and he pulled out a chair and sat along the side of the floor. "Go ahead," he motioned and I went to the front of the class. I had dreamed about this, but was not expecting it so quickly. I knew the Korean phrases to say to start class, but not necessarily the correct order in which to say them. My master would yell at me from the side with every mistake. It was horrifying.

When I counted out for the class, he would yell that I was "too fast," then "too slow." "Who taught you that," he would ask. The one-hour class seemed like an eternity. I was sweating more than the students. This is where I learned how to multi-task. I would be counting kicks, and the phone would ring, or someone would walk in.

You learn quickly how to delegate and manage time. Every Saturday for almost 2 months we did this. I would teach, and he would point out mistakes from the sideline. Then one Saturday, I received the biggest compliment he had ever given me. He did not show up. He trusted me to run class on my own.

Everything changed for me, being on that side of the floor. I wanted to teach so much. I was only a blue belt, so I did not have that much wisdom to share. But that changed in time. In time, my training would take me to Korea for competition.

I would end up moving to Korea to live, train, perform, and tour as a member of the Korean Tigers Professional Demonstration Team for several years. Back in the states, my experiences in Korea, and working in ad agencies, enabled me to build the world's largest martial arts school. This year we celebrated 22 years of business and our 12,000th student.

Thirty-something years of experience and earning an 8th degree black belt, gave me the *title* of master or grandmaster. But it was when I had compiled the experience and skills to pass to my students, with the intention to hold nothing back, to teach all that I know, and provide opportunity for even greater growth, to strive to make them better than I could ever dream – that I *became* a master.

Master Rondy is the owner of White Tiger Taekwondo and Martial Arts – known as the world's largest super school, located in Cary, NC, USA. The 24,000 sq. ft. school just celebrated its 22nd anniversary and enrolled its 12,000th student. Master Rondy lived in Korea from 1994-1996 as a member of the Korean Tigers Professional Demonstration Team.

Today, she is the Program Director and instructor at White Tiger, is a columnist for Taekwondo Times Magazine, serves on the Kukkiwon Advisory Board, and the U.S. Taekwondo Committee. Master Rondy also travels the world to share her marketing and public relations background to help other school owners achieve their dreams.

Master Rondy McKee can be reached at,
MasterRondy@gmail.com
fb.me/GrandmasterRondy
www.WhiteTigerTKD.com
www.WhiteTigerGlovalliance.com
www.facebook.com/WhiteTigerTKD
www.facebook.com/MasterRondy

Master Rondy McKee

The Importance of Effective Self-Defense
Max Massiah

Decades ago, leading up to the period of the early 80's, the average child, female, and elder were able to walk the streets and neighborhoods in relative comfort, without tension and fear. Now this would be deemed as foolhardy in many places, and not realistic in regards to how crime, violence, drugs and alcohol have escalated with almost a turbo-like speed. The results in the streets (and even indoors) unequivocally become very unpredictable, unsafe locations to be in, for your own well-being and safety.

Being mugged or bullied, experiencing domestic assault and abuse, or being unexpectedly attacked by a drug-crazed addict (whose imagination unfortunately zeroes in on the closest, most vulnerable-looking pedestrian, as the one who somehow has *his* money or drugs for safekeeping), is a real possibility in today's world.

This has become the order of the day for many unsuspecting and unprepared people, whose only defense is – no defense. They are simply left to the mercy of the ungodly and emotionless, to have their way, rendering their victims unconscious, bleeding, in severe pain, or fatally wounded.

Let's look at a general situation. You are an honest, decent, hard-working family man (or woman). You don't believe in violence, and you wish those who do would just leave you alone. You are a God-fearing person, so you convince yourself that you are protected by your beliefs. Nothing and no one will harm you. You also feel that those things only happen to the people you read about in the newspapers or see on the news channel. Situations of violence or assault have probably never happened to you, so you feel immune to such.

Now, look at a wall 10 feet away, place your hands over your eyes, and with speed, run towards the wall until you are stopped by the wall. You should not feel any pain or even fall down, because you are protected by your beliefs. What? Your beliefs did not protect you from hitting the wall? That should wake you up to the reality of the streets. Beliefs don't protect you; your knowledge and skills will.

I grew up as a skinny youth, so skinny that if someone mashed my foot, I would let it go for fear of getting into a fight. I grew up as a very quiet boy. I tried hard to be as insignificant as possible. I was aware, however, that my elder brother and I both had exceptional speed when we kicked and were as light as cats whenever we sparred or roughhoused with our schoolmates.

The few times we got into fights could not be considered as such, as the other guys (mostly bigger than us) just could not find us to land a punch, even though we were right there when the punch or kick was thrown. Most times, they just gave up after having a busted lip or bloody nose, realizing it was almost impossible to land a single blow.

Then in 1972, at the age of 11, my life took a significant turn when my brother and I were introduced to Karate. It was just what we needed. That was 46 years ago. What's uncanny is the fact that, today, at my age, I have an even deeper appetite to learn, to be innovative, and to teach.

In today's society, with morals, scruples, respect, decency, love, care, and consideration *not* being considered, bullyism has grown to enormous proportions. Lawlessness has imbedded itself into the underworld *and* our everyday world. Now it's moving at such a rate that you may not have to go out in the streets for it to find you – it may visit your very doorstep. So, the questions are, "How prepared are you? What can you do?"

Learn an effective form of self-defense. It would automatically lessen your vulnerability to harm by 80%. The Maxido Adult Self-Defense System is one such program. It's a no-nonsense system of self-defense that does not teach its students to fight.

We teach our students to finish fights. A fight should be finished in no more than four seconds.

Accepting the fact that the adversary has intentions to harm you is enough motivation for you to respond without emotion, immediately thrusting you into the mindset of "better him than me," whilst applying a chosen technique.

I implore Maxido students to ignore the submission techniques, as the attacker may beg surrender, only to resume his attack upon being let loose. We head straight to dislocation or breakage, with no sympathy. I stress the point that an adversary with a knife or gun is automatically entitled to two or more breaks of his limbs.

What is significant about Maxido is the fact that an elderly person in his 70's can render a 25-year-old thug helpless. The techniques are designed to be more effective against stronger and bigger assailants because it uses their strength against them.

A prospective student, Kojo McPherson, who weighs approximately 195 pounds, upon visiting to inquire about training, was reluctant to join the Maxido system. But he was convinced and registered immediately after a female yellow belt student (5'1" 115 pounds) subdued him in 3 seconds when he grabbed her arms. He is now a yellow belt student and married to Maxido. The system was specifically structured for the vulnerable such as businessmen, law enforcement and security specialist, seniors, and women.

The Maxido motto of "Pain Application for Bullies" is applied without exception, sympathy, or sentiment. Each technique is learned and applied with a concentration of submission, dislocation, or breakage of mainly the arm, shoulder, elbow, or wrist. It is intended for use on the evil-minded and ungodly. The techniques are based upon modern-day approaches and attempts by the adversary such as being grabbed by either one or both hands, rear-neck choke, grabbed from front or back, stick-ups with gun or knife, etc.

The benefits of learning self-defense are not only in learning to defend one's self, they also stimulate your mental confidence in any and everything that is a part of you. One specific, under-rated realism is the mental and physical protective shield that goes up.

Let me break it down so you can grasp what this means. In the same way an aggressive dog senses your fear and is encouraged to attack as he becomes aware that you are fearfully intimidated with the prospect of being bitten, the bully or mugger senses the fear you emanate based upon your actions and movements.

When one is prepared with reasonable or great understanding and knowledge of the defense techniques at his disposal, his mental and physical confidence radiates, so he is not targeted by the evil-minded, who mainly attack those in whom they sense fear.

I live in Guyana, South America with a population of just over 700,000 within 83,000 square miles. As in most countries around the world, violence, crime, guns, and illegal drugs abound, but bullying, domestic violence, assault, and murder top the list of its occurrences.

I just received news of a murder/suicide of a couple in the county of Berbice, Guyana. A female moved from the home of her abusive husband and returned in the company of a police officer in order to obtain her belongings. The husband had a history of abuse, yet the policeman left the woman in the house with the man, while he waited outside. That was enough space and time for the man to slit her throat, just before slitting his own. Talk about confirmation of a situation!

This brings my blood almost to the boiling point and confirms the reason I founded the Maxido system. I have five daughters, two biological sisters, among many other "sisters," a wife, and my 81-year-old mother. I pray daily not to be placed in a situation where I have to respond to anyone who attempts to, or does, physically harm them.

I am angered when violence and pain is meted out to innocent people. The general imagination would be miles off in trying to assess the anger that evolves from my thoughts of retaliation. I sincerely do not wish to be labeled as the world's cruelest protector of his family.

I pray for the day when the world will wake up to the reality that, in the dangerous world we live in, learning effectual self-defense and being able to protect one's self and family is of the *UTMOST PRIORITY*. It may just save your life or the life of someone you love.

The Secret of Maxido Self-Defense

In traditional systems, one tends to intercept the attack; the practitioners more or less anticipate and try to stop it. With Maxido, it is an entirely different approach. A mindset of implementing the EOS (Element of Surprise) is injected into the purpose and success of an effective response.

To begin with, the defender appears to surrender or submit to the aggressor due to fear. He may even beg, shudder, and appear to cry, and/or urinate or defecate upon himself from utter fear – all a strategy to get the aggressor to relax. The defender wants to appear defeated giving the aggressor a false sense of accomplishment. He believes that his victim has surrendered in fear for his life, with no thoughts of retaliation. That is the basis of Maxido.

Now the Maxido student has the perfect opportunity to turn the tables around, to unexpectedly apply his technique with swiftness, precision, and intention to get it right the 1st time. The tables are turned, and the aggressor then becomes the defender, and the Maxido student, who appeared to be defeated, is now the victor in less than four seconds.

The objective is to deter the aggressor, by either dislocation or breakage of the upper limbs – specifically parts of the arms which are either wrenched out of the sockets, or direct breakage of the bones and joints of the arms.

The uniqueness of Maxido is that it uses the joints and the positions of how the body is structured against itself. Without the requirement of very much physical strength, a female weighing 110 pounds or a small-built elder in their 70's, can apply the techniques to an aggressor weighing twice their weight with a devastating effect. The grade of intent and purpose of the aggressor – bare handed, knife, or gun, determines whether he/she is automatically entitled to be upgraded to a recipient of two or more breaks.

In plain talk – a Maxido student isn't taught to "fight." They are taught, with the aid of strategy and the use of the element of surprise, to deter and disable in just a few seconds.

The thought of hesitation, sympathy, or leniency is not entertained. The aggressor should not be a further threat to the Maxido student or anyone else. Their evil-minded ways are quickly placed in repentance. Learn to defend yourself and understand when to do so and how much force to use.

Verney Massiah, aka "Max" Massiah, was born in the South American country of Guyana. He started practicing martial arts at the age of 11 in 1972, with Sensei Danny, a 2nd Dan black belt in Shotokan (deceased 1976). In 1976, at the level of purple belt, he was enlisted into the Guyana National Service (GNS), a para-military organization, where he learned basic military skills.

During the four years away from the dojo, he continued training in base camps, which were in the deep interior of Guyana, hundreds of miles from city life. In 2014, he was promoted to the rank of 2nd Dan black belt by one of Guyana's *most recognized martial arts pioneers, 9th Dan Master Frank Woon-A-Tai.*

Being tested by Grandmasters Dennis Warren, Darius "Two Bears" Ross (aka Tali Yona Quosa Ukuwiyuhi), and Sifu Alan Goldberg, he was elevated to the rank of Godan and the title of Shihan (5th degree black belt) and presented with a Letter of Credence in September of 2017.

In 2017, he founded the MAXIDO ADULT SELF-DEFENSE SYSTEM in Brooklyn. He now conducts seminars in the USA and in Guyana. He also has a dojo in Guyana. He has a total of 46 years of continual martial arts training.

Master Max Massiah can be contacted by email at: maxmassiah@yahoo.com.

Master Max Massiah

The Martial Arts Revolution and Mind Control Theory
Jeff Scott

The study of martial arts can be traced back some 40,000 years ago. Wall carvings and etchings were discovered in the early 1900's in The Caves of Altamira, depicting organized groups of people doing fighting drills using hand and foot techniques in what appears to be a monastery type setting.

This suggests that the religious monasteries were not just peaceful places of inner study of self-fulfillment through enlightenment, but also sites for preparation of war against neighboring provinces. For me, this was actually corroborated by the original founder of Tang Soo Do (Soo Bahk Do), Grandmaster Hwang Kee, in his book, *Tang Soo Do Soo Bahk Do,* published during the 1940's.

As usual, territory was the motive in many disputes, prompting wars between provinces and the shifts in power and domination went on, as they do in modern times, ad nauseam. The most amusing farce about this is depicted in the drama, *Kung Fu,* in the 1970's staring David Carradine.

The show attempted to relay to the public that these monasteries were like martial arts universities of higher learning, and everything was based around peace, live and let live, and self-study enlightenment through intense physical combat training.

In reality, they were institutes of higher learning in the martial arts to be used to wage unending wars against other provinces. So in effect, you can call these Kung Fu and Ninja Masters the "Special Forces" for the particular province, not peace-loving priests.

Asian martial arts were almost non-existent in this country until the 1960's. Even then, there were few recognized, nationally known studios. There were some noted, great and legendary masters such as Gene Lebelle (Judo), Ed Parker (Kempo), Robert Trias (Okinawan), Robert Chaney and Jhoon Rhee (Tae

Kwan Do), and a little further into the 60's, many greater legendary names such as Bruce Lee, Chuck Norris, and Joe Lewis came on the scene. The evolution of the arts really started to pick up momentum.

I began training in the devastating street fighting art of Kajukenbo in 1972, in San Jose, California. I believe it's the most effective self-defense art even until this day. Every two letters denote a differently incorporated system, thus making it the first "mixed martial art." The Ka (Japanese Karate), Ju (Judo Jiu Jitsu), Ken (Kenpo), and Bo (Chinese Boxing) were its expansive components.

From the first day, one is taught to explore raw reactions to lethal attacks of fists, feet, knives, clubs, and other available deadly weapons. You overcome your fears of fighting by learning hundreds of intermixed defensive skills. Learning how to get hit is as important as hitting your attacker, because you come to the realization that you can be badly beaten, yet still survive.

It makes more sense than the many mixes of kicking and punching combinations taught in Korean martial arts schools, which seem to be planning and choreographing fights which haven't even occurred yet. This was one of Bruce Lee's major complaints about classical and traditional styles.

My training in Kajukenbo was under some truly tough individuals. Max Togisala, Raymond DeCoito, Larry Brown, and in command of our system was legendary master Adriano Emperado from Hawaii, and Joe Halbuna from Pacifica, California. Also, we were visited by martial arts legend, Sifu Al Dacascos, who later urged me to pursue instruction in kicking skills as I displayed a propensity for it.

There were three-hour sessions of nothing but drilling on every possible scenario that might occur with intense contact going on the entire time. At times, it was full on gang fights, without pads, which appeared to be an almost out of control brawl. The instructor's aim was to get everybody comfortable with being in the "eye of the hurricane." The slips, blocks, parries, elbow, and hammer fist strikes, made you become very proficient at deadly striking in very close quarters, while using your attacker's own momentum against him.

I made it up to first degree brown belt by fall of 1975, just missing black belt testing as I moved to Southern California to attend the University of California, Santa Barbara. This is when Sifu Al Dacascos told me the names of several Korean instructors to seek for kicking expertise. Among them was Jeong Sook Lee (7th Dan Tang Su Do) who I later appeared with on *Black Belt Magazine's* cover for July 1978 issue.

I became the senior instructor of the Santa Barbara studio learning much about conditioning and training from Master Lee. However, our relationship was strained and tenuous. By 1978, I was ready to move back to San Jose to open my own studio, as I had a different vision of what I wanted to teach. This was completely forbidden by the extremely traditional Tang Soo Do Federation I'd been under for years.

After opening my studio, Ed Parker contacted me to fight in the Long Beach International Tournament. Also, he wanted to set up a "meet" with Chuck Norris and me. I'd met Norris before and was aware of his thinking and incorporating other arts with Tang Soo Do. The meet went well, and since 1979, I have had a lifelong personal and professional relationship with Master Chuck Norris. We hit it off like family, and he began to include me in his personal life.

We spent hours discussing the evolution of martial arts in America. He had me come to many federation gatherings, and I impressed him, as well as many other board members, with my intense work ethic. The Kajukenbo toughness made it easy to overpower higher rank black belts who were shocked by the speed which I overtook them. Master Lee's excellent tutoring of my kicks gave me the best of both worlds. I had a great outside striking attack and charged at the right moment, when their legs were all extended, doing high, unrealistic head kicks.

Our Chuck Norris System was based largely in Kang Soo Do, but Master Norris believed in power over all other fighting qualities. He constructed a lot of forms and self-defense techniques that were Shotokan based, believing that he was blending the best of both worlds – upper body power striking and superior outside kicking attacks.

The early 1980's saw many schools starting to realize the days of traditional training, in one's thought process of how to move, were over. Indeed, after I formally joined the Norris Federation, I started holding seminars where experts of many disciplines would come to Las Vegas and share their ideas with our predominately kicking style. The game changer was Royce Gracie and the Machado brothers, who taught clinics at our seminars with eye opening effectiveness at penetrating and taking any of us down.

Since then, the Gracie's and Gene Lebelle have changed the face of training, because it's now widely accepted that one should be able to fight inside, as well as outside. This showed me how much of a visionary Chuck Norris truly is, because this was unpopular thinking in those days.

And anyone who defected from their traditional art was ostracized for daring to blend many systems together. But those of us under the Norris System had seen what we thought of as completely ineffective sparring and street fighting techniques by today's standards, and knew it was time to evolve.

The early 1980's also saw the formation, by Master Norris, of the United Fighting Arts Federation. This philosophy was meant to develop students mentally, emotionally, psychologically, and physically. Master Chuck Norris was quoted as saying, "Karate is the vehicle by which we promote mental and psychological growth of our students."

Also, we were going to now approach basic martial philosophy as American, not Oriental. The Oriental training had been largely circular and non-linear. Now it was to be non-circular, linear thinking, with an emphasis on moving towards an opponent to cause a reaction, and thereby, create an opening, rather than wait to be attacked and simply defend.

Along with the new philosophy of movement was a change in our thought patterns towards training in general. Our new American mindset training emphasized goal setting and its achievement by having a totally positive approach to training and measurable results in a short period of time. This is when Chuck Norris, Marcus Wynne, and I came up with an idea and concept for *Black Belt Magazine*, which emphasized mental training as the vehicle for accelerated improvement over a short period of time.

We researched Scientology, physics, biology, and several other disciplines starting in 1982. By 1983, we formulated our affirmation and visualization techniques. At the core of the whole concept was PMA (Positive Mental Attitude).

Also, one must dismiss negativity, as it can develop into negative imagery planted into the subconscious. And for a desired goal to be realized, an image must be created in the mind, then pursued until completion in order to build confidence.

Visualization is the conscious creation of an image within the mind and was strongly emphasized and encouraged by Master Norris. An image of what a student wants to achieve, or improve, is implanted in the subconscious and can shift the visualizer's entire psyche toward fulfillment of that mental picture.

At the deepest levels of the mind, the brain and central nervous system can't distinguish between something imagined and an actual occurrence. An example of this would be walking in an alley and suddenly getting an adrenaline rush because the

361

shadows ahead shift. Although there is no real threat, the mind perceived what it thought was a real threat.

Training the mind to see and hold the positive self-image visualization, shifts the self toward becoming that image. Holding the image of a positive, self-disciplined person, and performing precise, powerful, Karate techniques, the visualizer becomes what he believes he is – a positive, self-disciplined person, performing precise, powerful, Karate techniques.

In essence, he creates himself. Now he must stretch out and throw the desired techniques to make it complete. This was a relatively new concept in psychology, which Master Norris is known to have used long before most athletes did.

Chuck Norris used PMA in competition, seeing himself winning by creating fight scene scenarios. He visualized opponents' weaknesses and created visions of counter attacking their moves. To be successful at PMA and visualization, one must break the habit of negative thinking and implant positive imagery at the deepest subconscious levels.

To tap into the subconscious mind, the visualizer must be in a relaxed, calm, and receptive state. To prepare, sit in a relaxed, cross-legged position, then close your eyes until you are relaxed. One method is to count your breaths as you breathe deep and fully.

Then, starting at the feet, consciously tense and relax all major muscle groups, going from the feet upwards, one section at a time. Start at the feet, then the calves, thighs, hips, genitals region, the stomach and lower back, chest and upper back, neck, and shoulders. Finish with the face, tensing and relaxing all small muscles, the jaw, and the forehead.

Some visualizers conjure the image of them walking down steps, and the deeper each step goes, the more they relax. They tell themselves they are becoming more and more relaxed, until they are completely relaxed. There's a sensation of floating, like you are lying on a waterbed or an air mattress in a pool.

At this point, one can create training visualizations. For example, to improve a side kick, begin by visualizing a proper leg chamber and kicking with a perfect release of power and snap. Concentrate on detail and see it as clearly as possible. Imagine and feel the muscles used to perform the kick. See it as clearly as you would see a television set.

Also, since sidekicks are taught in four stages (chamber, kick, rechamber, set down), imagine the whole kick being reduced to just one step, without a stoppage, in your mindset. It is crucial that, whatever you wish to do, you must see it as clearly as though it is happening in front of you. It's not easy to cultivate; distractions and negativity will try to intrude, but with persistence, anyone can visualize at a deep level.

To improve sparring skills, visualize yourself with an opponent, moving confidently, countering his techniques. See yourself launching powerful, unstoppable attacks. This training will enable any student to overcome tension that comes with inexperience.

Another mind technique we used, which came from Master Norris, was using affirmations. This uses specific phrases to generate positive images. Many people are self-defeated by focusing on all the pitfalls that might prevent them from goal achievement. Phrases like, "I'll never be able to do this," will become a self-fulfilling prophecy. If you tell yourself that you're a failure, the subconscious mind will strive to achieve the negative goal.

Affirmations replace negative "tapes" with positive ones. The student constantly monitors his negative thoughts and ideas with positive catch phrases, because it is negative thoughts and self-doubt that can passively implant themselves unconsciously. Positive statements reinforce a student's image. For example, the student working on a sidekick would say, "Each day, my sidekick is stronger," and, "Each kick is more powerful." The fastest way to achieve your mental training goal is combining visualization and affirmations. While in a calm receptive state (as described earlier), repeat your affirmations while visualizing an image to go with it. Repeated affirmations will engrain themselves in the subconscious mind.

While running my Norris affiliate school in San Jose, California, during the 1980's, my students and I both used visualization and affirmations in our training. Each one would write down exactly what he or she wished to improve on or achieve. Then, each night, they practiced their visualization and affirmation techniques on their own, keeping track of the frequency they did it.

Also, they'd say affirmations aloud to themselves before and during class. Some would record their affirmations on tape and play them before sleeping and again upon awakening. Others would write their affirmations on small signs and place them where they could see them, (i.e., car, bathroom mirror, refrigerator door.

I would see results in three weeks, because 21 days of consistent, conscientious, mind training resulted in measurable, overall performance. Some students saw good results in shorter periods of time, but our research showed three weeks to be about average. Using these techniques can enable some students to cut learning time in half.

Daily physical and mental training generates a feeling of confidence and positivity. Eliminating the self-defeating habits of negative thinking, one can develop far beyond what they first thought possible. The key is *daily consistency*, because it is not enough to generate positive imagery for only 21 days. Rather, it is a lifetime task to develop a positive mental attitude. A great life starts with a mental visualization of what you want to do or be.

Master Jeff Scott is a 46-year-old veteran of the martial arts, both training and teaching. His interest in martial arts spawned with his seeing Bruce Lee in the Green Hornet series in the 1960's. His first studio was a Kajukenbo school in San Jose, from 1972-1975. He then moved to Southern CA where he trained in Tang Soo Do.

Within five years, he had a fateful meeting with legendary star Master Chuck Norris, and formed a lifelong bond that still exists today. He and Master Norris achieved worldwide notoriety with their mind control series, published in 1984, and 1990. He also appeared on Black Belt Magazine's cover in July 1978. He still resides in San Jose and is a 6th degree black belt.

Master Jeff Scott

Bushido

Long-Term Consequences of Fighting
Marc Stoner

Each night I awake with what feels like 10,000 voices of fire, aching throughout my body, not so gentle reminders of my martial past, when I was a martial artist and a competitor. I'm finally seeing the only option. Some of this seems trite and maybe even contrived, but it's not, it's real, it's honest, and it's forward.

Aches and pains in my feet, my joints, my hands, and my back are all gentle reminders of the training, the time, the effort, and the thousands of break-falls. It is the after effects of the innumerable kicks – the front kicks, the sidekicks, the roundhouse kicks, the inside crescent, the outside crescent, the mule kick, the snap kick, the ball kick, the edge kicks, the bridge kicks, all of them.

The gentle, throbbing reminders in my legs, feet, elbows, knees, hips, and lower back, take me back to a time when I was conditioning my hands in the sand and rocks, punching the heavy bag nonstop, the speed bag work, and the light bag work, all for one purpose.

The purpose was to prevent violence, to protect, to bring me to a place where I had a sense of control in an uncontrollable, chaotic environment. It was harsh training in order to survive, or even overcome, possible violent attacks, the violence which is forced upon us at different times in our lives, in different places. And so, I began my martial arts training, many years ago, as a 14-year-old boy, 5' 5" and barely 122 pounds.

One night, my best friend and I were in a hurry to get home and avoid violating our curfew, so we hitchhiked. At some point, a car stopped in the road, the door opened, and my best friend jumped into the car. The driver got out and stood there looking at me. Instantly, I realized that this was a trap and that we were in a very bad situation. I looked to my right, and there was a wall of hedges, three feet wide, almost impenetrable. To my left, across the street, was a hill that went up at an angle, about 10 feet high. Behind me was the road at a 45-degree angle, with a half mile slope.

To run away from this man, from this serious situation, I would have to take one of these options. Then again, I considered the fact that my best friend just jumped into a car full of strangers. I decided to take the other option and join him, survive, and deal with whatever came next, so I got in the car. For years, I thought this was the stupidest thing I had ever done, but now I realize, without a doubt, it was probably one of the most courageous.

Once inside the car, the gentleman who got out to look at me, turned around and started beating us with his fists and kicking us with his legs, in a close quarters situation. As we drove down the road, he used my face as a punching bag and then stopped and started kicking me in the face.

He took us to a desolate area, pulled over, and started to drag me out of the car. My best friend stepped on my back, jumped out of the car, and ran away as fast as he could.

My abductor took me to the edge of the road, draped me over the guardrails and then proceeded to kick me in the groin until I was unconsciousness. The last thing I heard was, "I think this one's dead."

They lifted me up and threw me over the guardrails, down into the ravine, where I later awakened in the dark. Beaten and confused, I climbed up out of the ravine to the side of the road, where I found my friend waiting. We walked the rest of the way home, stunned from what had just happened.

I hid from my father for the next two weeks because of the bruises on my face, on my neck, on my jaw, my black eye, bloody nose, swollen lips, and chest bruises from the heal kicks. I hid so that he wouldn't see it, because I didn't want to have to explain to him what happened to me.

My sister eventually told my father what happened and about a week and a half later, he asked me about it. I told him I fell down the stairs, an excuse I would use for years, but the truth was that I had been physically assaulted, bullied, beat, and left for dead by men twice my size, and at least 5-6 years older than I was. All for the purpose of entertainment and fun. It was just a Friday night for them, with nothing more to do than perhaps go out and physically assault some young men. This event began my journey into the martial arts.

It seems many of my associates in the martial arts, as I have learned, have had similar experiences. Some worse than mine, some not as bad. Maybe they were bullied, maybe someone slapped them in the face, punched them in the stomach, or kicked them in the groin. Whatever it was, it was an alpha male positioning.

My story is a little different. I'm no stranger to violence. I have known it from the early days of my life, probably due to the unhappiness of parental arrangements.

After multiple phone calls to martial arts schools in my local area, and my father's reluctance, although he was a first degree black belt in Japanese Jiu-jitsu, I began martial arts training on my own, with no support. He refused to teach me or allow me to attend any of his educational classes.

I was put into a Judo class, which was taught as a sport. It's a martial art that basically strengthens you and teaches you the skills of throwing, choking, and arm bars, and for a decade of my life, I studied and practiced Judo.

I went to many tournaments and lost spectacularly, that is until the day when I began to win. I went on to receive a bronze medal in the Junior Olympics and went to the Olympic trials, competed at Indiana University and gained a spot at the Pan American games. After that, I joined the army and became the post champion. Ten years after I started, I finally received my black belt!

Yet there still was a sense that I was incomplete, a sense that violence would find me, and when it did, I would be unprepared. I went on to study Minna Jiu-jitsu under Frank Collage at the Mayfield Academy in Cleveland, Ohio. I studied with him for over 4½ years.

I studied and trained with him, wondering to myself how I could be prepared for each and every possible attack, each and every violent situation that may befall me. I never really saw the overall picture. It was not until years later that I would understand this, as I was too deep into thinking, "What if?"

Now, looking back from a grandmaster point of view, I realize how different I perceive the martial arts now compared to how I did then. One of the biggest differences, I would have to say, is how I see the anatomy of a fight – how a fight starts, who wins a fight, etc. What are the statistical chances that, if I take my time to do this, I'll be able to win, survive, or overcome the odds in a fight?

I've reviewed dozens of training videos and been to countless classes, in hope of finding a real answer. I tried to not worry so much about the "what if's" and simply focused on being able to overcome any situation, no matter how big the opponent or how vastly outnumbered I was.

Realistically, I have to say that violence always begets violence. I believe that violence has its own spiritual signature. Then it calls like Ulysses' sirens to other people who have similar signatures.

Often, violence erupts from one violent act to another violent act. Many times men, who desire to do violence and wickedness to one another, are just trying to prove their masculinity. When you're younger, it's about who's the strongest, who's the quickest, who's the bravest, like gun fighters in an old western movie. If you have that tough guy reputation, then another must find you to see if he is better.

In the anatomy of a fight, certain things happen. One of them is posturing. Imagine you are sitting at a bar with your friends, talking and having a good time, and you look over and see a pretty girl. You catch her eye, smile at her, maybe send her a drink, and just acknowledge the fact that you're interested in her.

Then some guy, who's playing pool halfway across the room, recognizes the fact that you're eyeballing his girlfriend, and now he feels threatened and has to come set you straight. Most of the time, these "setting straight" events involve some bad language, some possible touching prior to the actual violent act itself, and normally, some sort of posture change to show dominance or a challenge.

There was a student I read about, who was doing his graduate work in Boston. He went to the jails every Friday and Saturday night and spoke to every single person who was arrested for fighting. He talked to them about how the fight started and who won the fight.

Most of the time, the fights were started by simply an exchange of words, then the guys puffed out their chests with their arms back, talking to each other like roosters in a courtyard, waiting to see who's going to start and how it's going to go. They were posturing up with threats to show dominance.

Interestingly enough, 80% of those fights were won by a sucker punch. The sucker punch, as most of you should know by now, is basically when you pretend to turn away, or act like the fight is over, your opponent relaxes, then you ambush him with a punch. It is a coward's punch. They distract you, and then they attack. Maybe a bottle upside your head or a pool cue to the back, but the truth of the matter is, it's never fair. That's it, it's over and done with!

In the other 20%, the fight was usually won by the guy with the best techniques, the best skills, and often times, the one who was the soberest. This is what most martial artists train for. If the guy who was blindsided survives the cheap shot, the fight has a lot to do with skill, drive, ambition, and the tenacity to finish the fight. When you're fighting somebody who just sucker punched you, or smashed something into you, it is a lot harder than if you were standing in the ring with the referee and two judges. At this point in time, chaos completely ensues any fight.

I once witnessed a fight where a guy was on top of another guy. I was just standing there in a bar having a drink, when suddenly the fight erupted. A much smaller man just beat the living daylights out of the bigger guy who had walked up to him and slapped him in the face.

The smaller man got the best of the big guy because of his skills and talent. He took him quickly to the ground, mounted on top of him, and began to ground and pound. But, another guy walked up, smashed the back of his head with a beer bottle, looked at the guy and said, "Look, I wasn't ready for this to end." For his amusement, he was more than willing to change the odds of who would win that fight. Of course, I felt that desperate need to intervene, but that's a completely different story.

I can only tell you that it's been my experience in life that violence will always be perpetrated by a man usually larger than you, because they don't usually target the biggest man in the room.

A bully doesn't want to lose, so he usually chooses a smaller victim. His simple attitude is usually that he wants to find a smaller, easier target so he can vent his anger, frustration, and hostility.

Alcohol makes this even more possible by reducing all the gates and gateways to a reasonable conversation or existence. Oftentimes, people in bars will find some guy there who feels the need to challenge them and the fight is never fair; fair fighting is only for rings, arenas, and for tournaments. Outside the ring, the fight is never fair and surprise is always the best advantage.

He who strikes first usually wins the fight, almost always. If you're in this kind of situation and you feel that it's time to strike, *remember that action is quicker and faster than reaction.* I would also like to repeat the words of Al Dacascos, who years later in Hollywood, I would train with, "Even when you win, you lose."

It was the first time I had ever heard that said by any grandmaster or master, yet I knew in my heart that it was absolutely true, from my years of experience with hand-to-hand combat, and close quarters battles with other people who always felt the need to express themselves in acts of violence.

Even when you win, you lose. Whenever you fight, like I said in the beginning, those silent reminders call to you in the middle of the night to remind you of that event with the heel kick to the chest, the dislocated fingers or toes, the ruptured tendons, the reconstructive surgeries, or the TMJ that you suffer with because of the multiple face-punches that you have received. They all remind us of the damage done.

At the end of the day, no one ever comes to your house and pats you on the back for the awesome job you did or for how awesome you were in that bar fight or street fight. The only thing that reminds you that you were there are the midnight calls and howls from your joints, arm and foot pain, as well as the back pains, which cry out to you reminding you how tough you once were.

We spend tens of thousands of hours training ourselves, kicking the heavy bag, and working with opponents in order to make ourselves better. It's all in preparation for the day that we may have to use our skills in a chaotic environment, against a vicious opponent who is taller than us, bigger than us, and maybe drunk or on drugs, and comes at us with a violent heart because of the emptiness inside of him.

373

The hatred that he needs to express comes in the form of an emotional release through physical violence. You may win, but at the end of the day, it doesn't change the fact that, even when you win, you lose.

The anatomy of the fight is straight forward. You must decide whether you'll stay and fight, whether you can de-escalate things, or simply walk away. Throughout the years, I have heard many grandmasters say that it is best to simply give in, refuse to fight, and walk away; the only thing that's hurt is your pride.

Guys will call you names because you're short or they will say something mean about you simply because they want you to engage. They will talk crap about your mother, your wife, or your girlfriend. They will say things that are unsavory, even about the best of people, just to get you to confront them and engage them.

My answer to that is, if you decide to engage, do it quickly, do it as fast as possible. Strike as many times as you can and fight unfair. You train hard, but remember that there's another guy out there who's bigger, badder, and will certainly be more than happy to vent his disapproval with life on you.

I had a friend named big Al Jonovich. Big Al was a big guy who loved to fight and had no problems with it. He liked to fight, as long as it was inside or outside of a bar; but in the ring or on the Judo mat was not his style. He was always afraid of looking bad and had a lot of anxiety about the fact that he might not win.

One day I watched Al, and let me tell you, it was an unpleasant experience at best. These guys were playing an arcade game in middle of the day on a Saturday. Al didn't know these other two guys; he was just in there drinking Catawba wine. These other fellows were drinking draft beer and playing their game Then Al joined in and played a game with them.
Al won and the one guy handed Al a draft beer. Al said, "No, I'm drinking Catawba wine." The guys said, "Well, we're

drinking drafts." They had bet a drink on the outcome of the game. At this time a draft beer was 25 cents and Catawba wine was 50 cents.

The guys refused to pay the extra quarter, postured, and challenged my friend. Al throat punched this guy, uppercut him after that, punched him in the abdomen with a left fist, and took the guy down with his right. He then picked the guy up, leaned him over the pool table, and pounded him about four more times, right in the face. His buddy, who had nothing to do with this, put his hands up and said, "Man, I got nothing to do with this fight."

Al said, "Too bad!" He grabbed the guy, picked him up and slammed him up against the jukebox in the bar. Then he punched him several more times, both in the face and in the gut, and the guy slumped to the ground.

The bartender looked at Al and said, "You can't come back here anymore, I don't want you doing this to my place, these are my steadies, you need to leave!" And with that, Al looked at me sitting at the table drinking my Pepsi cola, shook his head, and we walked out the door. And that fight was over a 50-cent drink. Actually, it was over a quarter. All that over one measly quarter!

There's always somebody bigger and badder than you! I have no idea what became of those men, but I had a whole new kind of respect for my friend and for what he could do; and a whole new way of thinking about him. Violence usually begets violence.

Later, Al would have a very bad night. He worked as a bouncer. And one night he was walking to his car when someone took a lead pipe to him and beat him in the head, shoulders, and in the face. It was not a fair fight, but maybe it was karma. The point is, real fights are never fair. Never fight unless you have no other choice!

Dr. Marc Stoner studied Judo at the Judo Academy of Pittsburgh, PA. with Tom Eshenbaugh. He also did his share of bare knuckle fighting. He studied Jujitsu with Frank Kovas and taught U.S. Army Special Forces where he was the Hand-to-Hand instructor for five years.

He also taught Judo for 10 years, Kajukenbo for 15 years, and more. He earned his 1st degree black belt under Mark Gerry, a 5th degree black belt under Ted Sotelo, and also studied under Professor Wally Jay. Marc is also a medical doctor and served as a Special Forces Green Beret.

Marc is available for uplifting inspirational public speaking at national conferences, including break out groups and process evaluation. You may contact Dr. Stoner at: Huunjin@gmail.com.

Master Marc Stoner

The Psychology of Street Survival
David Furie

The urban jungle of cities like New York City, Chicago, or Los Angeles, has its own characters and some unique struggles which come with living in such a hard, demanding environment. Intelligent people understand that your environment has a lot to do with the way that you think, the way that you conduct yourself, and how you carry yourself during your everyday routines, work, and basic tasks. These are the efforts which are carried out every day to achieve your goals and directives for your well-being and your survival amongst your peers.

As a child growing up in New York City, speaking of myself and others who I had the chance to grow up with, street kids and street workers, we all did many different jobs and different tasks to be able to earn money during the 60's and 70's.

Not all of these jobs were legal, but we thought they were necessary in order to have the opportunity to be able to do what we wanted in life. I wanted to train in the ways of martial arts to make myself stronger and smarter within the oppressive environment that is New York.

The power which I was aiming to achieve was to be greater, stronger, and superior to others. With this, what I mean is to be smarter, more cunning, more deceptive, and more capable to be driven and motivated to complete any task that was taken on. To be respected, mainly by others on the streets, is what the street life, or what I call the fury of the street, required to be powerful among other street people.

It is understood and recognized as basic terms of mutual respect of power, but is not always a materialistic advantage. The psychology and the forces of one's true drive, is to be able to deal with the stress, along with the competitive edge over other people who are trying to do the same thing, the ones who are fighting for the same piece of the pie. This is a tremendous responsibility in the city.

Going back to my youth, Brooklyn, New York in the 60's was, and still is, a very dangerous place. The danger factor, which comes when walking in certain areas within Brooklyn, as well as in the Bronx, New York City, and Harlem during certain times of the day or at night, is a very big deal.

Survival requires a certain mindset. It requires one to know his environment. Knowing the faces and the body language of others in your area plays a big role in the psychology of your own state of security when you are simply walking around, trying to live your everyday life.

Many people leave the city environment because of the danger of being constantly confronted. The stress of walking outside and having to deal with other people acting aggressively towards you, plays a big role, psychologically, in the way people react towards one another.

Street survival is not a difficult thing to do or a difficult state of mind; it all mainly depends on your belief in yourself and your capability of dealing with others, psychologically, while avoiding the use of physical force.

When confronted by an aggressive person or situation, one has to first remain calm and avoid getting stressed out. You must try to resolve the situation as quickly and firmly as possible.

I strongly believe that eye contact is essential when dealing with people in stressful situations. One has to be able to read the situation and analyze right away, the intentions of the person or people who are confronting you.

A lot of times, on buses and trains in the cities, people are confronted in confined spaces, under multiple stressful circumstances.

The weather can be a major factor as well. If it is hot, cold, or raining, the atmosphere plays a big part in the psyche of the aggressors. Being aware of these factors is 80% of one's power.

I mentioned eye contact and body language, along with the assessment of your environment. What is the correct way to deal with the situation at hand? It is best to be able to look at the face of your adversary and try to resolve the situation calmly. So that you understand, sometimes, not everything goes by the book or as we would want it to.

The other side of the coin, as we say on the streets, is when you see that there is no civil resolution. In these cases, be the first to resolve the situation by walking away. Words are one thing, but never let anyone assault you physically.

With all my experiences, I found that the best way to resolve a physical situation is to be the first to hit or to subdue the aggressor. On the streets we call it being street smart. The only way that you acquire this knowledge is by being around the streets, which I do not recommend for most people.

In the martial arts world, as in the world of a professional soldier, we understand what being tough really is, and it doesn't mean that you have the right to go around beating people up or taking advantage of people because you have the physical capability to do so. To a professional, being tough means to endure, to survive, and to overcome any obstacle which is put before you – to deal with it on your own terms at any given time.

I understand that writing and explaining the psychological aspect of street survival is easier to read than to actually go out and do while, at the same time, dealing with your own feelings and insecurities. In the professional world, we call that the fear factor.

The best knowledge that I can give to anyone, from all my experiences around the world, is to always practice patience and be understanding to yourself and others, because anything that we do physically, we pay for in the end. Before I close out this chapter, I would like to mention that it is best to believe in yourself and practice martial sciences which are suitable for your overall self-development of spirit, mind, and body.

Grandmaster David Furie is one of the top martial arts masters in the country, holding a 10-degree black belt. He had a long, prestigious career in the Special Forces, as well as in the martial arts. He has used his training and expertise to devise his own unique fighting style and philosophy by incorporating the knowledge of self, the environment, and the enemy.

Grandmaster David Furie

About Dr. Bohdi Sanders

Dr. Bohdi Sanders is a multi-award winning and bestselling author. His books, *Modern Bushido: Living a Life of Excellence* and *Men of the Code*, both hit #1 on Amazon. Seven of his other books have also been best-sellers and were also ranked in the Top 10 on Amazon. Dr. Sanders has been a martial artist for over 34 years and has trained in Shotokan Karate, Krav Maga, Ninjutsu, Combative Knife, and Escrima with noted martial artists Master Bob Allen, Sifu Al Dacascos, and GM Harry Greene. Dr. Sanders is a
5th degree black belt in Shotokan Karate. His work has won national book awards and been recognized by several martial arts hall of fames. He is the author of:

- *Modern Bushido: Living a Life of Excellence*
- *Men of the Code*
- *Warrior: The Way of Warriorhood*
- *BUSHIDO: The Way of the Warrior*
- *Defensive Living: The Other Side of Self-Defense...and more!*

Dr. Sanders' books have received high praise and have won several national awards, including:

- The Elite Black Belt Hall of Fame Inductee in 2017
- Lifetime Achievement Award from The Elite Black Belt HoF
- #1 Bestseller Amazon.com: Men of the Code 2015
- #1 Bestseller Amazon.com: *Modern Bushido* 2013
- The Indie Excellence Book Awards: 1st Place Winner 2013
- USA Book News Best Books of 2013: 1st Place Winner 2013
- IIMAA Best Martial Arts Book of the Year 2011
- U. S. Martial Arts Hall of Fame: Author of the Year 2011
- U. S. Martial Artist Association: Inspiration of the Year 2011
- The Indie Excellence Book Awards:1st Place Winner 2010
- USA Book News Best Books of 2010: 1st Place Winner 2010

Looking for More Wisdom?

If you are interested in living the warrior lifestyle or simply in living a life of character, integrity, and honor, you will enjoy The Wisdom Warrior website and newsletter. The Wisdom Warrior website contains dozens of articles, useful links, and news for those seeking to live the warrior lifestyle.

The newsletter is also a valuable resource. Each edition of The Wisdom Warrior Newsletter is packed with motivating quotes, articles, and information which everyone will find useful in their journey to perfect their character and live the life which they were meant to live.

The Wisdom Warrior Newsletter is a newsletter sent directly to your email account and is absolutely FREE! There is no cost or obligation to you whatsoever. You will also receive the current news updates and new articles by Dr. Bohdi Sanders and others martial arts masters as soon as they are available. Your email address is never shared with anyone else.

All you need to do to start receiving this valuable and informative newsletter is to go to the Wisdom Warrior website and simply sign up. It is that simple!

You will also find special package deals on all of Dr. Sanders' books on The Wisdom Warrior Website! You will find The Wisdom Warrior website at:

www.TheWisdomWarrior.com

Also, be sure to find posts by Dr. Sanders on Facebook. Dr. Sanders posts enlightening commentaries, photographs, and quotes throughout the week on his Facebook pages. You can find them at:

www.facebook.com/Bohdi.Sanders

Sign Up Today!

Copies of *BUSHIDO: The Way of the Warrior* are available
from Amazon at: www.amazon.com/dp/B075TH53C9. Those
who would like signed copies of *BUSHIDO* can get them from:
www.TheWisdomWarrior.com.

Copies of *Modern Bushido* are available from Amazon at: https://www.amazon.com/dp/B008S26INK. Those who would like signed copies of *Modern Bushido* can get them from:

www.TheWisdomWarrior.com.

Copies of *Men of the Code* are available from Amazon at:
https://www.amazon.com/dp/B017JA1ZUM. Those who would
like signed copies of *Men of the Code* can get them from:

www.TheWisdomWarrior.com.

Copies of *Defensive Living* are available from Amazon at: https://www.amazon.com/dp/B009EF7U8M. Those who would like signed copies of *Defensive Living* can get them from:

www.TheWisdomWarrior.com

www.SwordXP.com

Copies of *The Warrior Lifestyle* are available from Amazon at:
www.amazon.com/dp/B00ELW2DVM. Those who would like
signed copies of *The Warrior Lifestyle* can get them from:

www.TheWisdomWarrior.com.

Copies of *LEGACY: Through the Eyes of the Warrior* are available from Amazon at: https://tinyurl.com/LEGACY-Al-Dacascos. Those who would like signed copies of LEGACY can get them directly from Sifu Al Dacascos.

390

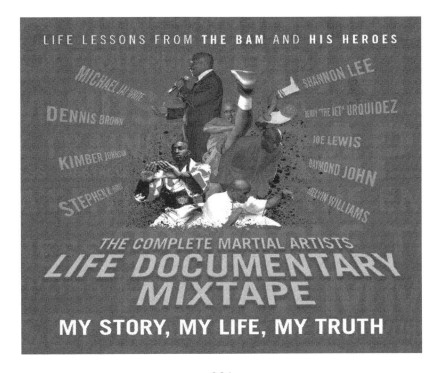

Secrets of the Soul
The Guide to Uncovering Your Hidden Beliefs

Best Seller
amazon.com

by Award Winning Author
Bohdi Sanders, PhD
USMAA Inspirational Author of the Year!

Copies of *Secrets of the Soul* are available from Amazon at:
https://www.amazon.com/dp/B009EF7OL0. Those who would
like signed copies of *Secrets of the Soul* can get them from:

www.TheWisdomWarrior.com.

To donate to this worthy charity, go to:

www.ThePeaceFund.org

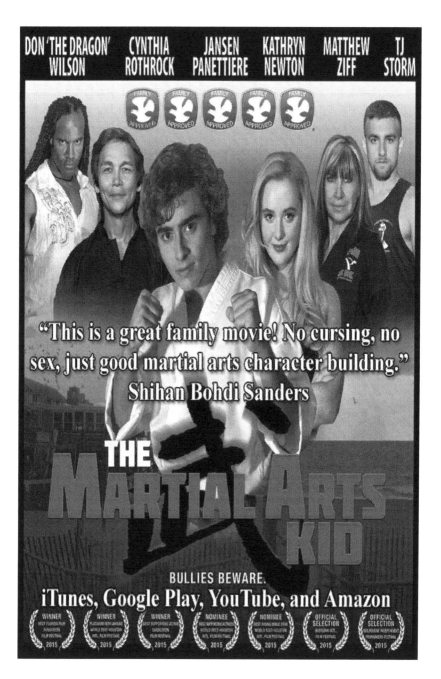

Be sure to check out our website for DVD's, updates on *The Martial Arts Kid II*, and for lots of interesting information:

www.MartialArtsKidMovie.com

Copies of *Warrior: The Way of the Warriorhood* are available from Amazon at: www.amazon.com/dp/B00ELWCALA. Those who would like signed copies of *WARRIOR* can get them from:

www.TheWisdomWarrior.com

396

You may Contact Doug Marcaida by email at:
Doug@DougMarcaida.com
You may Contact Fred Mastro by email at:
Fred@MastroDefenceSystem.com

Copies of *Warrior Wisdom* are available from Amazon at: https://www.amazon.com/dp/B009F27CQY. Those who would like signed copies of *Warrior Wisdom* can get them from:

www.TheWisdomWarrior.com.

Copies of *Martial Arts Wisdom* are available from Amazon at:
https://www.amazon.com/dp/B00M1T7QDC. Those who would
like signed copies of *Martial Arts Wisdom* can get them from:

www.TheWisdomWarrior.com.

400

Copies of *Men of the Code* are available from Amazon at:
https://www.amazon.com/dp/B017JA1ZUM. Those who would
like signed copies of *Men of the Code* can get them from:

www.TheWisdomWarrior.com

To join or for more information contact:

www.HaeMuKwan.com

Copies of *Wisdom of the Elders* are available from Amazon at:
https://www.amazon.com/dp/B00ELW2AT2.
Those who would like signed copies can get them from:

www.TheWisdomWarrior.com.

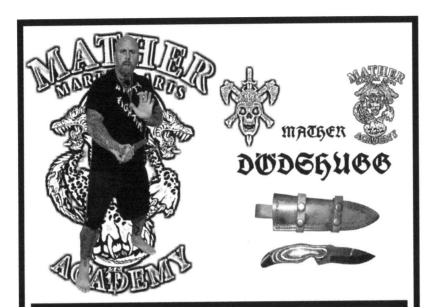

Get the rest of the Secrets of the
Martial Arts Masters Series!

SECRETS
of the
Martial Arts
MASTERS

Bohdi Sanders, Ph.D.
Foreword by Grandmaster Eric Lee

Get the rest of the Secrets of the
Martial Arts Masters Series!

SECRETS
of the
Martial Arts
MASTERS

Bohdi Sanders, Ph.D.

Foreword by Grandmaster Eric Lee

Secrets of the Martial Arts Masters Volume 3
Get Your Copy on Amazon at:
https://www.amazon.com/dp/1937884236
or get a signed copy from:
www.TheWisdomWarrior.com

408

27236847R10244

Made in the USA
San Bernardino, CA
27 February 2019